EL ALAMEIN 1942

AUSTRALIAN ARMY CAMPAIGN SERIES / 33

EL ALAMEIN 1942

MARK JOHNSTON

Published in 2025 by Hardie Grant Custom, an imprint of
Hardie Grant Publishing, on behalf of the Australian Army History Unit.

Hardie Grant Custom (Melbourne)

Level 11, 36 Wellington Street
Collingwood VIC 3066, Australia
www.hardiegrant.com.au

Hardie Grant acknowledges the Traditional Owners of the Country on which we work, the Wurundjeri People of the Kulin Nation and the Gadigal People of the Eora Nation, and recognises their continuing connection to the land, waters and culture. We pay our respects to their Elders past and present.

A catalogue record for this book is available from the National Library of Australia

El Alamein, 1942
ISBN 978-176145243-7
Publishing Directors: Courtney Nicholls and Christine Dixon
Project Editors: Shahirah Hambali and Mahalia Brooks
Series Editor: Garth Pratten
Editor: Courtney Page-Allen
Art Director: Dallas Budde
Design: Robert Bertagni
Cartographer: Catherine McCulloch
Printed in China by Leo Paper Group

CONTENTS

SERIES EDITOR FOREWORD

EL ALAMEIN IS THE 33RD TITLE published in the Australian Army Campaign Series. Commencing in 2006 and spanning over a century of Australian Army operations, the Campaign Series is one of the most sustained endeavours in Australian military history publishing. It is also the third series of books produced by the Australian Army specifically for the purposes of professional military education.

The Army's first professional education series consisted of six volumes written by Colonel Eustace Keogh between 1954 and 1965 to assist officers preparing for the military history examinations that were then required for promotion. The second series was instigated in 1990 by then Chief of the General Staff, Lieutenant General John Coates, as the basis of an Army-wide history education program for Army officers; four volumes were published by Training Command between 1991 and 1995. The current Campaign Series similarly resulted from an initiative by the Strategic Advisory Group to the Chief of Army, Lieutenant General Peter Leahy, to promote an understanding of military history among the Army's future generation of commissioned and non-commissioned leaders. These three series are united not only by a recognition of the value of the study of history to the military profession but by the imperative to provide clear, concise accounts of the Australian Army's operations accompanied by a wealth of supporting illustrations, organisational charts and maps.

The Campaign Series does not seek to derive explicit lessons from history but rather explore the factors shaping the outcomes of military operations: tactics, techniques and procedures, weapons and other technology, logistics, command and leadership. History does not repeat but it does rhyme. As Paul K Van Riper, one-time Commander of the US Marine Corps Combat Development Command, observed, 'The vicarious experiences provided through study of the past enable practioners of war to see familiar patterns of activity and to develop more quickly potential solutions to tactical and operational problems'. Context is critical to forming judgments – there are no single factor explanations. The Campaign Series thus also encompasses the political aims, national strategy and campaign objectives of the operations it examines alongside the characteristics of the operational environment.

Unlike a lot of Australian military history, the Campaign Series does not beat a nationalist drum. As Keogh once noted, 'our history is full of great military myths, most of which we thoughtlessly accept at their face value'. If we reduce history to a set of shallow clichés, we deny ourselves both an insight into the true complexity of war and military operations, and the chance to profit from that experience. The Campaign Series questions decisions, outcomes and established narratives, and embraces the perspectives of allies and adversaries alike.

Above all, the Campaign Series is grounded in the human experience of war. As Keogh observed, 'the basic material which the soldier uses in … [their] … profession is human nature – men and women. They must know how people react to the stresses of war, and how they react to danger and adversity, to triumph and disaster'.

Although intended for a military readership, the accessible style and attractive presentation of the Campaign Series has made it popular with a more general readership. I am delighted the partnership between the Australian Army History Unit and Hardie Grant is enabling the Campaign Series to continue to educate Australia's soldiers and encourage a more sophisticated understanding of the Army's history in the wider community.

Associate Professor Garth Pratten SFHEA FRHistS
Series Editor

PRELUDE

AT EL ALAMEIN IN EGYPT IN 1942, Australians made a decisive contribution to one of the great turning-point battles of the twentieth century.

To British Prime Minister Winston Churchill, Alamein 'marked ... the turning of the "Hinge of Fate"'. He acknowledged that 'the magnificent forward drive of the Australians, achieved by ceaseless bitter fighting ... swung the whole battle in our favour'. Yet this major part of our nation's heritage is little known in the Australian military, let alone the wider community. Very few serving Australian soldiers know what Australians did at Alamein, or who General Morshead was, even though they have probably heard both names: Alamein Company at RMC, for example, or Morshead Drive in Canberra.

Alamein was one of the few places where Australian troops made an undeniably significant historical contribution, but it was in some ways part of a bygone era. It was the last time that Australians fought conventional operations in a large-scale formation context: that is, fighting as a complete division, beside other divisions, within a corps. Yet it also brings out many themes still relevant to the military today. The war in North Africa has been called 'pure' warfare, where freedom of manoeuvre was comparable to that in a naval battle and where many of the lessons are eternal. An enormous number of books have been written about leadership and command in North Africa, and these lessons have value for current leaders. The fighting at Alamein put tremendous pressure on leaders from the highest to lowest levels within the Australian force, and how they responded is a major theme of what follows. Australians nearly always fight alongside allies and under allied command, and British leadership of Australians at Alamein is a major theme.

Both sides in the battle fought in coalitions and this had profound implications for Australian plans and performance.

Another major theme is adaptation and learning, for the Allied victory at Alamein represented the culmination of two years of attempts to match the Germans' own successful adaptation to the demands of desert warfare. Alamein was a campaign where profound lessons were learnt about infantry-armour cooperation, air-ground liaison and artillery support, among others.

It was also a hugely testing campaign for participants. The personal experience of war is a major strand in this book. That personal experience includes the three Australians who were awarded the Victoria Cross (VC) for their actions in the battle. The fighting at Alamein was on a truly epic scale, with hundreds of thousands of men involved. Thinking of Homer's account of the fabled siege of Troy, one British general described the Australians' efforts at Alamein as 'homeric'. Names such as the Hill of Jesus (Tel el Eisa), Trig 29, the Saucer and the Blockhouse should be part of Australian military folklore.

The Alamein campaign had three main stages – the July fighting (often called First Alamein), in which Australians won and held Tel el Eisa and other vital ground on the coast but in which they also suffered some costly rebuffs; the 'static phase' in which patrolling, Operation Bulimba and training under General Montgomery were the main elements; and the great battle of El Alamein (Second Alamein) in which the Australians captured and held more crucial ground (notably Trig 29 and the Blockhouse) before Rommel was forced to admit defeat and retreat for the last time. This book's organisation follows that order of stages.

ACKNOWLEDGEMENTS

PROFESSOR PETER STANLEY alerted me in 2021 to the Army History Unit's interest in a volume on Alamein in their campaign series and he encouraged me to offer to write it. I'm grateful that he did so. I am also thankful to have been able to draw on the substantial sections he contributed to the 'Alamein book' we wrote together more than tweny years ago. Phil Bradley, who has written several superb books for the same series, also gave me valuable advice early in the process.

Garth Pratten, as series editor, went through the manuscript with the proverbial fine-tooth comb, challenging many parts of the traditional account that I had long taken for granted, offering new insights and getting me to provide more detail on matters that needed to be explained better or more fully. His advice on the last chapter, on insights, was profoundly important. At times I was perturbed by the need to keep fine-tuning the book, but it is now very much tighter and more informative thanks to Garth's work.

Catherine McCulloch produced a beautiful set of maps, and I thank her for her patience in following the numerous instructions and directions that Garth and I sent her. Jason Smeaton at the Australian Army History Unit was a helpful guide through the process of bringing the book to fruition, ultimately with Hardie Grant. Courtney Page-Allen and Ian Hodges did a superb job copyediting and making suggestions for Hardie Grant, for whom Courtney Nicholls was an efficient and encouraging publishing director.

Many photos in this book come from private collections, and for these I'm grateful to all donors, especially David Pearson, Paul Oaten, Peter Bannigan, Peter Stanley, Alan Sandbach, Ted Carter and Peter Burness. Bryce Abraham gave valuable advice on decorations, as did Craig Tibbitts on casualties.

Thanks as always to my wife Deborah for her vital support during the writing of this book.

ABBREVIATIONS

ADS	Advanced Dressing Station
AGH	Australian General Hospital
AIF	Australian Imperial Force
Arty	Artillery
AT	anti-tank
AWL	Absent without leave
AWM	Australian War Memorial
Bde	Brigade
BHQ	Battalion Headquarters
Bn	Battalion
BRA	Brigadier Royal Artillery
CCS	Casualty Clearing Station
CO	Commanding Officer
Coy	Company
CPL	Corporal
DAK	*Deutsches Afrikakorps* [German Africa Corps]
DCM	Distinguished Conduct Medal
Fd Amb	Field Ambulance
FOO	Forward Observation Officer
HQ	Headquarters
Inf	Infantry
lt	Light
IWM	Imperial War Museum
LT	Lieutenant
LTGEN	Lieutenant General
MC	Military Cross
ME	Middle East
MJC	Mark Johnston's Collection
MG	Machine gun
MM	Military Medal
NAA	National Archives of Australia
Ops	Operations
Pnr	Pioneer
PTE	Private
RAA	Royal Australian Artillery
RAE	Royal Australian Engineers
Regt	Regiment
RMO	Regimental Medical Officer
RSM	Regimental Sergeant Major
RTR	Royal Tank Regiment
SGT	Sergeant
TNA	The National Archives (United Kingdom)
TEWT	Tactical exercise without troops
VC	Victoria Cross
WO2	Warrant Officer Class Two

FIGURES

MAPS

MAP SYMBOLOGY LEGEND

MILITARY

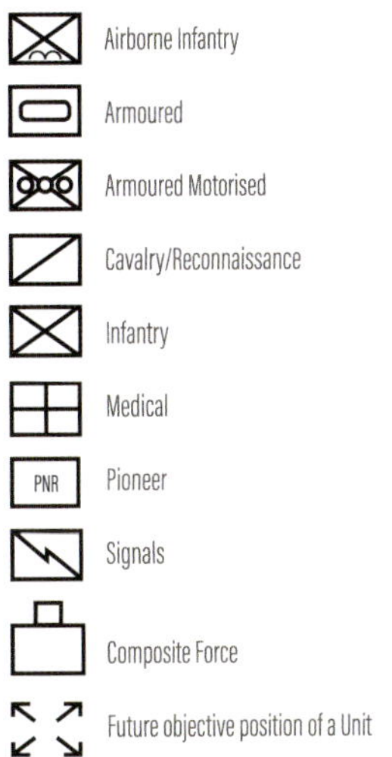

- • Detachment
- •• Section
- ••• Platoon
- I Company
- II Battalion
- III Regiment
- X Brigade
- XX Division
- XXX Corps
- XXXX Army
- XXXXX Army Group

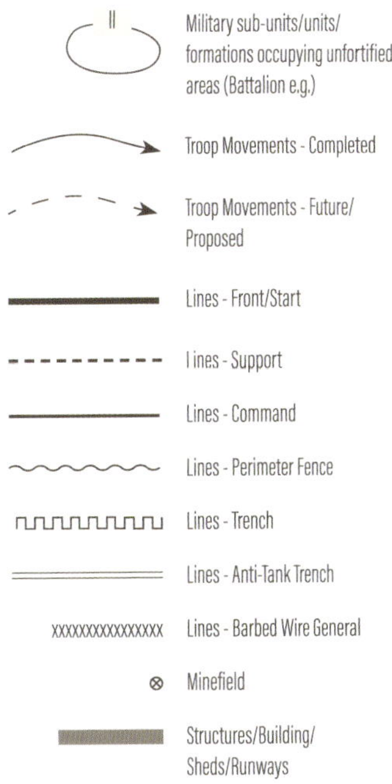

CIVILIAN

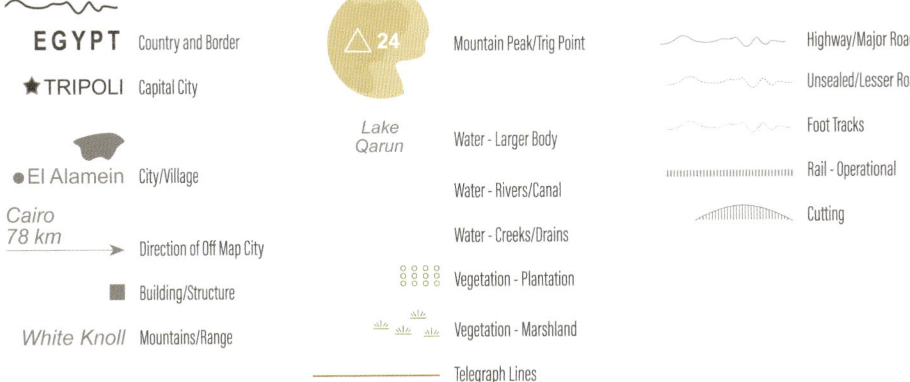

Note on map colours: contour colours represent difference in elevation, they do not necessarily represent specific heights.

PART 1

THE JULY BATTLE

Australians, probably of the 2/32nd Battalion, in their dugout in mid-July.
(IWM E14449)

FRANCE
Sarajevo
CORSICA
Ajaccio
Rome
ITALY
Durrës
Taranto
Brindisi
ALBANIA
Salon
SARDINIA
Valona
GREEC
Cagliari
Palermo
SICILY
Cori
Ionian Sea
Bizerta
Algiers
Tunis
ALGERIA
Valletta
MALTA
TUNISIA
Gabes
Gulf of Gabes
Mediterran
Sabratha
Tripoli
Gargaresc
Misrata
Benghazi
Gulf of Sirte
Er Regim
Sirte
Beda Fomm
En Nofilia
Bir El Merduma
Agedabia
El Agheila
LIBYA
0 100 200 300 400 Kilometres
0 100 200 300 400 Miles

Map 1: The eastern Mediterranean

CHAPTER 1

AUSTRALIANS AND THE DESERT WAR

TO JULY 1942

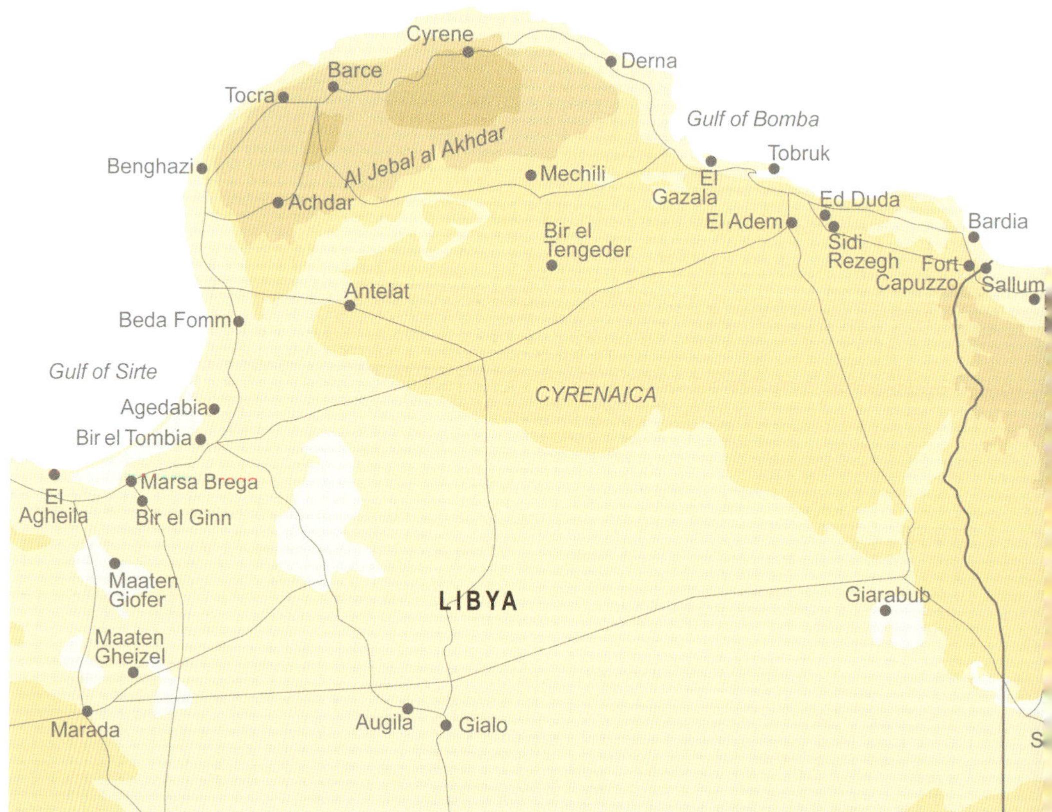

(Below)
Map 2: The Western Desert

THE BATTLES OF EL ALAMEIN had their origins in German and Italian ambitions. Nazi Germany's conquest of Poland and France was built on combined arms operations, emphasising mobility and speed. On 10 June 1940, with French defeat imminent, the Italian leader Benito Mussolini declared war on France and the United Kingdom. His goal of creating a new Roman empire was directed largely at North Africa, where Italy already controlled Libya. In the second half of 1940, Britain held off the German bid for air superiority in the Battle of Britain. Preventing an invasion of Britain was one achievement, but defeating the Axis was quite another challenge. The Mediterranean was the one land theatre where the war could be taken to the Axis, with the possibility of knocking Italy out of the war, while safeguarding the Suez Canal as a route to the Indian Ocean.

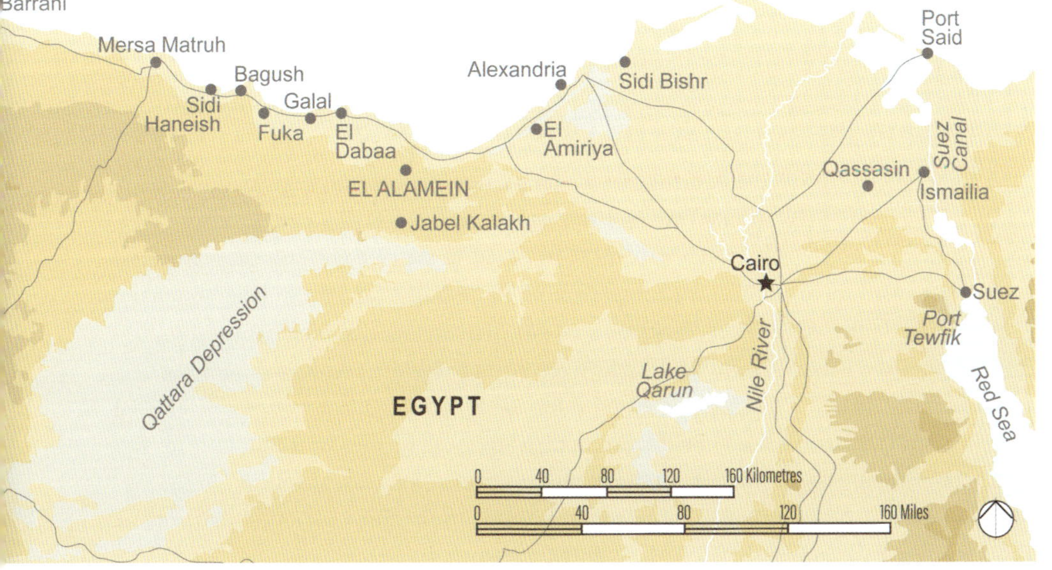

Britain's land operations for the next two years focussed on the Western Desert of North Africa. The British were not fighting alone: the North African campaign would feature army divisions drawn from Australia, India, New Zealand and South Africa, and smaller units from other parts of the Empire, such as British Central Africa. The Australian, Indian and South African forces were all-volunteer, and the New Zealand one largely volunteer, and this was reflected in their quality: the Australians and New Zealanders were generally rated the best troops in the Allied army in the desert. There were also allies from occupied countries, including Free French, Polish, Greek and Czech servicemen.

In 1940, Italian forces in Libya posed a threat to British interests in Egypt. Although Egypt was officially independent, the Suez Canal was vital to Britain, which in 1939 invoked a clause in the Anglo-Egyptian Treaty of 1936 that enabled British forces to occupy Egypt in the event of war. Alexandria was the main base of the British Mediterranean fleet throughout the war, while the headquarters of the Commander-in-Chief of Middle East Command was in Cairo. Palestine and Transjordan were British administered territories dating from the carve-up of the Ottoman Empire after the First World War.

In September 1940, Hitler offered a Panzer (armoured) division to Mussolini but the *Duce* was lukewarm, saying only that Panzers and Stuka dive-bombers might come in handy for the final attack on Alexandria. In fact, the Italian incursion into Egypt in September 1940 ended in disaster at Sidi Barrani in December. This established one of the themes of the campaigns culminating at Alamein: the inferiority of the Italian armed forces to the British and German, and the fact that quality usually mattered more than quantity. Churchill tended to be preoccupied with quantity, but quality was crucial in matters such as equipment, morale, command, intelligence, training and logistics. This theme was often most apparent in relation to *German* high quality, but also improving British quality and, closer to home, Australian quality. Having the bigger forces was no guarantee of success.

Australians enter the North African campaign

After General Archibald Wavell's British forces defeated the Italian 10th Army at Sidi Barrani, his Western Desert Force (under Lieutenant General Richard O'Connor) invaded Libya. The 6th Australian Division – the first division raised in the Second Australian Imperial Force – provided the main infantry component of O'Connor's force from late December. At the fortified town of Bardia on 3–5 January 1941, the 6th Division fought Australia's first land battle of the Second World War. Tanks were often a decisive factor in desert warfare, and at Bardia British Matilda tanks working alongside Australian infantry proved a winning combination. The Australian and British forces then advanced further west and, in a two-day battle commencing on 21 January, captured another Italian fortress, at Tobruk. In the two battles of Bardia and Tobruk in January, the Australians took more than 60,000 prisoners. Their 6th Division comprised fewer than 20,000 men.

ROMMEL

The Axis effort in North Africa will always be identified with Erwin Rommel. Hitler's choice of Rommel to command the 'blocking detachment' he sent to Libya in February 1941 proved brilliant. Rommel had earned the coveted *Pour la Mérite* medal (equivalent to the VC) in 1917 as a dashing and innovative infantry commander at Caporetto, where he led a daring attack that captured 9000 men and 81 guns. Commanding the 7th Panzer Division in France in 1940, he was credited with capturing 10,000 POWs, 100 tanks and twenty-seven guns in the first week. Rommel was a master of the *Bewegungskrieg* (war of movement) that was essential to German success early in the war. It reached its apogee in June 1942 with his capture of Tobruk – which resulted in his promotion to the rank of field marshal – and invasion of Egypt. Historians debate his limitations. In a campaign where supplying far-flung forces was crucial, Rommel took little interest in logistics. As German Major General Johann von Ravenstein told his captors, 'The Western Desert may be the tactician's paradise, but it is the quartermaster's hell!'[3] Rommel also preferred being on the move at the front, checking on and directing the forward troops, rather than at his headquarters – leading some to criticise him as unsuited to command an army. At Alamein in October, he was not at his best, probably partly due to ill-health. His repeated daylight counterattacks frittered away his armour. He was also deceived into believing that the main thrust of the Eighth Army was to come from the Australians in the north.

The success of the deception at Alamein was undoubtedly related to his high evaluation of Australian troops. In his first written reference to them, he described prisoners he saw from the 9th Division as men 'who without question represented an elite formation of the British Empire'.[4] When first mentioning their role in the July 1942 campaign, he wrote of knowing Australians 'only too well' from Tobruk.[5] Australians respected Rommel as a capable and honourable opponent, and his concept of a 'war without hate' benefited Australian prisoners of the Germans.

Undated photograph of Rommel using a field telephone at 'a desert bunker'.
(AWM P00869.008)

In February, the Australians entered the major city of Benghazi. They had advanced nearly 600 kilometres in a month. Their advance was then halted and they were withdrawn for operations elsewhere.

British forces were within striking distance of the last Italian possessions in Libya, notably Tripoli in Tripolitania (the western region of Libya). The Germans had reason to worry that if all of Libya fell into Allied hands, the whole southern flank of the Axis would be exposed to seaborne attack. In February 1941, Hitler reluctantly sent a 'blocking detachment', initially comprising the 5th Light Division, to Libya to prevent it from falling into Allied hands. Hitler made a fortunate selection of commander for this force: Lieutenant General Erwin Rommel, who had been a highly successful panzer division commander in the French campaign.

Hitler insisted that Rommel defend Libya east of Tripoli and that his force's purpose was defensive. This 'Afrika Korps', as the German forces came to be called, officially comprised the 5th Light Division and, from May 1941 onwards, the 15th Panzer Division. In August, the 5th Light Division was renamed the 21st Panzer; and a third division, the 'Afrika' or 90th Light Division, was added in late 1941. The Afrika Korps was a 'child of chance', for Hitler was not interested in colonial acquisitions outside Europe. It was not specially trained or equipped for desert operations.[6]

To honour a political commitment from the British government, Wavell had sent some of his best troops, the veteran 6th Australian Division and the New Zealand Division, to Greece, where German invasion seemed imminent. The 6th Division was replaced in Libya by the inexperienced 9th Australian Division.

British intelligence intercepts, known as Ultra, informed Wavell that Hitler and Mussolini wanted Rommel merely to prevent the British from taking Tripoli, but Rommel became increasingly confident that the British were too weak to attack. He sent out reconnaissance forces within hours of landing and, ignoring orders not to advance beyond Tripolitania, advanced further and further into Cyrenaica (the eastern region of Libya), driving confused British and Australian units before him. Following the capture of Mersa Brega on 1 April, 'the Afrika Korps exploded over Cyrenaica like a bomb-burst'.[7] O'Connor was captured. By mid-April, the British were back at the 'wire', the border between Libya and Egypt, with the exception of one location: the sole base in Libya still in British hands was Tobruk, which Rommel's forces surrounded on 11 April 1941.

The Siege of Tobruk

Tobruk's Italian-built defences were manned by 15,000 Australian infantry (most of the 9th Division and a brigade of the 7th), while 8,000 British troops provided most of the supporting arms and services. At least twice as many Axis troops surrounded Tobruk as defended it, and an eight-month siege began.

During this siege, the 9th Division's men became world famous as the 'Rats of Tobruk'.

Many were lucky to be in Tobruk on 11 April, having in previous weeks been part of the so-called 'Benghazi Handicap', in which Rommel's forces had chased and narrowly missed capturing a large part of the division and the rest of the British forces west of Tobruk as they retreated ignominiously from the vicinity of Benghazi.

The 9th Division's origins were no more promising than this hasty withdrawal. Its main elements were only determined in February 1941, when the least-trained and most recently enlisted Australian Imperial Force (AIF) brigades, some of which were incomplete, were regrouped under the command of the recently appointed Major General Leslie Morshead. Two of the division's three brigades, the 20th and 26th, were transferred from the 7th to the 9th Division in this regrouping, much to the annoyance of the men concerned. Add to this a lack of training and equipment, a lack of headquarters staff to support the new commander, as well as the fact that men in the formation had been told that the reorganisation was only temporary, and the prospects for esprit de corps and success against Rommel seemed grim.

Despite being forced to learn its trade 'as an apprentice on the job', the 9th played the central role in preventing Rommel from capturing the fortress.[8] When the Germans tried their usual Blitzkrieg tactics, the defenders defeated them in April and May. Panzers were allowed to pass through the defences to be destroyed by British artillery further back, while the diggers defeated the accompanying German infantry. Moreover, Morshead proved an able and aggressive commander. Insisting that the defenders 'besiege the besiegers', he sent

Map 3: North African 'See-Saw' 1940–1942

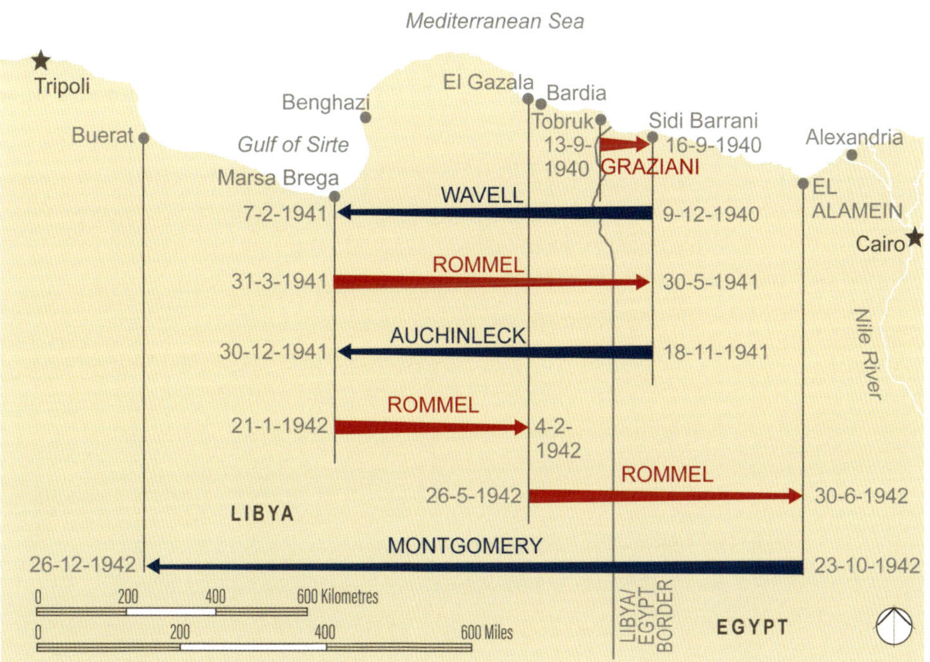

SIR LESLIE MORSHEAD

In 1915, Leslie Morshead served as a captain and major at Gallipoli, where he was wounded at Lone Pine. In 1916, he was appointed to command the newly raised 33rd Battalion, which became recognised as one of the First AIF's best battalions. Charles Bean described the Morshead of 1917 as 'the nearest approach to a martinet among all the young Australian colonels, but able to distinguish the valuable from the worthless in the old army practice'.[9] Between the wars, Morshead became branch manager of a passenger cruise line, but also served enthusiastically with the militia, rising to the rank of brigadier. At the outbreak of war, he was given command of the Second AIF's 18th Brigade. When the officer originally commanding the 9th Division, Major General Henry Wynter, fell ill in January 1941, Lieutenant General Sir Thomas Blamey appointed Morshead in his place.

Consequently, Major General Morshead's new men first got to know him during operations in the siege of Tobruk. They called him 'Ming the Merciless', after a cartoon villain, for he was still a martinet. He was also a fine leader, showing imperturbability, organisational skill, vigour and aggression as commander of the division and, between 14 April and 22 October, of the entire Tobruk fortress and its diverse garrison. Early in the siege, he told his subordinate commanders, 'There'll be no Dunkirk here ... There is to be no surrender and no retreat'.[10] He was determined to yield no ground, to dominate no-man's-land, to organise defences in as much depth as possible and constantly to improve those defences. His tactics enabled the defenders to survive Blitzkrieg-style attacks in April–May. His operational contribution caused Rommel much frustration, preventing him from invading Egypt in 1941.

Morshead was knighted in early 1942. One of his officers wrote home in April 1942: 'We have the best General of the lot in Sir Leslie Morshead and he compares very favourably with other Generals outside the A.I.F.' On the other hand, some of the attacks and raids that Morshead initiated in Tobruk were costly failures. Alamein would add to the impression that his approach to problems was sometimes unimaginatively 'last war', and he drove his men to the limit of endurance. Nevertheless, Alamein cemented Morshead in the 9th Division's affections. After returning to Australia, he was in March 1943 appointed a corps commander.

At Alamein, as in Tobruk, Morshead stood up for Australian interests, and more particularly for his troops, on many matters – including awards; unrealistic attacks; lack of British air, armour or artillery support; and any suggestion of a piecemeal dispersal of his division. He had to deal with fewer complaints about Australian indiscipline in 1942 than in 1941, but German propagandists tried to play on that reputation by referring to Morshead and his men as 'Ali Baba and his 20,000 thieves' when they returned to the desert in 1942.[11]

Lieutenant General Morshead speaks with Winston Churchill, British Prime Minister, at 9th Division Headquarters, El Alamein, 5 August 1942. (AWM P01997.009)

out many reconnaissance and fighting patrols, especially at night. Morshead's insistence that the Australians dominate no-man's-land had numerous benefits: making it difficult for the Axis to concentrate infantry and artillery up close preparatory to attacks, or to reconnoitre the defences, and also assisting the British artillery and enabling the defenders to pinpoint the Axis artillery.[12]

Tobruk was a thorn in Rommel's side, for while it remained in British hands, he could not safely advance into Egypt and it denied him a deep-water port to shorten his supply lines. The aggressiveness of the garrison ensured that he could not leave the siege to Italian troops alone and prevented him from building up strength on the Egyptian frontier. Tobruk dominated German thinking, and Rommel's planning was devoted in 1941 to taking Tobruk rather than invading Egypt. So the Tobruk garrison became a constant threat to Rommel's strategic plans, and provided a tactical example of how British forces could defeat the Axis. The Australians were greatly assisted by British and other Commonwealth forces, especially artillery.

The spirit of the 'Rats' was never broken, but the commander of the Australian Imperial

Force, Lieutenant General Sir Thomas Blamey, became increasingly worried about the siege's effect on the garrison's physical and mental health. At his prompting, supported by the Australian government, the Australians were replaced in September–October. The 2/13th Battalion, left behind because of air raids, helped in the landward relief of Tobruk in December.

Operation Crusader

That relief was part of Operation Crusader, launched on 18 November 1941 by the newly created Eighth Army. This offensive pre-empted a major attack on Tobruk that Rommel had long been preparing.

(Above) German troops pose in a trench somewhere in Africa, in one of a series of photos that once belonged to a German officer captured at Alamein in October 1942. German troops would fight well throughout the Alamein operations. (AWM P03091.008)

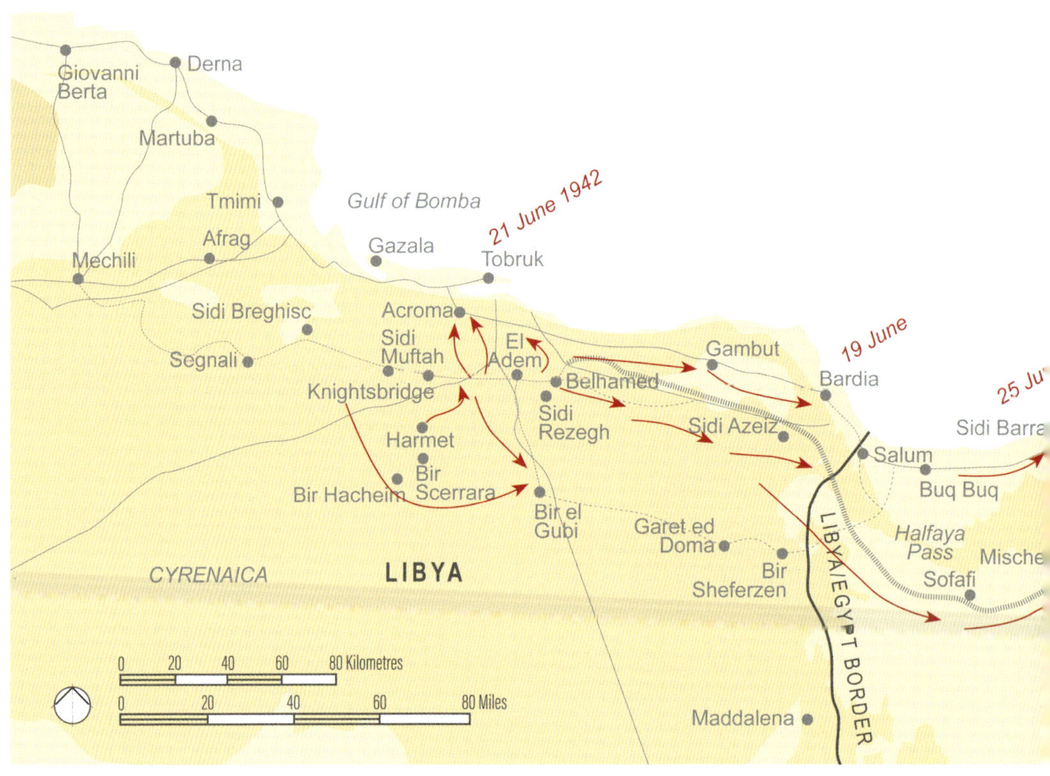

Rommel initially thought Crusader a mere raid, but on recognising its real magnitude, threw himself and his men vigorously into the battles of Sidi Rezegh. The Eighth Army sustained such casualties that its commander, Lieutenant General Sir Alan Cunningham, called for General Claude Auchinleck to come forward and advise him. Auchinleck sacked Cunningham and replaced him with Lieutenant General Neil Ritchie.

Rommel's losses in these battles, partly from an impulsive 'dash to the wire' (the Egyptian frontier), as well as supply problems, forced his withdrawal on 8 December. Tobruk was relieved.

That December also saw Japan enter the war, which soon resulted in the departure of the I Australian Corps, including two of the three Australian divisions in the Middle East. By contrast, in early January 1942, Rommel received more tanks and fuel. Air support and U-boats had arrived too, and had an immediate impact. Rommel regrouped for another surprise attack. On 21 January he pre-empted Auchinleck's advance into Tripolitania by striking east to Mersa Brega. His newly named *Panzerarmee Afrika* took the British by surprise. Rommel captured Benghazi before pausing near Gazala.

Under pressure from Churchill, Auchinleck agreed to launch a major attack in June 1942, but Ultra signals intelligence revealed that Rommel planned to attack in May

Map 4: Rommel's advance into Egypt

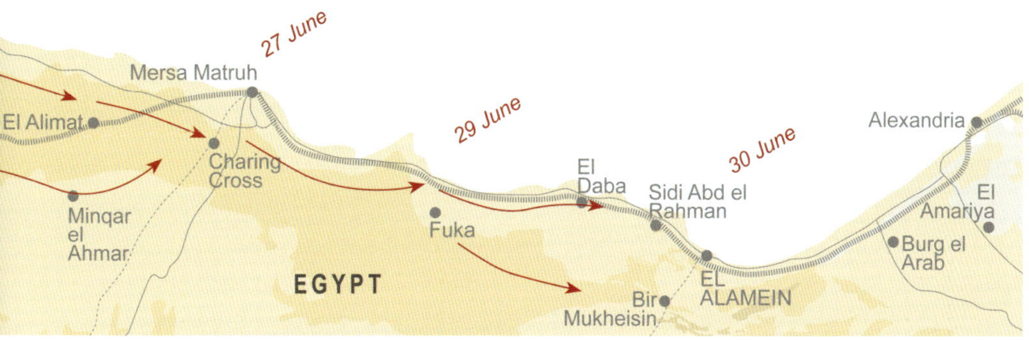

(Operation Venezia), and Auchinleck made defensive preparations. Rommel's forces outflanked Bir Hacheim and defeated Ritchie in the battles of Gazala.

The Fall of Tobruk and Rommel's invasion of Egypt

On 21 June 1942, after a day's fighting, Rommel took Tobruk. This was a catastrophe: here and at Gazala the British suffered between 50,000 and nearly 100,000 casualties, most of them prisoners. Churchill was demoralised. The 9th Australian Division, manning the Turko–Syrian frontier, was dismayed. Rommel – recently promoted to the rank of field marshal – advanced into Egypt. Auchinleck, now in personal command of the Eighth Army, was unable to halt him at Mersa Matruh, the abandonment of which signalled the low-point of British fortunes in the Middle East.

There was an air of gloom, or even panic, in Cairo as the British fell back another 200 kilometres to the El Alamein line which, because of its proximity to the impassable Qattara Depression, offered an opportunity to defend against Rommel's outflanking tactics. No-one could know that the back and forth, highly manoeuvrable period of the desert war was nearing its end, and that conditions at Alamein would reintroduce battles of attrition. The 9th Division, ordered back to Egypt in late June, would be heavily involved.

CHAPTER 2

'9 DIV' RETURNS TO THE DESERT

7–10 JULY 1942

AT THE BEGINNING OF JULY, General Auchinleck's front line stood in defensive positions at El Alamein, an area extending some 65 kilometres south from the Mediterranean coast to the Qattara Depression. His XXX Corps held the northern sector, XIII Corps the southern sector, of this area that was soon to become a vast battlefield. Relatively narrow though it was, the area was too wide to be held by a continuous line, so the British forces were spread among defended areas called 'boxes', vestiges of earlier failed defensive tactics at Gazala. Alamein itself was a siding rather than a settlement, through which ran the railway and coast road from Alexandria.

Although on departing Syria many 9th Division soldiers were hoping they were headed for Australia, by 30 June they knew they would be returning to Egypt. There were signs of panic among British troops coming in the opposite direction, and many Australians expected to be fighting on the defence again, as at Tobruk. However, in the first three days of July other British forces held Rommel's attack in the first stages of what has become known as 'the First Battle of El Alamein' or 'First Alamein'. Auchinleck wrote at this time, 'I plan to defeat the enemy and destroy him'. The destruction of Rommel's army was his priority in the operations described in the next two chapters. The arrival of the Australians would give him fresh troops for taking the initiative.

Thus, although the Australians would have much defensive fighting in the months ahead, their initial and main role would be offensive. The division was a powerful formation at full-strength and with two battalions of corps troops attached. Nevertheless, it was not accustomed to fighting the open battles that lay ahead, and especially to fighting alongside tanks, an essential element of combined arms warfare in the desert. As Auchinleck once told Churchill, 'infantry cannot win battles in the desert as long as the enemy has superiority in armour'.[13]

Generals Morshead (left) and Auchinleck (right) with Ramsden (centre) at 9th Division headquarters during Churchill's visit on 5 August 1942. Auchinleck and Ramsden would soon be replaced. (AWM 024764)

9TH DIVISION ORGANISATION

The 9th Australian Division that fought at Alamein comprised about 17,000 men. As an infantry division, it constituted infantry supported by artillery, engineers and other arms and services units. It was based on three infantry brigades, each of three battalions, and numbered '20th', '24th' and '26th'. Each brigade had a supporting field regiment of artillery, field company of engineers, field ambulance and other smaller units. Together, these units formed a 'brigade group', which British commanders to mid-1942 saw as semi-independent forces ideal for desert operations. Senior Australian commanders were not enthusiastic about this notion, seeing it as dissipating the division's strength and compromising the long-held Australian belief that Australian national formations should be kept intact. Most units of the 9th Division had the prefix 'Second'. For example, one infantry battalion was the Second Fifteenth, written '2/15th'. There was another battalion in the home based militia forces called the 15th, and the term 'Second' was used to distinguish the two. The numbers, brigade groupings and states of origin of the nine infantry battalions of the 9th Division were as follows:

Figure 1:

9th Australian Division Order of Battle
23 October 1942

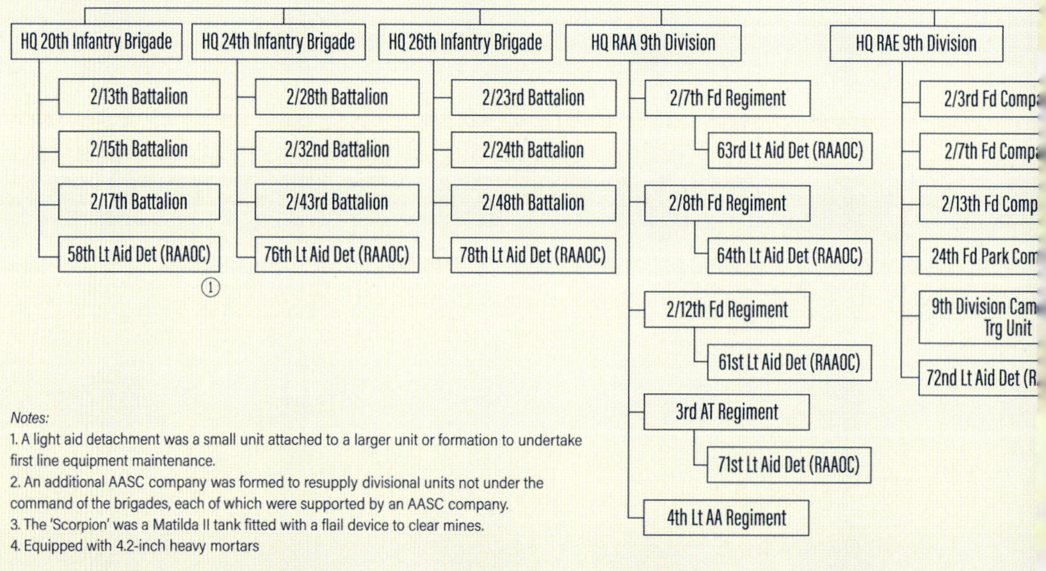

Notes:
1. A light aid detachment was a small unit attached to a larger unit or formation to undertake first line equipment maintenance.
2. An additional AASC company was formed to resupply divisional units not under the command of the brigades, each of which were supported by an AASC company.
3. The 'Scorpion' was a Matilda II tank fitted with a flail device to clear mines.
4. Equipped with 4.2-inch heavy mortars

Unless otherwise indicated, all force elements are Australian

20TH INFANTRY BRIGADE

2/13th Infantry Battalion	New South Wales
2/15th Infantry Battalion	Queensland
2/17th Infantry Battalion	New South Wales

24TH INFANTRY BRIGADE

2/28th Infantry Battalion	Western Australia
2/32nd Infantry Battalion	All states (initially formed from service units in the UK)
2/43rd Infantry Battalion	South Australia

26TH INFANTRY BRIGADE

2/23rd Infantry Battalion	Victoria
2/24th Infantry Battalion	Victoria
2/48th Infantry Battalion	South Australia

Each battalion contained four rifle companies – designated A, B, C and D – and a Headquarters Company which undertook tasks such as transport and anti-aircraft work. Units not in or supporting brigades were 'divisional troops', including the 9th Division Cavalry Regiment (an armoured reconnaissance unit), the 2/3rd Anti-Tank Regiment, the 2/4th Light Anti-Aircraft Regiment, the 2/2nd Machine Gun Battalion and the 2/3rd Pioneer Battalion.

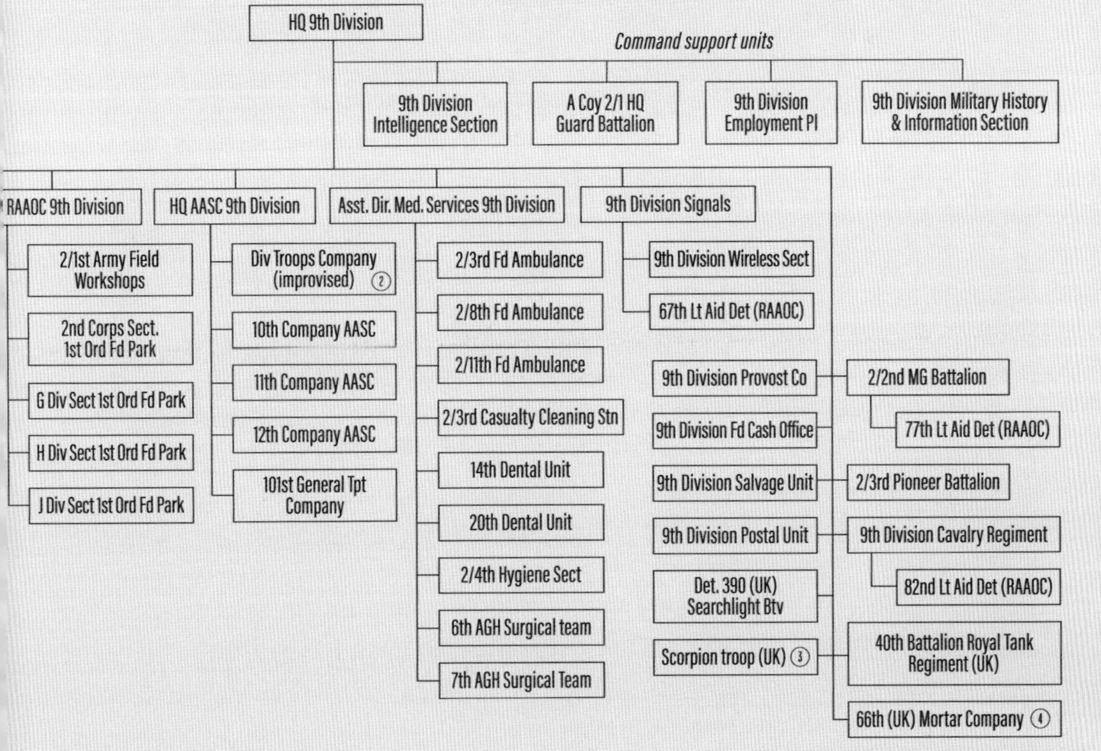

Night raid: Australians enter the fighting

The first Australian action in the desert in 1942 was a familiar type for Tobruk veterans: a night raid on 7–8 July. Captain Mervyn Jeanes of the 2/43rd Battalion took a 'fighting patrol' of four officers and sixty-four other ranks of his company, together with six battalion stretcher-bearers and twenty sappers of the 2/7th Field Company, to destroy enemy guns, vehicles and troops on a ridge about 2 kilometres from the British front. Jeanes made painstaking preparations for the raid, reportedly hiding in a wrecked tank for much of the previous day to observe the area of the proposed attack. Conducted on a very dark night, the raid was brilliantly successful. The Australians destroyed four German anti-tank guns, six to eight vehicles, and one field gun. They killed fifteen enemy troops, wounded up to twenty-five and captured nine men and a machine gun. Lieutenant Gordon Combe, who led one of Jeanes' platoons, wrote to his wife afterwards that he was 'immensely proud of [his men], most of them are just plain common people it might be said, but they were gallant and heroic in this action'.[14]

Men of the 2/43rd Battalion who had participated in the successful raid of 7–8 July pose in a Bren carrier they had recaptured that night. (IWM E14448)

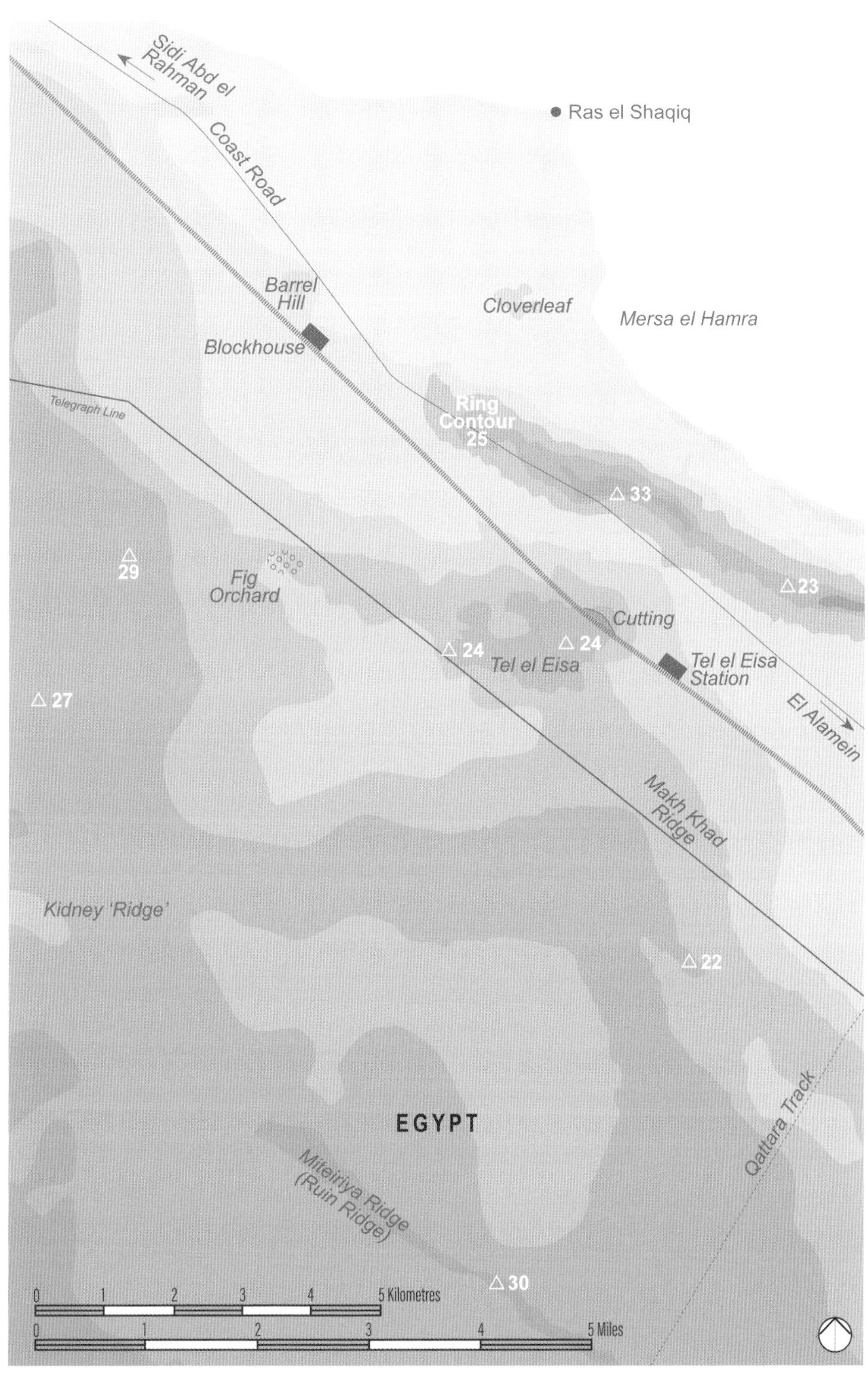

Map 5. Area of Australian operations at Alamein, July–November 1942

SAFEGUARDING AUSTRALIAN INTERESTS: NATIONAL COMMAND AUTHORITY

Australian forces in the Middle East operated within a British force and under the overall direction of British commanders. Nevertheless, as commander of the Second AIF, Lieutenant General Blamey had to follow a charter set out by the Australian government and based on that drawn up in the First World War. The charter insisted that he ensure that the AIF be recognised as an Australian force under a commander directly responsible to the Australian government, that he communicate directly with that government, and that he make sure the force was not split up without his consent. Questions of policy regarding the AIF's deployment were to be decided by the UK and Australian governments in consultation, although the force would come under 'the operational control' of the Commander-in-Chief in the theatre in which it was serving. In February 1942, before leaving the Middle East, General Blamey informed General Morshead that he would become GOC, AIF (Middle East), and advised him not to permit any piecemeal splitting of Australian forces from the main formation.

Blamey had clashed heatedly with British General Auchinleck over this principle when in 1941 he had insisted that Australian forces be relieved from Tobruk. Morshead's resolve was tested when the 9th Division returned to Egypt in July 1942. He was informed that the division was to be formed into battle groups, and that one brigade was to be sent to the front immediately. Conscious that his brigades were not yet fully equipped, he ordered that the 24th Brigade be made as ready as possible, but also visited Auchinleck. According to Morshead, the C-in-C treated him brusquely:

> **Auchinleck:** *I want that brigade right away.*
> **Morshead:** *You can't have that brigade.*
> **Auchinleck:** *Why?*
> **Morshead:** *Because they are going to fight as a formation with the rest of the division.*
> **Auchinleck:** *Not if I give you orders?*
> **Morshead:** *Give me the orders and you'll see.*
> **Auchinleck:** *So, you're being like Blamey. You're wearing his mantle.*[15]

Rather than wait for this issue to be resolved at the inter-governmental level, Auchinleck agreed that the entire 9th Division should be brought forward as soon as possible. Morshead reluctantly agreed to the temporary detachment of a brigade. Morshead spoke up again later that month, arguing that British plans for the Ruin Ridge assault were unrealistic and put too much faith in British armour. Auchinleck 'exploded' on hearing this, while the XXX Corps commander, Major General William Ramsden, privately described Morshead's attitude as 'bloody-mindedness'.

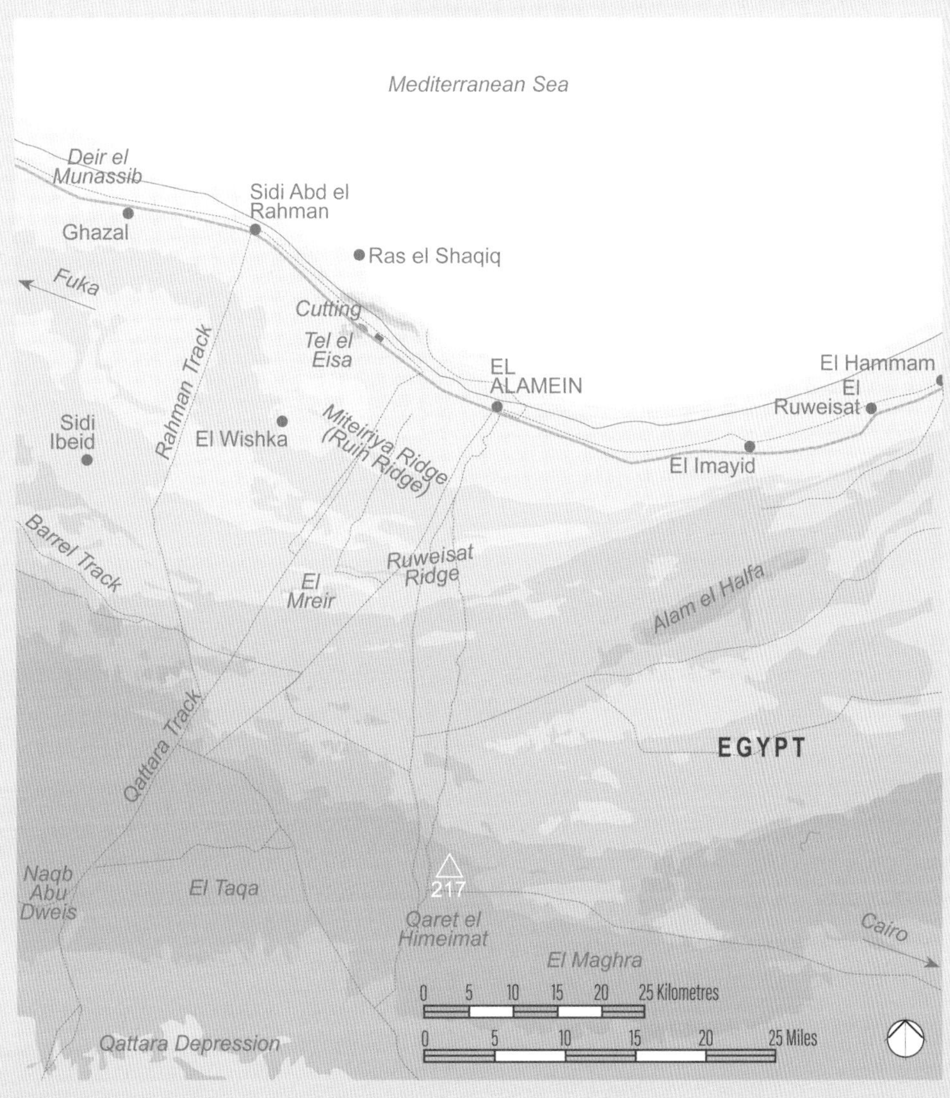

Map 6: El Alamein Area

At an outwardly civilised meeting in Ramsden's caravan, Auchinleck offered Morshead a British infantry brigade to help and the Australian agreed, despite continuing scepticism. Auchinleck's Chief of Staff saw 'political reasons' behind Morshead's objections. He was right, and the challenge of looking after the interests of a national force within a larger coalition is an enduring one for Australia. Morshead spoke up for the security of the national force entrusted to him, as well as the wellbeing of its members. This outwardly civilised meeting symbolised a 'gulf of misunderstanding' between Britain and Australia, allies who otherwise admired and respected each other. The arrival of Lieutenant General Bernard Montgomery would help to close this gap.[16]

The 7–8 July raid had benefits disproportional to its size. Prime Minister Curtin praised it in the Australian Parliament as marking the fact that the elements of the AIF still in the Middle East had gone into action, news that was welcomed by units throughout the Eighth Army. The New Zealanders sent warm congratulations on the Australians' successful return to action; the commander of the Armoured Corps signalled, 'Well done, a great start for the Australians and a most useful raid'; and the corps commander said, 'Fine show, thank all who participated'. Rommel reacted too, sending reserves to the area and ordering troops to be more alert.[17]

10 July – battle for high ground

The 9th Division's large-scale operations at Alamein began on the night of 9–10 July and involved the 26th Brigade. Morshead later wrote proudly that as preparation 'even battalion commanders had participated in the constant night patrols which had gained much valuable information about the enemy's positions'.[18] The brigade's 2/24th and 2/48th Battalions were sent to capture key ground in XXX Corps' northern sector, the object being also to promote Auchinleck's project of destroying Rommel's army, starting with the weak Italian formations. The first objective was a ridge nearly 5 kilometres long, which provided excellent observation of the generally flat surrounding area and also shielded the coastal area from Axis surveillance from the west. This ridge had three main features. At the eastern end and about 3 kilometres from the British lines was Point 26, some 1200 metres south of the coastline. About 4 kilometres away at the ridge's other end was its highest point, Trig 33, while about halfway between these two heights, on a saddle, lay Point 23. After capturing this ridge, the Australians were to move south and take Tel el Eisa Ridge and railway station.

The two attacking battalions each had a squadron of British tanks in support, as well as Australian machine gunners, anti-tank gunners and sappers. There would also be plentiful artillery and air support for the attacks on this eminently defensible ground.

The 2/48th Battalion, a South Australian unit which had acquired a great reputation in Tobruk, was ordered to take Points 26 and 23, setting out at about 3.40am. The recently arrived commander of the 2/48th, Lieutenant Colonel Heathcote 'Tack' Hammer, chose to attack Point 26 without artillery support. This decision achieved its purpose, as the Italians holding the point were completely surprised: some, in pyjamas or undressed, had to be roused from their beds. Four hundred were captured.

Artillery did support the attack on Point 23, but here, too, the Italians were soon overrun and by 5.55am, five minutes ahead of schedule, the Australians held this objective. Sergeant Tom 'Diver' Derrick described his company advancing in 'one long extended line, Captain Shillaker performing splendidly in the centre of the two fwd Platoons'.[19] Derrick himself was credited with capturing, through 'his own personal courage and leadership', three Fiat machine-gun nests and 100 Italian soldiers.[20]

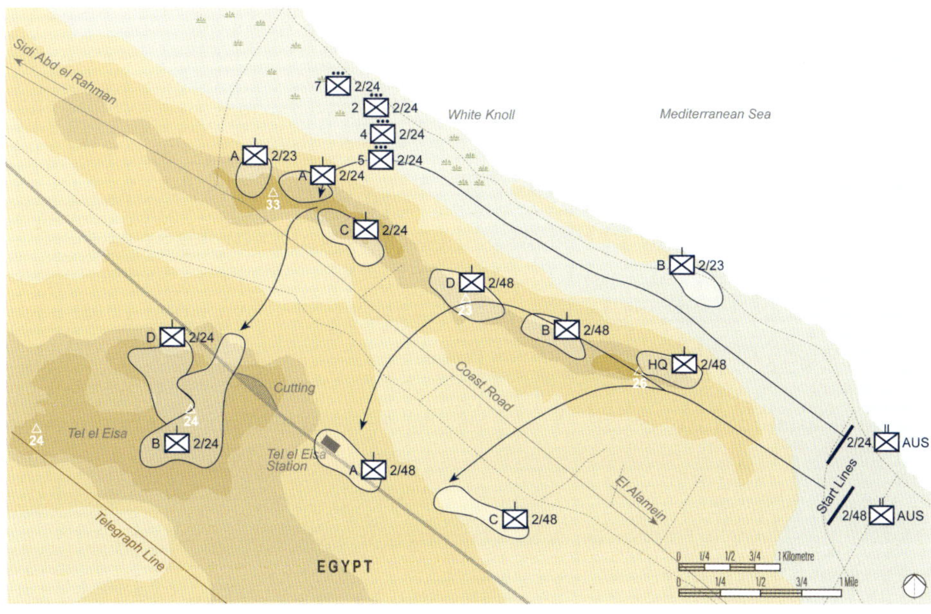

Map 7: 26th Brigade attack, 10–12 July 1942

One of 900 Italians captured on the night of 10–11 July was the Commanding Officer of the 7th Bersaglieri Regiment. (IWM E14394)

AUSTRALIANS AND ITALIANS AT ALAMEIN

Australians at Alamein were generally disdainful towards Italian troops. This attitude originated with the Italian defeats at the hands of much smaller Australian forces early in 1941, and was reinforced in many cases by personal experience in the siege of Tobruk. The first battles against the Italians at Tel el Eisa, where many were caught literally asleep, did nothing to change that contempt. Australians scorned the Italians for their supposed unwillingness to fight them face-to-face. They were said to be afraid to face the bayonet: no Australian would have been surprised by the story of the young Italian who fainted on seeing four Australians charging at him through the murk. Even if they did put up a fight, Italians often enraged their opponents by firing at advancing Australians and then trying to surrender at the last moment, when it was clear they could not halt the attack. An Australian non-commissioned officer (NCO) wrote that, at Alamein, 'on one occasion we attacked a position held by Ities and they fought like hell right up until we were 3 yds off them then they brought their hands up and called for mercy (they never got much)'. Their docility reached the point when some were permitted to drive vehicles to the Australian positions, or even their prison camps. In the last days at Alamein, an Australian infantryman declared of Italian prisoners: '... the Ities are the worst of the lot, underfed, miserable, and too bomb happy to be any good'.

The lack of respect extended to Italian organisation, as exemplified when an Australian described enemy entrenchments thus: 'These positions were *typically Italian* ... we took cover and put up with the stench and rubbish'. At the battle's end, salvage units concentrated on German equipment rather than Italian. Recalling one Italian gun with wooden wheels and dated 1907, one man tellingly concluded with a comment that captures the typical Australian mixture of contempt and pity: 'the tired looking dead Italian reclining against the wheel with the flies buzzing into his open mouth looked as if he'd been made in that year too'.

Some Italian units fought well against the Australians, notably in the 17 July fighting, but Australians then and since have been reluctant to acknowledge successful enemy forces as anything but German. As had been the case since Bardia in January 1941, the Italian artillerymen also earned Australian respect for fighting steadfastly, often until their guns were taken at bayonet point. On 17 July, for example, some fought to the death.

Italian leaders had, since first meeting the Australians, depicted them as barbarous and brutal. Various Italian accounts described Australian soldiers as drunk when in action. An Italian artillery captain only a few hundred metres from fighting involving Australians wrote in his diary at the height of the October battle

at Alamein: 'Hand-to-hand fighting is going on. The Australians, *roaring drunk on whisky*, are like madmen ... The wounded, both German and Italian, have horrifying tales to tell'. An Australian artilleryman dismissed such accusations, made by German propagandists too, saying: 'Under Ali Baba's battle-restrictions we get one bottle of beer per man per three days!' Italian accounts generally depicted Australians as terrifying, relentless and careless of life.[21]

Italians captured in the Australian advance of 17 July. Italian troops generally fought effectively on that day.
(PHOTOGRAPHER: EDWARD ERNEST SMITH, AWM 024535)

The 2/24th simultaneously launched its assault on Trig 33. Its route lay not across the ridge, but via sand dunes near the coast, from which it was to swing south and seize that high point. Trucks and tanks became bogged down on the way to the start-line when they fell through the thin crust on top of a salt marsh but eventually, through what the brigade report called 'superhuman efforts', the advance began on a one-company front.[22] The 2/24th also surprised some pyjama-clad men, but enemy resistance gradually stiffened. A lone platoon sent forward an hour before the rest of the battalion to clear the dunes met severe opposition. Lance Corporal Jack Holman and his section captured four machine guns and their crews. The battalion's Bren (or Universal) Carriers were armed with an unorthodox assortment of anti-tank guns, including guns 'scrounged' from light tanks, and machine guns, including Vickers and Besas – 'anything but Bren Guns', says one account. The drivers of these vehicles, which some Germans mistook for tanks, used their mobility superbly and captured two troops of anti-tank guns with a daring frontal assault.[23]

The opposition which the 2/24th defeated in the sand dunes included a prize of enormous value. A highly efficient German intelligence unit, Intercept and Intelligence Company 621, had set up among the dunes, mistakenly imagining that they were safe behind an entire Italian division. In their encounter with the 2/24th, they tried to fight it out, apparently because their commander, Captain Seebohm, had been criticised previously

View looking northeast from Trig 33 in 1997. At far right is Point 26, now the site of a German war cemetery. The 2/24th advanced along the coast here on the night of 10 July. (AUTHOR'S COLLECTION)

for not using his unit in action. Now he was mortally wounded; some sixty-nine other men captured; invaluable vehicles, equipment and documents destroyed or confiscated; and the unit's effectiveness shattered. In this success alone, the 2/24th had unknowingly made a massive contribution to victory. The main body of the 2/24th now followed the original plan and swung left towards Trig 33, which they captured with ease by 7.45am.

Half an hour earlier, the 2/48th had begun the attack towards its next objective, the Tel el Eisa station area. Even before it began advancing from Point 26 it came under heavy artillery fire, which intensified as it moved closer. Following orders to silence the guns, Sergeant 'Tex' Weston led his platoon in a direct advance across open ground, supported only by 3-inch mortar fire. When close enough, this small group charged, bayonets fixed. The enemy guns caused casualties, but their crews were captured, largely because of the inspirational courage of the Thompson submachine-gun wielding Weston. Corporal Jim 'Spud' Hinson and his section braved point-blank fire to charge and take two guns and their detachments at bayonet point. Through bold, aggressive action, this one platoon captured 106 men, mostly Germans, and at least four guns. The 2/48th advance continued until it had occupied Tel el Eisa station and ground to its east. The battalion came under heavy shelling but could only dig in a few centimetres in the hard ground. British tanks and Australian machine gunners and anti-tank men came up to join them.

THE CAPTURE OF COMPANY 621

In the words of one British authority, the Australians' capture of Intercept and Intelligence Company 621 (Nachrichten Fernaufklaerung Kompanie 621) on 10 July 1942 was 'quite the most important intelligence coup of the entire North African campaign'. The company had since April 1941 been intercepting British radio traffic and, through its members' growing expertise in translating English jargon and identifying call signs, provided Rommel invaluable information on the locations and intentions of British formations. This information was radioed directly to Rommel from the Company's positions near the front. Three rifle platoons of the 2/24th Battalion and the battalion Carrier Platoon overcame strong resistance in areas identified as a German 'Rest Camp' and the 'White Knoll'. To one of the Australians the Germans all seemed to be bronzed giants, wearing diminutive shorts. A German officer from 621 Company, Lieutenant Wischmann, was with Rommel when news came that the unit was out of contact. Rommel asked Wischmann to show him on the map where the unit was located. Furious, Rommel said: 'Then they are done for'.[24]

An armoured radio car from Nachrichten Fernaufklaerung Kompanie 621.
(WORLDWARPHOTOS.INFO/GALLERY/GERMANY/ARMORED_VEHICLES/SDKFZ_221_222_223/SDKFZ-260-NFAK-621-DAK)

As 10 July drew on, it became increasingly obvious that Rommel was determined to recapture the crucial ground just lost to the Australians. There were five or six aerial attacks on the Point 26 – Trig 33 ridge, and the Australians repulsed probing infantry and tank attacks on Trig 33 from the west. The first really threatening attack came at 2.30pm, when ten tanks advanced towards the forward 2/48th companies south of the Trig 33 ridge. The tanks emerged through the artillery fire and reached the foremost Australians near the station. Unprotected by anti-tank mines, the men had to 'lie doggo' while the tanks ran over their slit trenches. The Australians fought back, though, using anti-tank 'sticky' grenades. Sergeant Bob Haynes jumped from his trench and placed a sticky grenade on a tank, which caught fire in the explosion. Its crew were shot down as they emerged. Haynes himself fell from a gunshot wound to the left chest, but survived to fight again. Opposition from Haynes and other infantrymen as well as the anti-tank guns and field guns forced the tanks to withdraw.

In the late afternoon, up to thirty tanks advanced on Trig 33. About eighteen drove across the saltmarsh from the west and north-west, but most became bogged. Australian anti-tank guns picked off many of these tanks. Gunner James McMahon did outstanding work as No. 1 on his gun, probably a 2-pounder, which he towed forward of the other guns. Three other members of the crew were wounded, as was he in the leg and hand, but he fought on, destroying two enemy tanks. Australian Vickers medium machine guns and British artillery drove off the infantry who continued to advance on Trig 33 after the tanks retreated.

That afternoon, intense enemy artillery fire fell on the two forward 2/48th companies near Tel el Eisa station. It foreshadowed another tank and infantry attack on the two forward

companies. With no anti-tank mines protecting the Australians, tanks drove among them at will. Company commander Captain Don Bryant remained in communication with battalion headquarters, calling in artillery fire and giving a running commentary. When asked about the situation at one stage he replied coolly, 'She's sweet', a comment that entered battalion folklore. He had led the company on to Point 26, and now inspired them to hold on against the tanks.

(Left to right)
Australian and South African anti-tank guns destroyed this Italian M13 tank as it made a lone sortie towards Trig 33 on 10 July. (IMAGE COURTESY OF TED BOYD)

Two craters, possibly former gun emplacements, near Tel el Eisa station, photographed in 1997. (AUTHOR'S COLLECTION)

Tel el Eisa station, site of heavy fighting in July 1942. On the right is the remnant of a 'Volkswagen' [Kubelwagen], the leading vehicle in a convoy of fifteen German vehicles destroyed while approaching the station on the night of 15 July. (PHOTOGRAPHER: FRANK HURLEY, AWM 013347)

GERMANS AND AUSTRALIANS

9th Division men rated the Germans their best adversary of the war. At Alamein many paid tribute to German martial skill. In July, a 2/48th Battalion soldier explained one of his unit's rare failures by saying that 'leaders' had made the usual mistake of underestimating that 'good fighter the hun'. At the height of the October battle, a private reported 'the noise and concussion terrific, if Jerry is not bomb happy he is not human ... she sure is a willing war, but Jerry is putting up a great fight'. As the battle neared its conclusion, Private John Butler wrote: 'There are strong pockets of resistance and one must salute these brave Germans who hold out'.

Butler never forgot that the Germans were the Australians' enemies, and commented bitterly on German propaganda that the 9th Division men were the world's second-best fighters: 'I suppose if we fired on ambulances, mowed down stretcher bearers, used the white flag illegally, used the anti-tank rifle on men and a lot of other despicable tricks, we would be the world's best'. Germans were also accused of booby trapping the dead of both sides and of pretending to surrender and then firing on their would-be captors. Moreover, Australians despised the Nazi political cause.

Australians felt themselves superior fighters to the Germans, especially concerning desert warfare staples: patrolling and night-fighting. They also had a psychological advantage in hand-to-hand combat, particularly with the bayonet. References to Hinson, Gurney, Gratwick and numerous others in this book are evidence of that. German troops at all levels respected Australian fighting qualities. In July, soon after the 9th Division's return to the desert, an Australian infantryman met a German prisoner who refused to accept that his captors were Australians: he believed that the Australians had gone home, but that English troops were continuing to 'dress up as Australians to frighten us'.

German prisoners could be truculent, and some received punches and bayonet prods. Normally, though, they were treated respectfully, not least because Australians believed that they themselves would be treated humanely if captured by Germans. The same applied to the war dead. An Australian captain killed at Ruin Ridge was buried by the Germans, who inscribed on a rough cross: 'A gallant Australian officer'. After the October battle, Australian cavalrymen tasked with reburying Australians buried by the Germans were impressed that on the chest of each corpse, the Germans had placed the personal belongings with which he had died. Germans also helped Australian wounded, notably at the Blockhouse in October. The Geneva Convention was rarely dishonoured in the desert war, and on occasions both sides withheld fire to allow wounded to be assisted.

Smiles all around as a young German prisoner poses with his Australian captors at El Alamein in July 1942.
(IWM AYY 238/2, STILL IMAGE AT 03:54)

Australians and Germans seldom met, but when they did, an air of mutual respect often prevailed. An Australian and his mates sat down and shared their food with some German prisoners during the October battle. 'Though we could not converse', he wrote later, 'all had a happy time and I remember considering how damned silly it was to be fighting coves just like ourselves'. Of course, in many ways Germans were not 'just like' Australians, but they did share many attributes, and the German was the enemy with whom Australians felt the greatest affinity.[25]

As the German tanks drove across the trenches, calling on the Australians to surrender, Corporal Jim Hinson again demonstrated inspiring leadership. Leaping from cover, this fine athlete raced to a Panzer and, after placing a sticky bomb, slid into a nearby trench and heard it explode. When an anti-tank shell hit another tank and set it alight, Hinson again left his cover despite heavy shelling, this time chasing down the German crew and capturing them.

Unmoved by the shelling and the German tanks, Sergeant Weston moved among his sections, instructing and encouraging them. Like Hinson, he captured the escaping crew of a destroyed tank. For his efforts on 10 July, Weston added a Military Medal to the Distinguished Conduct Medal (DCM) he had earned at Tobruk. He had lost the weapon that had helped him gain the earlier decoration: a tank ran over the Tommy gun on which 'Tex' had notched a record of each of his kills. Weston, a tall, muscular 30-year-old tractor driver, would be badly wounded at Alamein, but still managed to carry a wounded comrade more than a kilometre to a dressing station. Hinson would get to wear his own DCM ribbon but be killed at El Alamein in October.

(Left to right)
Lieutenant Colonel 'Tack' Hammer (centre) and Sergeant 'Tex' Weston (right) congratulate Corporal 'Spud' Hinson on his immediate award of the Distinguished Conduct Medal. (AWM 024750)

Australian infantrymen at Tel el Eisa. These 2/48th men are posing in front of a captured 'Iti truck' towing a Breda 20mm anti-aircraft gun. (IMAGE COURTESY OF PAUL OATEN AND JAMES HOLNESS)

German infantry advancing at Alamein. One Australian said of such an attack: 'The Germans came forward in small groups, rifles slung, looking for all the world like spectators drifting away from a minor football game'.[26] (AWM 042394)

Tanks attacked a platoon of Australian machine gunners near the station, deliberately trying to crush them by making sudden turns and dropping the tracks into the trenches. One tank track scraped Sergeant John Cockram's back, crushed his water bottle and mess tin and bent his rifle barrel. It later emerged that the track had broken three of his vertebrae, but now Cockram sought revenge. He chased the tank and stuck an anti-tank grenade on it, only to realise, when there was no explosion, that he had not pulled the pin. When the platoon commander was mortally wounded, Cockram took over.

Another machine gunner, Sergeant Gus Longhurst, ignored the bullets from German tank machine guns and the calls for surrender and, jumping from his trench, chased a tank 50 metres. He was a fine rugby player but could not reach it. Nevertheless, as the tanks headed towards the station, anti-tank guns destroyed several and he brought his Vickers machine gun to bear on one escaping crew. They took cover in a trench but, in a remarkable feat of strength, Longhurst lifted the 43kg weight of the entire gun and tripod and, with the help of Private Bill Selmes, fired about 150 rounds at them. The crew surrendered. Longhurst's bravery inspired those around him, but the devout Christian also impressed them when, changing from avenger to Samaritan, he used his field dressing to treat the most seriously wounded German.

At about 7.30pm, the Germans mounted a really determined tank and infantry attack. They forced one of the 2/48th companies back, but a resolute counterattack by one of the battalion's other companies, shouting, 'Come on, Australianos!', pushed them back to their start-line. Sergeant Tom 'Diver' Derrick damaged two German tanks with sticky grenades here. In his diary, Derrick said his company 'had all performed splendidly', including the 70 per cent who had previously seen little or no action. He ascribed their success mainly 'to the old brigade (originals) who were just as good and calm as Tobruk days'.[27]

The Australian official historian, Barton Maughan, described 10 July as a turning point in the desert war, and indeed in the entire war in the West. He said this on four grounds. One was that the attack was a first successful push west against Axis forces at Alamein, who were now further east than ever before in North Africa. Another was that the Australian attack disrupted Rommel's plan for an attack of his own, further south. A third was that the attack took the most commanding feature in the coastal sector of the front; and the fourth was the overrunning of the key German intelligence unit, Company 621.[28] Maughan's claim was an exaggeration, but 10 July was a day of great achievement for the 9th Division, including not only the infantry but also the artillerymen and machine gunners, many of whom were fighting their first battle. Australians had captured important ground and a key intelligence unit, inflicted more than 1000 casualties and destroyed up to twenty-two tanks, all at a cost of fewer than 100 men. Unfortunately, that casualty list would swell as 'First Alamein' continued.

British historian Niall Barr comments that Auchinleck's use of the Australians in this area committed the 9th Division, one of the Eighth Army's most potent infantry formations, to operations in a relatively small area of the Alamein front for the foreseeable future.[29] Then again, the Australians' role as an immovable object and later a formidable spearhead on the 'right of the line' would ultimately prove hugely beneficial, even decisive, for the Eighth Army.

TEL EL EISA – THE HILL OF JESUS

Australian soldiers of the 26th Brigade used the term 'Tel el Eisa' or 'The Hill of Jesus' to describe the site of the whole of the July fighting, even though Tel el Eisa was only one of several important ridges over which Australians fought in that month. It was often confused with the Trig 33 – Point 26 Ridge, which lies closer to the coast and is much more photogenic. Indeed, Tel el Eisa barely deserved the name 'hill', for unless one was on it, one could scarcely see it. However, Tel el Eisa was the site of some of the fiercest fighting in that month, because it afforded an excellent view over the surrounding terrain and was thus tactically significant. The Tel el Eisa station was easily identifiable, as was the railway cutting which ran through part of the ridge. The ridge was sometimes called Point 24, at other times the Double 24 feature, because it contained two points 24 metres in height. More than 500 Australian casualties were sustained in fighting for this low ridge.[30]

This photograph, from the collection of a 2/48th Battalion soldier, is captioned 'scene after break through on Hill of Jesus'. The area is dotted with graves, apparently German. (SLSA PRG1737/2/47)

CHAPTER 3

TEL EL EISA RIDGE TO RUIN RIDGE

11–28 JULY 1942

FOR THE REMAINDER OF JULY, Auchinleck and Rommel would each seek to make a conclusive penetration of the other's line and force him to retreat. At the same time, each would seek to regain quickly any lost ground and prevent the other from breaking through. Auchinleck, as we have seen, also intended to destroy enemy formations.

By 6.30am on 11 July, the 2/24th Battalion, supported by anti-tank gunners and machine gunners, had captured East Point 24 on Tel el Eisa Ridge, taking 260 prisoners on the way. Both sides had artillery observation over this ridge, and Australian casualties mounted during the day. Three Australian and two Commonwealth artillery regiments drove off several German infantry and tank attacks. The 2/8th Australian Field Regiment, fighting its first battle, gave crucial support, largely because of its forward observation officers (FOO) near East Point 24 and the railway cutting. When one FOO, Captain John Elder, was wounded, his assistant, Gunner Alan Kinghorn, took over. Kinghorn had no experience shooting with live ammunition but shot his troop and his battery for four hours, until relieved by Lieutenant Tom Smith. Thirty minutes later, shrapnel knocked Smith unconscious, and Kinghorn again took charge, this time for three more hours.

The railway cutting at Tel el Eisa, scene of heavy fighting in July 1942. Photographed from south of the railway line in 1997. (AUTHOR'S COLLECTION)

All day the 36-year-old Tasmanian played a vital part in holding off enemy tank and infantry attacks on the 2/24th.

The 2/8th Field Regiment's observation post party supporting the 2/48th at Tel el Eisa station also suffered. After their officer, Lieutenant John Steer, dragged a phone and cable to the railway cutting to support the 2/48th, shellfire inflicted a wound so serious that his leg was later amputated. His assistant, Lance Bombardier Charles Dennis, took over. This was only his second day in action, but despite constant shelling and machine-gun fire, Dennis called in fire from his troop that was vital to the infantry.

Late in the day, a company of the 2/24th went from Trig 33 to reinforce its single company on Point 24. A company of the 2/23rd took its place on the forward slopes of Trig 33. The next day, 12 July, this company faced the full brunt of German artillery, followed by up to 2,000 infantrymen of the 21st Panzer Division. A shell burst mortally wounded the company commander, Captain George Anderson. The company Bren gunners forced enemy infantry to ground but suffered casualties and were joined by three fresh Bren gunners from the 2/24th.

The Germans launched a major infantry and tank attack on the Trig 33 ridge in the late afternoon. It lasted more than two hours and was repelled, with the enemy leaving behind some 600 dead. Australian artillery, which fired about 9000 rounds, received much of the credit, but a platoon of machine gunners from the 2/2nd Machine Gun Battalion was also critical to the defence of Trig 33. Corporal Vic Knight and his section of two Vickers guns had already won attention on 10 July when they carried their guns across Trig 33 under fire, set them up in the open and provided invaluable support against the enemy infantry. Now, while covering the southern slopes of the ridge, news came that enemy forces were advancing on the right. Knight moved his section over the ridge, through intense enemy artillery, mortar and machine-gun fire. On arrival, they had no time to dig in, but set up their guns (initially two, later three) in the open and fired bursts of 100–150 rounds at the enemy infantry debussing from their half-tracks. Closely packed and advancing in waves, the Germans presented a fine target, though they had support from 'a veritable hail of fire' from mortars, artillery, tank guns and small arms. Whenever the enemy fire got too close, Knight moved the guns backwards or forwards on the ridge. They moved seven times in the course of the day. Knight displayed an inspiring nonchalance as he stood and directed the deadly fire of his machine gunners, some of it hitting targets as distant as 4500 metres. Firing at that range required the guns to be shooting almost vertically. The machine gunners used oil, water, soup and urine to keep the guns going (partly in the cooling jacket, mainly poured into the working parts) over several hours of firing.[31] At nightfall, Knight and the gun crews – apart from two wounded men, one of whom Knight had carried out – could finally dig in. The four guns of his platoon had fired nearly 80,000 rounds that day.[32]

VICKERS MEDIUM MACHINE GUN

The water-cooled Vickers medium machine gun was famously reliable, but was also very heavy and cumbersome to move, making it best suited to defensive work. It played a prominent role throughout Australian operations at Alamein. The 2/2nd Machine Gun Battalion had its initiation to battle in July 1942, when on the first day of fighting two guns were vital in defending the newly won Trig 33. The following day, 11 July, four of its guns fired nearly 80,000 rounds, hitting targets more than 4 kilometres away. Too often in the July fighting though, after capturing ground Australian infantry lacked the firepower to hold it against the inevitable German counterattacks. As a result, in August a medium machine-gun platoon comprising four Vickers was added to each infantry battalion.[33] This firepower proved valuable in the October battle, when detachments of the 2/2nd Machine Gun Battalion continued to do sterling work, alongside the infantry battalion guns, at crucial places such as Trig 29 and the Saucer.

CALIBRE
0.303in (7.7mm)

WEIGHT
Gun, without water — 15kg
Gun, with water — 18.14kg

TRIPOD
22.67kg

BARREL
72.4cm long

RATE OF FIRE
450–550rpm (cyclic)

FEED DEVICE
250-round fabric belt

SYSTEM OF OPERATION
Recoil

Two members of the 2/2nd Machine Gun Battalion man a Vickers machine gun at Tel el Eisa in July 1942. These men fired virtually without pause for two vital days on Trig 33. Hot cartridge cases burned their arms and they had to add urine to the gun's water-jacket to cool it. (AWM 041953)

(Top to bottom)

Bombardier Archie Muffett commanded one of two 2/3rd Anti-Tank Regiment's 2-pounders that destroyed seven German Panzer III tanks, including this one, near Tel el Eisa station on 14 July.

(IMAGE COURTESY OF TED BOYD AND DAVID PEARSON)

This is probably one of three 'guns mounted on porteaux' that Tom Derrick saw attacking the 2/48th on the night of 15 July. He destroyed one of these vehicles – an Sd.Kfz. 10/4 self-propelled AA gun – with a sticky bomb.

(IMAGE COURTESY OF PAUL OATEN AND JAMES HOLNESS)

Australian anti-tank guns of the 2/3rd Anti-Tank Regiment were also important on these days. Gunners had to show cold-blooded courage in waiting for enemy tanks to come within range. Those tanks with 75mm and 50mm guns outranged the Australians' 2-pounders (40mm) and 6-pounders (57mm). Moreover, the tanks' machine guns could inflict havoc among the gunners, whose only protection came from gun shields and whatever concealment and cover they could find for their guns in the desert – digging in was vital. On 13 July, when German tanks and infantry approached Tel el Eisa from the south-west, Bombardier Richard Cotterill and his 6-pounder anti-tank gun crew destroyed four enemy tanks.

The Australians were not doing all the fighting on the Eighth Army front. A major Axis attack on the South African division south of the Alamein Box (an area prepared for a deliberate defence) on 13 July could, if successful, have enabled Rommel to attack the Australian positions from behind. The South African and Australian divisional artillery provided mutual support wherever possible in the July fighting, and the 2/7th and 2/12th Australian Field Regiments (firing from east of El Alamein) helped to drive off this attack.[34] Lance Bombardier Bill Cutler, whose 2/12th Field Regiment Observation Post was shelled three times that day, spoke truly of the period since 10 July: 'The initial onslaught and the continuing action has called for superhuman efforts from the men on the guns'.[35]

According to Rommel's official report on 13 July, the afternoon's attacks at Tel el Eisa came to a standstill in front of 'concrete fortifications, which were defended stubbornly by the 9th Australian Division'.[36] There was no concrete. Rommel launched powerful tank and infantry attacks against the Tel el Eisa area on 14 July. During a tank attack that evening, three of Cotterill's detachment (prominent the previous day) were killed or wounded, but destroyed three more Panzers before the remaining gunner was killed and their gun put out of action. Though wounded himself, Cotterill attached himself to the nearest infantry unit and acted as a runner to the company commander till the attack was driven off. Nevertheless, by day's end the hard-pressed Australians had abandoned Point 24 and withdrawn to Trig 33. Again, the anti-tank gunners did exceptional work, two guns knocking out seven Panzers before the Germans retreated from the station.

An Australian bombardier who witnessed the German tank attack from an observation post on Point 26 found the day 'unforgettable'. He described a 'Wagnerian' scene, featuring 25-pounder guns firing from all around the coastal sector; enemy tanks; smoke and dust; and aircraft filling the skies, fighting each other and dropping bombs that drowned out all the other frightening noises. Feeling exhilarated but 'desperately frightened', he could scarcely believe the nonchalance of the 2/48th infantrymen he could see. With the enemy less than a kilometre away, officers strolled around posts and two men sat on the edge of a trench, 'drinking beer as though they were at a drive-in theatre'.[37]

In the early hours of 15 July, a German column comprising a tank and three vehicles mounting guns approached the 2/48th positions near Tel el Eisa station. Amid a confusing firefight, Tom Derrick ventured out and placed a sticky grenade on the rearmost vehicle, which exploded with a blast so powerful that it knocked 'Diver' over.

THE 2-POUNDER GUN

Originally designed for the Cruiser Mk. I tank, the 2-pounder was the standard British and Australian infantry anti-tank gun at the outbreak of war. By July 1942 it was obsolete. Nevertheless, at Alamein this 40mm gun continued to be an important Australian weapon in that month's fighting and beyond, for it armed the anti-tank platoons of the infantry battalions, and its 6-pounder replacement was only just being issued to the 2/3rd Anti-Tank Regiment that month. The 2-pounder was inadequate against the frontal armour of the Panzer III and IV tanks, and detachments had to wait patiently and courageously for enemy tanks to come within 500 metres before opening fire. The weapon was very heavy, thanks mainly to its carriage, which allowed 360° traverse, and also had a relatively high silhouette – a problem in flat terrain, where opening fire tended to raise a dust cloud. Its detachments suffered heavy casualties in July, but also inflicted casualties on German and Italian vehicles. On 14 July, for example, two of the 2/3rd Anti-Tank Regiment's 2-pounders destroyed seven German Panzer III tanks near Tel el Eisa station, for the loss of one gun.

CALIBRE
40mm

WEIGHT
814kg

PROJECTILE
2 pounds (0.9kg) AP

EFFECTIVE RANGE
914m

CREW
4

MUZZLE VELOCITY
792m/sec

RATE OF FIRE
22rpm

Australian gunners of the 2/3rd Anti-Tank Regiment man a 2-pounder gun at Tobruk in 1941.
(PHOTOGRAPHER: THOMAS FISHER, AWM 020760)

The enemy directed a huge volume of shelling, including airburst, mortar and machine-gun fire on the forward slopes of Trig 33 that morning, and at one stage a section of thirteen Australian machine gunners were almost the only Australians who had not fallen back. Four were killed, three wounded and three later evacuated with shock. After six German tanks approached within 400 metres and opened fire with machine guns, the Australian machine gunners eventually withdrew. Returning meant almost certain death, but Lance Corporal Eric Brandrick went back through this fire to rescue a seriously wounded man and then made a second trip to rescue another. The unaccompanied German tanks later retreated, allowing the Australians to reoccupy the forward slopes.

On 16 July, two companies of the 2/23rd Battalion were sent, with five British tanks in support, to recapture East and West Points 24 of Tel el Eisa Ridge. When the foremost platoon was pinned down by close-range fire from an enemy post at the railway cutting, Lance Corporal John Bell led the reserve section to a flank. He leapt over an embankment into the cutting and, while his comrades threw grenades, used his Tommy gun to inflict heavy casualties. The platoon captured at least thirty Germans. The Australian company suffered casualties from mortar fire as it crossed the cutting, but by 6.30am it had taken East Point 24.

Captain Keith Neuendorf now led the second company towards West Point 24. Intense enemy fire was inflicting casualties, but Neuendorf was coolly courageous as he directed return fire. While trying to communicate with the tank commander, his hand was shot away. Undaunted, he pulled out one of his bootlaces, and with help from his runner tied it as a tourniquet. In his good hand he took up an Italian pistol. He continued to show inspiring

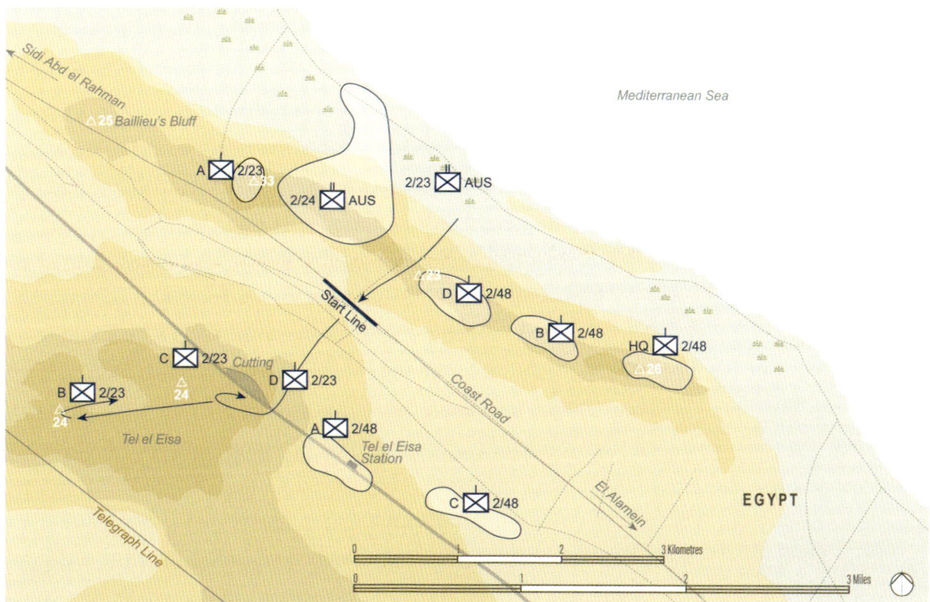

Map 8: 2/23rd Battalion attack on Tel el Eisa, 16 July 1942

leadership – one moment calling his men on, the next ordering them to ground, while he remained standing. Amidst the shells and bullets, he was wounded a second time, but continued regardless, directing the tanks against nests of resistance. Eventually, while he was walking back after helping a wounded man, a salvo of shells killed him. His body was found days later, pistol still in hand.

By the time Neuendorf was killed, the Australians had occupied West Point 24. They were deluged by close-range shelling and machine-gun fire while digging in. They also took so many prisoners they could barely cope: 601, forty-one of them Germans. Despite this success, the 2/23rd commander, Lieutenant Colonel Bernard Evans, decided that the Australians' newly won ground was untenable, and pulled them back to salt flats near the coast. Ninety of the 200 Australian participants in the attack were killed or wounded. Thus ended the 26th Brigade's operations, for a time. The brigade had captured vital high ground west of Alamein and near the coast, inflicting about 2,000 casualties and taking 3,708 prisoners.

Fighting for new ridges

The next day, 17 July, saw the 24th Brigade enter the fighting for the first time since the 7–8 July raid. Rommel's forces were engaged in fierce fighting around Ruweisat Ridge, where on 15 July they had inflicted 1400 casualties on the New Zealanders. The 24th Brigade's task was to prevent even more casualties in the centre by maintaining pressure on Rommel further north. Trig 22 on Makh Khad Ridge would offer useful observation, as would Miteiriya Ridge (Ruin Ridge) further south.

Commonwealth tanks and artillery provided support to this demanding and complex night operation. One company of the 2/32nd overshot its objective by 1400 metres. In confused and heavy fighting, the battalion captured, lost and recaptured Trig 22.

Vital to their consolidation of this position was a squadron of the 9th Division Cavalry Regiment, operating seven Crusader tanks and fifteen Bren carriers. This force commanded by Captain Henry Fyffe was, according to his MC citation, fighting the 'first Tank action ever fought by an Australian Unit' (though Australian light tanks had fought in Libya and Syria), and much depended on him. It also depended on his tank crews, like Trooper Bill Masterson, a gunner in a Crusader tank. During the advance, Masterson's tank suddenly came upon a well-concealed enemy anti-tank gun just 30 metres away. Masterson opened fire with his Besa machine gun, which eliminated two gunners, but then the Besa jammed. He could not clear it, and as the remaining gunners were bringing their gun to bear on the tank, he fired the 2-pounder main armament. This scored a direct hit on the anti-tank gun, knocking it out. This was one of several anti-tank and machine-gun posts that Fyffe's squadron eliminated. Under intense shelling, Fyffe confidently directed the disposition of his vehicles, often on foot. When the unit suffered tank casualties, he personally organised the evacuation of the wounded.

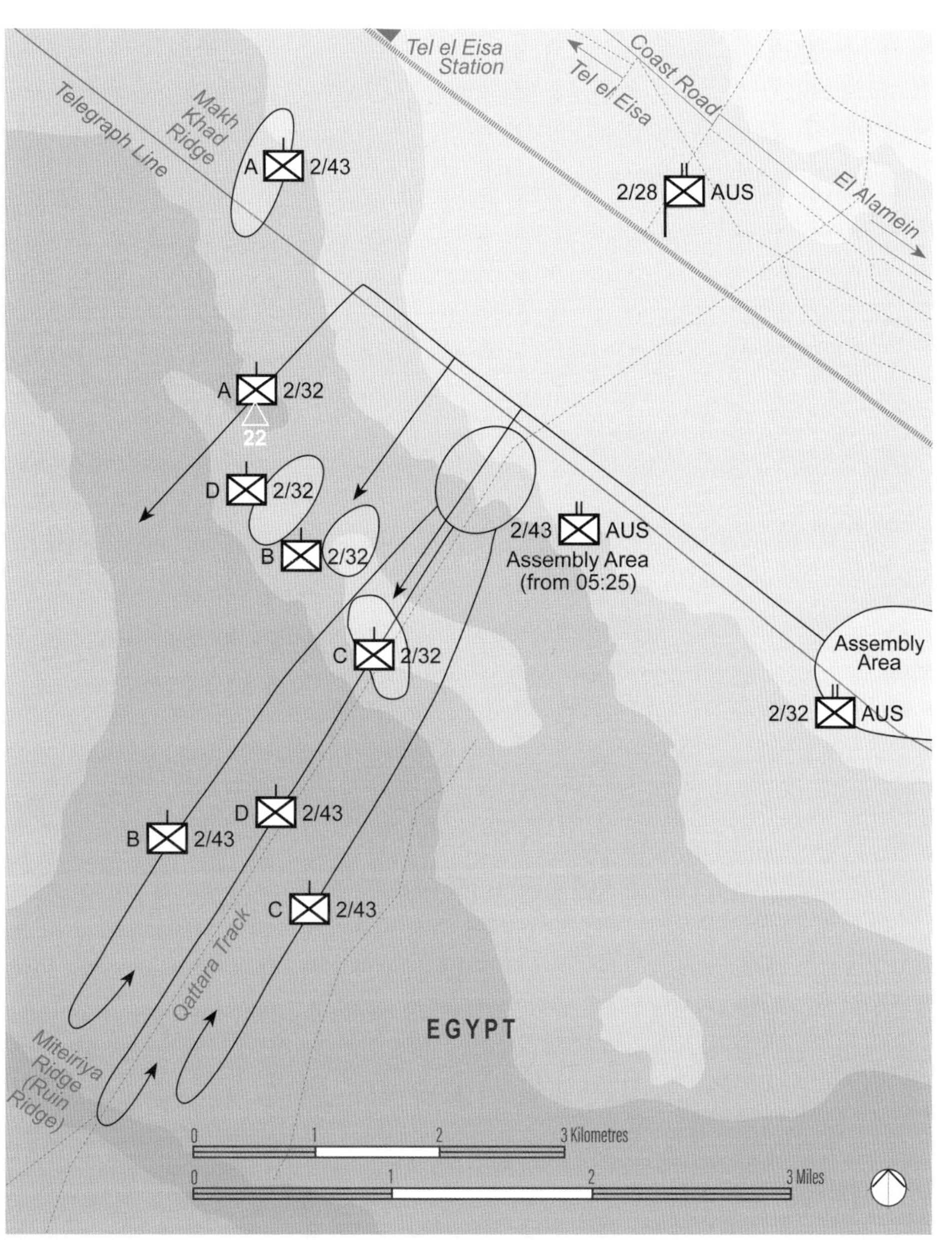

Map 9: The 24th Brigade attacks, 16–17 July 1942

The 2/43rd passed through the 2/32nd on Trig 22 at about 6am, tasked with marching the further 5 kilometres towards Ruin Ridge. At the meeting with the commander, Brigadier Arthur Godfrey, at which the 2/43rd was given this demanding objective, the battalion commander, Lieutenant Colonel Bill Wain, had not questioned his task, but before leaving he reportedly told Don Jackson, the brigade major, 'Don [this with a characteristic stutter], we'll all be killed!'[38] It was daylight and even before passing through the 2/32nd the battalion came under extremely heavy artillery fire, including airburst shells from the dreaded '88' guns.

One of the 2/43rd platoon commanders, Eric Grant, later recalled that as the advance continued, 'I could see the results of our intensive training; the discipline was marvellous, and in the midst of the shelling the formations held as though on a training exercise'.[39] Another platoon commander in the same advance, Gordon Combe, told his wife, 'The troops moved on relentlessly, digging cowering Italians out of their holes and sending them back [as] prisoners. It was nothing short of thrilling to witness the magnificent courage of

Trig 22 on Makh Khad Ridge. Mr Raouf Elmalky, curator of the German War Cemetery, is standing next to the Trig marker and pointing out the ground to Dr Peter Stanley in 1997. The terrain in this area was very rocky.
(AUTHOR'S COLLECTION)

our men'.[40] Within minutes, Combe would be seriously wounded in the face. Captain John Gordon and his company on the left met stiff resistance from the Italians confronting them. In the section on the far left of the advance, all but one man, Private Hollister Dean, were hit. Dean fought back with his Bren, wiping out an enemy machine-gun post and keeping the flank secure. John Gordon, aged just 23, led his company on to the objective, taking 400 prisoners en route. He then personally led them in attacking enemy artillery batteries that were firing at the battalion at close range. His men took another 150 prisoners and captured the gun positions, but soon enemy tanks and infantry were menacing the whole battalion. Lacking anti-tank guns to fight back and low on ammunition, the battalion had to withdraw to Makh Khad Ridge.

The courage shown by the 2/43rd men was magnificent, but their leaders' judgement in sending them in a daylight attack in full view of the enemy was questionable. Little wonder that one lieutenant called it 'a bitch of a show' in his diary and asked a series of questions: why the lack of fighter air support, why tanks were in amongst the infantry drawing fire, and why the objective was so distant. 'Why a hell of a lot of things', he concluded, before adding a common soldier's lament: 'what's the use! One will never know'.[41]

On Makh Khad Ridge, the pressure on the 2/32nd Battalion then intensified. At 10am tanks and armoured cars attacked the Australians. Among the anti-tank guns that forced the attackers back was an unusual one manned by an extraordinary soldier. Corporal 'Curly' Leeson of the 2/32nd had developed a reputation in Tobruk as a fearless patroller. The 23-year-old electrician's labourer from Queensland had got an abandoned 20mm Breda anti-aircraft gun working and received permission to use it. During this counterattack he came under machine-gun, anti-tank and mortar fire, but managed to knock out two, probably three, enemy vehicles. Eventually an enemy anti-tank shell struck his gun and knocked him out of the gun pit with a face wound. Undaunted, he repaired the gun and resumed firing. He later left the pit to rescue a man he had heard was lying exposed under fire. In doing so, he was wounded more seriously, in the hip, but returned to the gun and used it against enemy aircraft. This irrepressible soldier would be killed on 31 October, at the height of the Second Battle of El Alamein, but his efforts on 17 July helped to consolidate the gains near Trig 22.

The 24th Brigade had taken more than 700 Italian prisoners and prompted Rommel to send in German tanks to prevent the loss of more ground. In the late afternoon, some of these tanks attacked again, overrunning several platoons and pushing the Australians back more than a kilometre. The situation was stabilised, partly due to the skill and courage of anti-tank gunner Lance Sergeant Dan Daley. Despite being wounded twice, Daley kept his gun working and destroyed six Panzer III tanks. He was the fourth Australian anti-tank gunner to earn a DCM between 10 and 17 July. On the night of 17 July the 2/28th regained the positions from which the other two battalions had just withdrawn. It then underwent heavy shelling, especially from 88mm airburst. The battalion suffered more casualties from airburst on that day than it had from shelling throughout its six months in Tobruk.

AUSTRALIAN ARMOUR AT ALAMEIN

The AIF infantry divisions in the Middle East included a cavalry (light armoured reconnaissance) regiment. The 9th Division Cavalry Regiment saw action in the Syrian campaign in June 1941, just two months after leaving Australia, and then accompanied the division to Alamein in July 1942. By then, its obsolete Vickers Mark VIb light tanks had been replaced with more modern Crusader Mark II and M3 Stuart light tanks. Sergeant Sutton Ferrier wrote of the Crusader he was commanding at this time: 'She is fast, heavy, got beautiful guns and has a magnificent engine with all the guts in the world'. His characterisation of the Crusader as 'the fastest and most powerful tank in the world today' was wide of the mark, but understandably he felt 'very proud of her

A Crusader tank of the 9th Division Cavalry Regiment, pictured in July 1942. (AWM 024483)

and my crew and we are very confident of doing a good job'.[42] For all the enthusiasm of Ferrier and his crew, the Crusader was no match for its main opponent in the desert, the Panzer III, in terms of firepower, armour or reliability. The Germans respected it for speed, though their anti-tank guns could knock it out with relative ease.[43]

The regiment's first action at Alamein was a raid on Sidi Abd el Rahman on 10 July, but this ambitious plan came to grief under artillery fire, aerial bombing and the threat of German tanks. The Crusaders did well on 17 July. On the eve of the October battle, the regiment had fifteen Crusaders and five Stuarts, but was held as divisional reserve throughout. It was chosen as advance guard for the 9th Division's advance to the west, and on 5 November drove past Sidi Abd el Rahman to the airstrip at El Daba. This was the furthest point west of Alamein that the 9th Division reached in the battle. However, the regiment was disappointed to be sent no further.[44]

CRUSADER MARK II

LENGTH
6m

WIDTH
2.64m

HEIGHT
2.24m

WEIGHT
19,305kg

CREW
3–5

POWER PLANT
Nuffield Liberty V12 340 hp (petrol)

ARMAMENT
QF 2 pdr Mk 1 (40mm);
1 x 7.92mm Besa machine gun

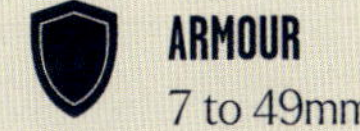

ARMOUR
7 to 49mm

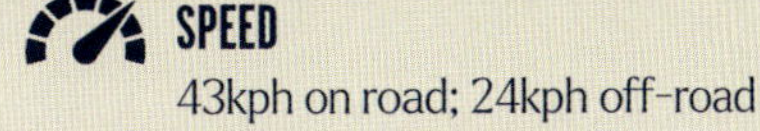

SPEED
43kph on road; 24kph off-road

22 July

The strain of the July fighting was intense. The 2/23rd Battalion suffered nearly 50 per cent casualties in the fighting for Tel el Eisa on 16 July, so it is not surprising that on 20 July, eight of its men refused to man a new post in the area of the cutting. They were subsequently court-martialled and imprisoned. The strain was about to intensify for the 2/23rd and many other Australians at Alamein.

General Auchinleck launched a series of hastily organised Eighth Army offensives on 21–22 July, and Australian troops were among those committed. These attacks, which involved XIII Corps advancing on the central bulwark of the enemy positions while XXX Corps attacked similarly strong defences in the north, were very ambitious. In a stormy two-hour conference with the XXX Corps Commander, followed by a discussion with Auchinleck, Morshead expressed his dissatisfaction with what he saw as unreasonable demands on his division, which he summarised thus: 'I did not like our plan because of wide dispersion and difficulty to support and pointed out that our immediate objectives were much more difficult than realised by Army and Corps'. In particular, he doubted that the British armour could achieve its assigned roles. Morshead was eventually persuaded to back down, but this was to have dire consequences for his men.[45]

In the north, the 26th Brigade was sent to secure the right flank by capturing the elusive Double 24 feature (Tel el Eisa), and Ring Contour 25, a position on the coast road that guarded the approach to Rommel's main command and supply base on the Alamein front. Considering the meagre forces allotted, these were impossible tasks, as Morshead had suspected. The 1st Tank Brigade and 50th Royal Tank Regiment were placed under the 9th Division's command, but their tanks were not allotted to the attacking companies. Instead, they had to be called to assist – a process that would prove disastrously slow. The 2/24th and 2/48th had to continue holding their current positions, so could only spare two companies each for their attacks. Major Charles Weir, commanding the 2/24th, looking from Trig 33 to Ring Contour 25 on the eve of the attack, reflected that this was a case of the British tactics referred to in a captured German document: it said the British would invariably try to capture high ground with as few troops as possible.[46]

Crossing their start-line before dawn, the 2/24th's companies came under machine-gun fire as soon as they advanced, but Captain Bill Mollard's company secured Ring Contour 25 with light casualties. However, as they began digging holes in the open rocky ground, heavy machine-gun fire swept their positions, while German troops seemed to be arriving from all sides. Seven of the company's eight corporals were killed or wounded. Sergeant Bill Hughes fought back. The platoon he commanded was on the objective, but pinned down by the fire of two German machine guns, 100 metres away. Hughes crawled forward, though still under fire, to a position where he could shoot back. With two rifle shots the 34-year-old disabled the No. 1 of each gun. These gunners were replaced by their No. 2s, but he dispatched both of them with two more shots. Nevertheless, the platoon had to withdraw. As it did so, Hughes heard cries for help from Corporal Bob Beecroft, some

150 metres away. Hughes went back and carried Beecroft until he was hit again and killed outright. Mollard's company now tried to hang on and maintain contact with the other company. That sub-unit was suffering too. Its commander and second-in-command were both wounded and evacuated, leaving Lieutenant Albert 'Bunny' Austin in charge. Austin, a 23-year-old schoolteacher from Murtoa, was a recent arrival and barely knew the men. However, aided by the one surviving NCO, Sergeant Gordon Annear, he held the scattered company together. When a withdrawal order came, Austin told Annear to assemble the able-bodied and accompany them back, while he stayed to gather and evacuate the wounded. The two companies suffered more than 100 casualties on 22 July; between them they were reduced to just 74 men. The 2/24th estimated that they had inflicted 250 casualties.

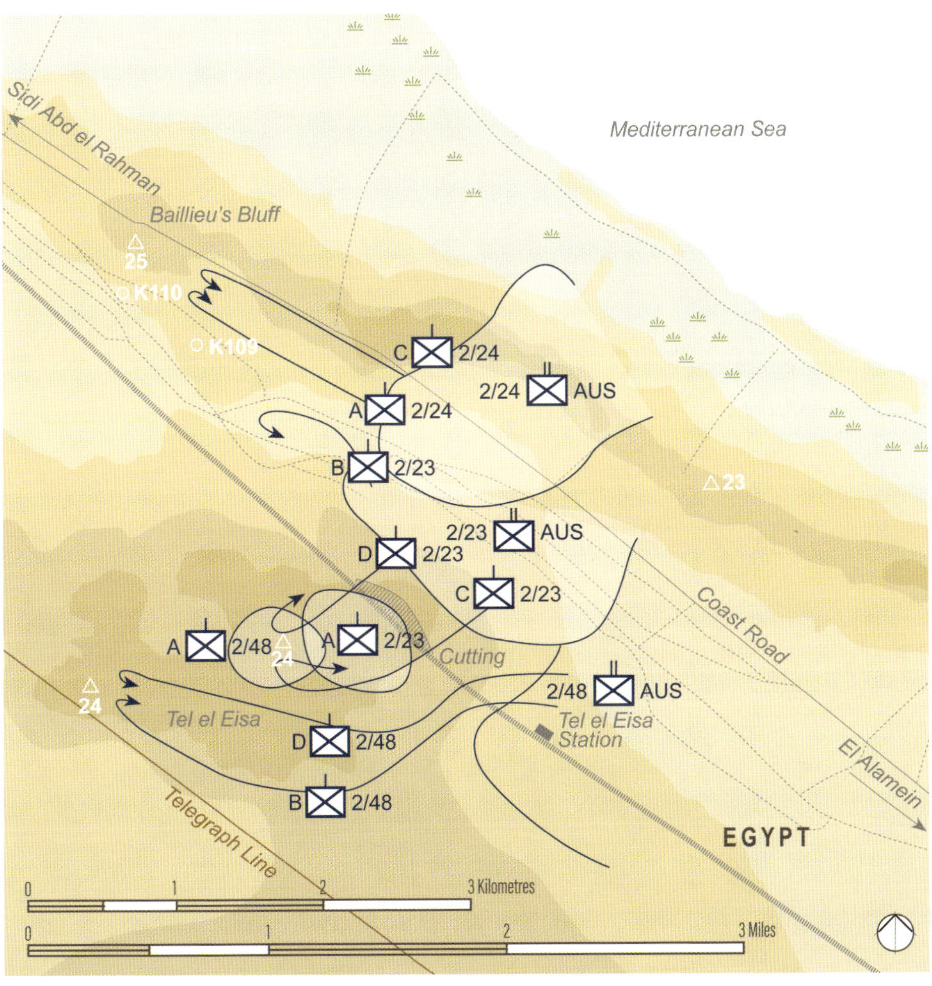

Map 10: 26th Brigade attack, 22–23 July 1942

GERMAN MACHINE GUNS

German machine guns are mentioned repeatedly throughout contemporaneous accounts of Alamein. Most of the awards for bravery won by Australians involved silencing 'Spandaus', a generic and inaccurate term used by Commonwealth troops for German machine guns. The main German machine gun at Alamein was the MG34, which was usually belt-fed, and had a rate of fire of 800–900 rounds per minute. It was the standard tank machine gun, too. The MG42, which fired up to 1550 rounds per minute, was reportedly first used in North Africa in May 1942, but its use seems to have been very limited. There appear to be no photographs of them in use at Alamein. The MG34 and MG42 were superb weapons, arguably the best machine guns of their time, and their actions remain the basis for those of modern belt-feed machine guns. Each could be mounted on a bipod (for mobility) or tripod (for sustained long-range fire). Australians usually treated German prisoners and dead with respect, but one Australian saw a comrade at Alamein lift up a dead German machine gunner by the ankles and kick him in the behind, saying, 'many's the time you've scared the tripe out of me'.[47] Australian troops used salvaged German or Italian automatic weapons whenever they got the chance to thus increase their firepower. There were seventy-one 'Spandaus' in the 9th Division on the eve of the October battle. They were especially useful supplements to battalion firepower.

MG34 on an anti-aircraft mount and with drum magazines. (AWM P01396.007)

Like the 2/24th attack, the 2/23rd assault faced fierce resistance and many of its officers were soon killed or wounded. Nevertheless, the unit took East Point 24. That feature was then shrouded in smoke from enemy artillery and mystery as to what was happening, as German infantry fought to recapture it. Private Ron Claffey drove a truck over the battlefield and brought in more than thirty wounded in his bullet-riddled and shrapnel-damaged vehicle. Three times he insisted on going through seemingly impassable fire, despite attempts to restrain him.

One company of the 2/23rd went forward on the right after seeing the 2/24th's success signal from Ring Contour 25. From there, Captain Mollard observed them struggling forward under fire so heavy that all but one of the officers and half the company were soon dead or wounded. In the week leading to 22 July, the 2/23rd lost all its company commanders, killed. Now all their replacements had become casualties. The 2/23rd also captured the cutting, but that day suffered more than 200 casualties.

While the 2/23rd fought for East Point 24, the 2/48th's two companies advanced in daylight on West Point 24. Both company radios were soon out of commission, and there was intense artillery and mortar fire. Three of the four officers in B Company were hit by 7am, and the sole survivor was out of communication on a flank. Sergeant Wally Pryor, a 26-year-old builder's labourer, took charge. He led the company into position and then, despite lacking maps, directed the defence of its new positions until 8pm. At dusk, with the enemy moving to surround it, he ordered the company to withdraw, taking the wounded. On getting back, B Company comprised just fifteen men.

The other 2/48th company had been pinned down by machine-gun fire and artillery fire, just 100 metres short of the enemy positions. In an astonishing act of individual initiative, Private Stan Gurney stood up and charged towards the nearest machine gun. After hurling a grenade from just metres away, he bayoneted a German who emerged and confronted him. Gurney and another soldier then ran into the post and together bayoneted two more Germans. Gurney then charged into a second post, where he bayoneted another two Germans and sent another out as a prisoner. As he charged yet another post, an exploding grenade knocked him off his feet. Undeterred, he got up, grabbed his rifle and entered the post, where he was last seen vigorously using the bayonet. He then disappeared from view. Gurney's action, later recognised by the posthumous award of the Victoria Cross, enabled his company to approach to within 150 metres of their objective, but again they became pinned down by fire. Private Herb Ashby, of the same company, was also outstanding that day. He commanded a section which became separated from the rest of the company early in the fighting. Nevertheless, he refused to retreat, despite intense enemy fire from in front and on the flanks and a seemingly impossible situation. In the late afternoon, a British Valentine tank was destroyed nearby and Germans captured its crew and two of Ashby's men. On Ashby's orders, the men still with him opened fire on these Germans, killing them all and rescuing the prisoners. He and his men inflicted casualties on the enemy in a period lasting at least 14 hours.

This Valentine was one of few seen that day. Lieutenant Colonel Hammer, the 2/48th's CO, called for British tank support at 7am but, to his fury, tanks did not arrive for four hours. The tanks withdrew twice, first on entering a minefield and later after losing two tanks to anti-tank guns. Hammer was later scathing in his criticism of the armour. In the entire action, the 2/48th lost 115 men killed or wounded, while estimating it killed sixty Germans. After the huge sacrifice of the three Australian battalions around Tel el Eisa, which for a time seemed to have been wasted, early on 23 July the Germans abandoned both Points 24, ground that would prove invaluable in the months ahead.

The 24th Brigade was also ordered into attacks on 22 July, advancing as on 17 July towards Trig 22 and Ruin Ridge. The 2/32nd took Trig 22 again, despite heavy losses that included sixty-six men captured. The 2/43rd Battalion's A Company supported the 2/32nd advance and was guided to its start-line by Lance Corporal Jim Maddocks of the 2/43rd Intelligence Section. The company commander was soon mortally wounded, and the leading platoon became pinned down. On his own initiative, Maddocks went forward and found the platoon. It was held by fire from in front and from a machine-gun post just 25 metres away to the right. Acting alone amidst this heavy fire, Maddocks grabbed the muzzle of a nearby unmanned 88mm gun and swung it around until it pointed at the machine-gun post. Bluffed, the strongpoint's fifteen Germans surrendered. Maddocks then moved back and brought up machine gunners who helped to consolidate the position. The company lost fifteen killed in this action.

Lieutenant Richard Cameron took forward thirteen machine gunners of the 2/2nd Machine Gun Battalion at dawn to support the 2/32nd's advance. He headed for the crest of a ridge allotted to them in planning but found it more than 300 metres from the nearest Australian infantry. Moreover, German machine gunners had got there first, and enemy mortars were firing on them from the ridge's reverse slope. Cameron had no time to dig in but ordered his two Vickers guns to set up in the open. When these guns got into

2/23rd Battalion officer Lieutenant Harold Gray writes home in the cutting in August, eight days after his company captured it in bitter fighting. (AWM 024703)

action, they silenced all but one of the 'Spandaus', which inflicted two casualties. Cameron crawled forward to a position where he could fire his pistol at the lone German gunner some 75 metres away. Eventually Cameron stood up and ran at the German, who rose on his approach before being shot down by another Australian. Cameron now grabbed the German machine gun and turned it on the mortar and anti-tank crews on the reverse slope. The gun soon jammed, though, and he ran back to his section through enemy fire.

The Vickers gunners kept firing throughout the morning, but with enemy airburst seeking them out, eventually they pulled back. By the time Cameron got back to the group after liaising with the nearby infantry, just five of his men were still on their feet. He reorganised them into two gun teams and, taking his own turn on the gun, kept them operating for the following 24 hours. For four hours his unit had been up to 450 metres in front of the nearest Australians. All but four of the thirteen men who went out in his section were killed or wounded. Cameron received a Distinguished Service Order, a rare award to a subaltern.

In the 2/28th's attack on Ruin Ridge, some fifty Australian infantrymen rode on British Valentine tanks of the newly arrived 50th Battalion, Royal Tank Regiment (50 RTR). This tactic, unpopular with the infantrymen concerned, seems to have come from Morshead.[48] For a time the drive was fun, but when enemy anti-tank and machine-gun fire started hitting the tanks, one Aussie reflected, 'Bloody hell! We're out here and he's inside'.[49] The riders jumped off and helped the other Australian infantry to dig in. The tanks drove on, hoping vainly for the infantry to follow. Communications broke down, until the infantry were able to call back the tanks. By then, twenty-three Valentines had been destroyed, largely on a minefield. To add to the tragedy of the event, the Australian infantry had made an embarrassing error: they had dug in on what they thought, from the presence of a derelict building, was Ruin Ridge, but was in fact 1800 metres short of that objective. The hastily improvised nature of the attack had precluded a prior reconnaissance or rehearsal with the tanks.

The theme of poor infantry–armour cooperation was a major one that day. An Australian soldier caught up in the terrible fighting at Tel el Eisa, and brought back from the front because he was on the point of nervous collapse, was heard to say as he lay back, 'If only we had tank support!'[50] Earlier that day, the New Zealand division had sustained such heavy losses in a battle where the British tanks failed to turn up on time that the New Zealanders soon resolved to turn one of their infantry brigades into an armoured one.

A 2/48th Battalion soldier, Private Bill McEvoy, looks over a destroyed British Valentine tank, possibly the one mentioned in the text as being lost while supporting the 2/48th on 22 July. Australians were often critical of British tank support, but they appreciated the courage of many individual crews, and on 31 October the 2/48th war diary would praise the magnificent work of the British tanks in the Saucer. (IMAGE COURTESY OF BILL MCEVOY)

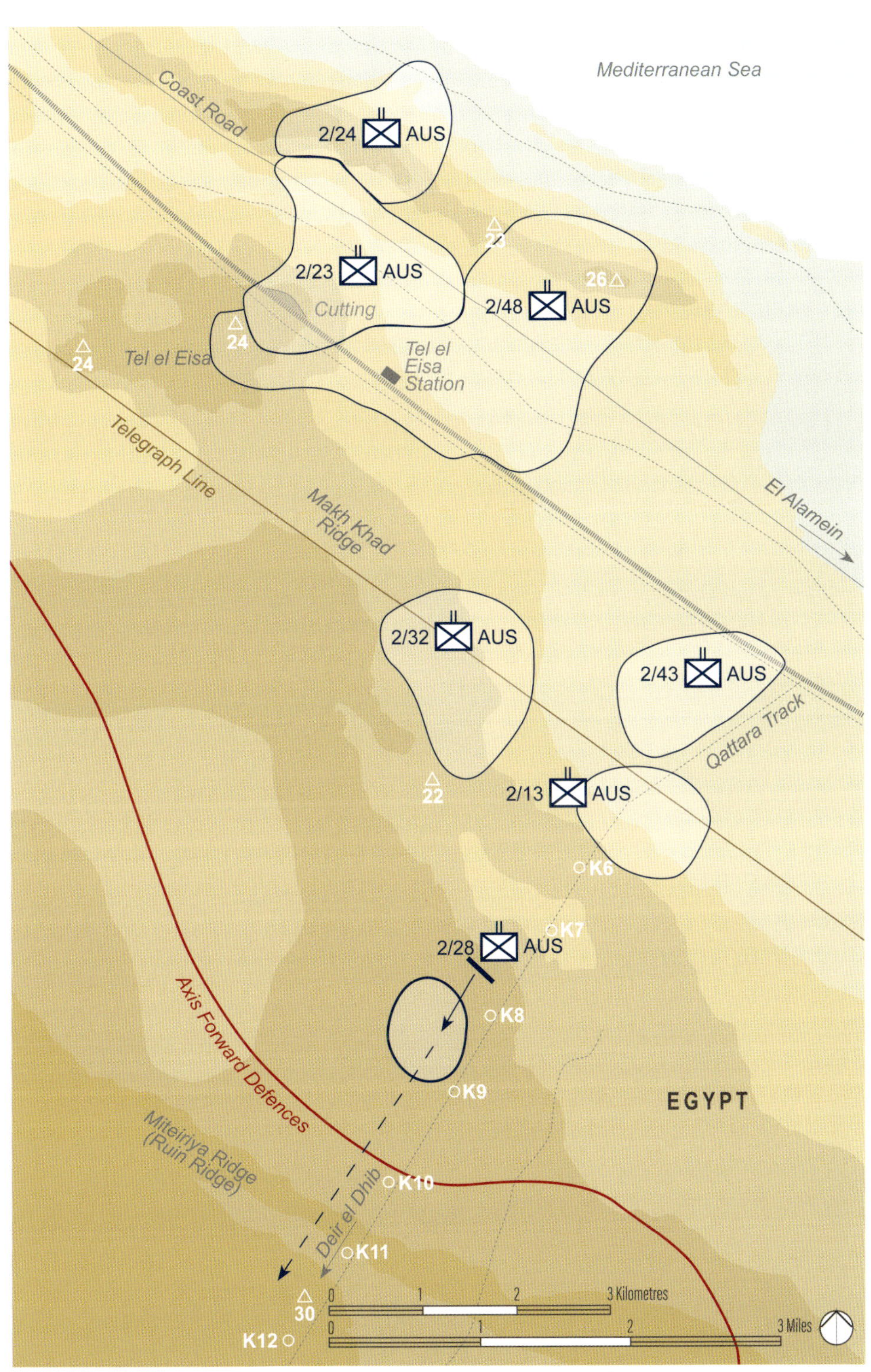

Map 11: Australian dispositions on the evening of 22 July 1942 and the 2/28th Battalion attack towards Miteiriya Ridge

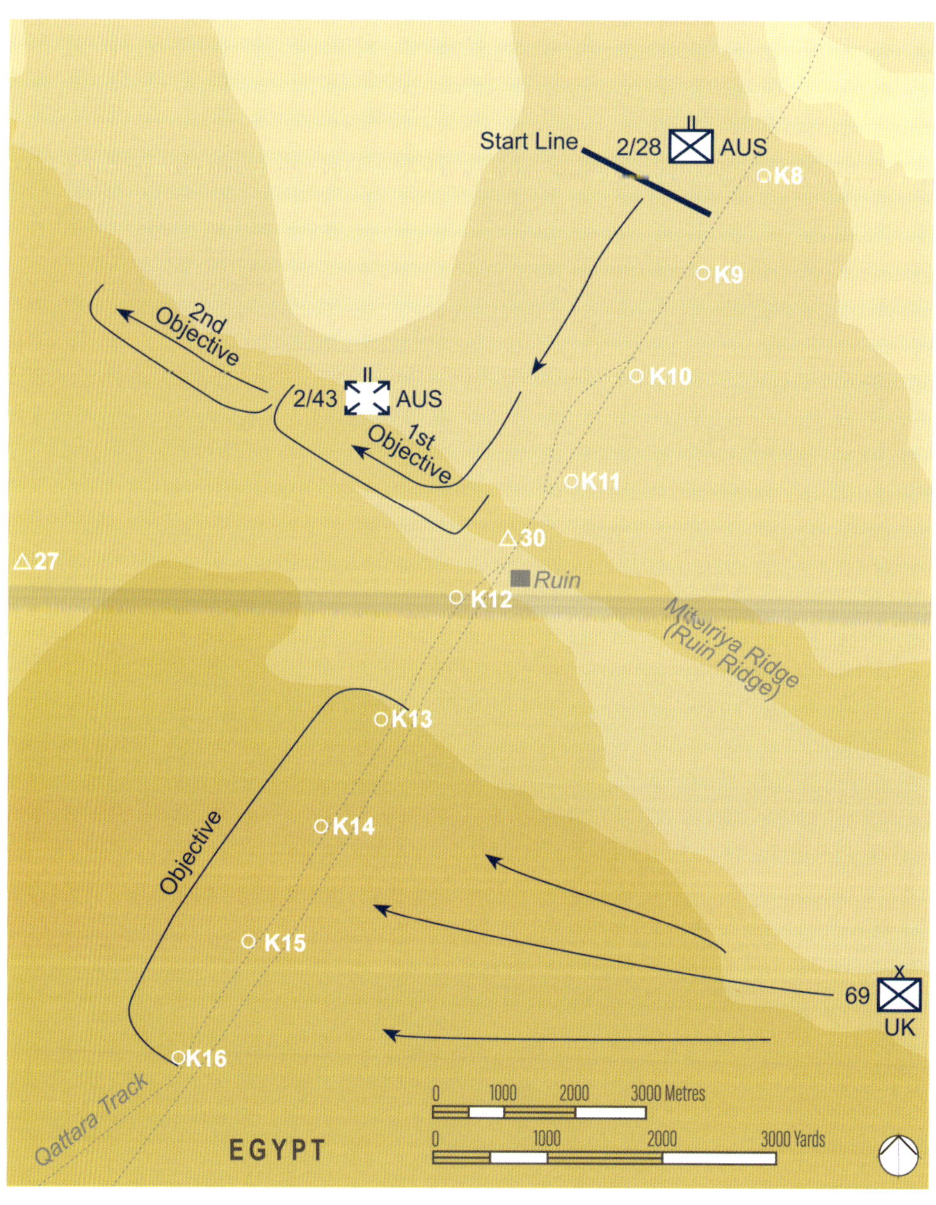

Map 12: Plan of attack – Miteiriya 'Ruin' Ridge, 26–27 July 1942

Disaster at Ruin Ridge

Auchinleck believed that he could 'break' his weakened enemy at Alamein and made a final attempt to achieve a breakthrough on Miteiriya Ridge between Ruin Ridge and Deir el Dhib on 27–28 July. Initially, he planned a night attack involving Australians with British tank support and artillery and South African engineers. Morshead, sceptical of the night attack on a narrow front and of armoured support, and willing to say so, again ran up against Auchinleck and the XXX Corps commander, Ramsden. Eventually, while the three drank tea in Ramsden's caravan, Morshead agreed to a revised plan that involved an additional British brigade, the 69th. However, while accepting his condescending superiors' plan, Morshead retained his doubts as to the British tanks' ability to arrive on time. The British commanders resented Morshead delaying the attack with his remonstrances but were ignoring the fact that Morshead represented not just part of the British Empire's army but also an independent allied government.[51]

There were last-minute changes in both the South African and the British brigades to be used in the attack, undermining some early liaison work. The Germans anticipated the attack and they, not the Italians Auchinleck had planned for, were there when the Australians advanced towards Ruin Ridge on the night of 26–27 July. The attack was two-pronged, poorly coordinated by British headquarters and not mutually supporting. The plan involved the 2/28th Battalion taking Ruin Ridge as the preliminary to the 69th Brigade advancing to support them, and the South African engineers lifting mines to allow a tank thrust through and behind enemy lines.

The 2/28th Battalion was determined to avenge its embarrassment of the previous week. The day before the attack, the 2/28th CO, Lew McCarter, concluded his orders: 'We must get on that ridge ... We must not be distracted by fire from the right flank. By dawn all our troubles will be over'. One of his NCOs, Sergeant John Kehoe, wrote later that the words 'We must get on that ridge' had motivated him throughout the action that followed.[52] As they advanced that night, many were hit by German small-arms fire, and when anti-tank fire hit a vehicle, disaster loomed as a dozen more were 'brewed up' by mines or AT guns. Yet the Australians reached the ridge, albeit with Germans all around them. WO2 Fred Holding was with the company on the battalion's left flank. At 7.30am the company's left platoon was pushed back by intense fire. Jumping from his weapon pit, Holding ordered the men not to withdraw beyond the ridge, instead personally leading them forward to their previous positions. Seemingly leading a charmed life, he moved continuously around the company area, ignoring intense machine-gun, mortar and artillery fire. The Western Australian battalion waited for the reinforcements due in the morning. However, the 69th Brigade's attack was meeting problems. Their unfamiliar route had been inadequately marked and the minefield not cleared. The British troops, many inexperienced and others exhausted, got lost and became pinned under heavy German fire. Two British battalions were virtually destroyed.

The 2/28th lost its wireless truck on the minefield, and static made its one remaining wireless unworkable. Despite brave individual efforts to get messages through about the unit's

(Top to bottom)
Four Australians, probably of the 2/32nd Battalion, in their dugout in mid-July. Three of them are Indigenous Australians, said to be former pearl divers. (IWM E14449)

dire state of communications and supplies, there was uncertainty at XXX Corps headquarters about what was happening. Concerned about whether the British tanks could negotiate the minefields, Morshead held back the tanks and Australian infantry that had been earmarked to support the 2/28th. So when tanks approached the 2/28th on Ruin Ridge that morning, they were not the Valentines the Australians were expecting. An Australian captain was killed driving out to meet them. The German tanks began rounding up the Australians, and only when they were closing in for the kill were the defenders able to get a radio message through to 'rock the artillery in'. Communications were not good enough to allow accurate direction of the guns. When McCarter signalled the brigadier, 'We have got to give in', the reply came, 'Tanks will be with you immediately', but that was simply not true, although 50 RTR moved out just as the 2/28th were on the point of capitulating. German guns soon destroyed twenty-two Valentines. The 2/28th Battalion lost 490 men captured, as well as sixty-five dead. Lieutenant Ray Stewart wrote of the survivors' reactions, veering between 'hot with anger, disillusioned, relieved and ashamed'.[53] The 2/28th suffered more than 500 casualties at Ruin Ridge, which would not fall into British hands until the October battle.

The Ruin Ridge debacle signalled the end of the July fighting, or the 'First Battle of Alamein'. Rommel's *Panzerarmee* had been halted on the Alamein line. Though tired after months of continuous fighting, both sides had made attacks. Australian troops had contributed to holding the Axis advances, but contrary to some interpretations of the Australians saving the Eighth Army in defensive fighting, its role had been primarily to attack. It had suffered some reverses, notably at Ruin Ridge and Ring Contour 25, but these were outweighed by successes at Trig 33, Tel el Eisa and Makh Khad Ridge. The ground won at Tel el Eisa and Trig 33 would be vital in the October battle – for example, it gave superb observation over much of the battlefield and provided a launching pad for attacks. The faith that Auchinleck had put in the Australians by sending them in there had been justified. He would not be in charge in October, for Ruin Ridge would prove to be his last fight. Under Auchinleck's command, the Australians had suffered the consequences of some poor decision-making. In early August, Morshead complained in his diary: 'Fighting always in bits and pieces and so defeats in detail'. He described 'Formations being broken up automatically' and concluded that 'it has been difficult and unpleasant keeping 9th Div intact'.[54] Criticism of British armour support – some justified, some not – was particularly strong in the 9th Division and the Eighth Army's other infantry formations. As the official historian says, 'German armoured formations almost always arrived where most needed, British almost never'.[55] The deficiencies of British armour did not entirely explain the deficiencies in planning and execution – Australian as well as British – that exemplified the July fighting. Much bravery and many lives had been squandered.

The 9th Division suffered 2,500 casualties in July: a high number in a battle almost unknown in Australia today. Both sides recognised now that they lacked the resources to make an assault that could penetrate the other's line. They sought to recuperate, bring in reinforcements and prepare for another round in the see-saw operations of North Africa.

Looking for survivors at Ruin Ridge, July 1942 – 65 men had been killed, 490 captured. (AWM 042488)

PART 2

THE OCTOBER BATTLE

Gunners of 2/8th Australian Field Regiment, Royal Australian Artillery, firing a 25-pounder field gun at a range of 9,800 yards on German positions on the coastal sector near El Alamein. One man is seen about to place a shell in the breech. A pile of empty shell-cases is in the foreground.
(AWM 024513)

CHAPTER 4

PREPARATION

AUGUST – 22 OCTOBER 1942

FOR ALL ITS HUMAN COST – including able officers and NCOS – and failure to bring the hoped-for conclusive breakthrough, First Alamein had made the 9th Division more self-confident and efficient.[56] Some important changes to battalion organisation followed the hard-earned experiences of the July battles. One of those lessons was the difficulty of holding ground once it had been won, and thus a need for more effective defensive firepower. In August, each battalion received four Vickers machine guns with which to arm newly formed machine-gun platoons. All battalions already employed large numbers of captured automatic weapons to provide long-range sustained machine-gun fire, and these were generally retained. The October battles would vindicate the use of sustained fire weapons at the battalion level, leading to the retention of the machine-gun platoon and a recommendation that each battalion have eight Vickers.[57] Another valuable addition to the defensive power of battalions came in the form of eight 2-pounder anti-tank guns issued to the anti-tank platoons (formed after Tobruk), which had previously depended on non-standard, often captured, weapons.[58]

Between August and 22 October, the 9th Division remained in frontline positions, but for most men this time was much quieter than July or late October. As in Tobruk, digging and patrolling were constants for the infantry, but supplies were more plentiful and men had more opportunities for genuine relaxation.

Prime Minister Churchill gives the 'V for Victory' sign to Australian troops lining the road to see him in August 1942. (IWM E15305)

(Above, top to bottom)
2/48th Battalion men striking 'patroller' poses for the camera. All are carrying Thompson submachine guns. The officer in the centre, Lieutenant John Gregory, is wearing a one-piece overall, or 'murder suit', as well as a cap comforter. Corporal Adams, on the left, would be Mentioned in Despatches in the South-West Pacific, where he would be wounded in New Guinea and Tarakan. Private Bill Southern, on the right, had been wounded in Tobruk, and would be again in New Guinea. (IMAGE COURTESY OF PAUL OATEN); Unit commanders gather around a sand map at 20th Brigade headquarters before the battle. (AWM P01614.018)

The British Prime Minister, Winston Churchill, visited Egypt on 5 August and travelled out to the front, first visiting the Australians on the coast. His visit resulted in Auchinleck being sacked and replaced by General Sir Harold Alexander, and Lieutenant General Bernard Montgomery taking over the Eighth Army. As soon as Montgomery arrived in Egypt, he too visited the Australians, with whom, as the son of a former Bishop of Tasmania, he claimed a special bond. Montgomery came to the Eighth Army determined to make whatever changes he thought necessary to bring victory. One of these was to ensure an improvement in the contribution of the British tanks. After Ruin Ridge, rumours circulated among other Australian units that 'the British tanks had "dingoed" it'.[59] After a conference in August, though, Morshead could write, 'Montgomery, bless him, has plainly told the Armour that it has to fight'.[60]

During this lull at the front, the 9th Division was on the coast, in positions from which it could repel an enemy attack but also prepare to attack. The 26th Brigade was relieved at Tel el Eisa by the 20th Brigade, which had been in reserve during the July fighting. Lieutenant John Thompson, of the 2/17th Battalion, confirmed through patrolling the existence of a major enemy defensive locality 5 kilometres west of Tel el Eisa station, south of the railway. The Australians came to know this locality as 'Thompson's Post'. The 2/17th Battalion spent forty-six days in contact with the enemy in August and September, its longest such period in the war. Every night it provided patrols of some kind, and this was typical of Australian units in this period. For example, in the 24th Brigade, the 2/43rd Battalion sent out one patrol every night, as well as manning numerous listening posts at night and observation posts by day. The listening posts were in no-man's-land, with a field telephone, tracer bullets and flares available to warn of danger. On average, each month every member of a 2/43rd Battalion rifle company undertook three patrols – reconnaissance or fighting. Lieutenant Colonel Evans, of the 2/23rd, justified his heavy patrolling program as a means 'of "breaking in" all ranks' in a unit with many reinforcements.[61] Of course, patrols served many other purposes. One was building the intelligence picture of the enemy's order of battle, dispositions and defences, especially minefields. Another was to prevent the enemy from improving their own picture of the Australians' changing dispositions ('security'). A third was maintaining a psychological edge, notably in night operations.

During a 2/43rd fighting patrol under Lieutenant Phil Adnams on 16–17 August, Sergeant Bev Allen and Tim Newton found themselves fighting twenty Italians around one sand-bagged pit. After their ammunition ran out, these Australians were captured – but when an expired flare gave a moment of darkness, both grabbed their weapons. Newton bayoneted a nearby Italian, a sight which horrified even the hard-bitten veteran Allen. It also prompted other nearby Italians to flee or raise their hands. This gave the patrol three prisoners, who helped the Australians renegotiate the minefields. When they reached their lines and found a good brew of tea waiting for them, the Aussies passed the first three cups to their prisoners. Adnams considered this 'a great example of the Australian soldier'.

The Australian casualties that night included a 19-year-old reinforcement on his first patrol.

MONTGOMERY AND THE AUSTRALIANS

Montgomery's arrival to command the Eighth Army in August 1942 was a turning point in the desert war. As a young lieutenant during the First World War, Bernard Law Montgomery had been wounded twice in 1914, when he had also earned a Distinguished Service Order (DSO). As a General Staff Officer in various formations, he was horrified by the human cost of the Somme and Passchendaele battles, and later stated, 'my war experience led me to believe that the staff must be the servants of the troops'.[62] By war's end he was a lieutenant colonel, and in the inter-war years rose to the rank of major general, commanding a division. Early in the Second World War he won a reputation with the 3rd Division and XII Corps as an outstanding trainer. When Churchill sacked Auchinleck, William Gott was originally named the commander of Eighth Army. Gott's death in a plane crash led to Montgomery's appointment. Montgomery's key qualities included decisiveness, seen in his readiness to weed out and replace inefficient commanders, an unusual ability to simplify and go to the heart of apparently complex problems, and a concern to maintain his men's morale and loyalty.

Montgomery's impact on the already high morale of 9th Division, which had not suffered as much as other units from the poor command decisions since January, may have been relatively small and less than his impact on their training. Nevertheless, he tried to improve Australian morale. When he visited the 9th Division on 14 August, he asked for a slouch hat, on the grounds that his father had once been Bishop of Tasmania, and Monty himself a schoolboy in that state. He wore the hat pulled down too far and covered with unit badges, and although some Australians saw this as comical, they appreciated the effort. Some British officers used the knowledge that Montgomery intended to travel in a tank to persuade him to discard the 'Australian bush hat' in favour of the black beret that became his trademark.[63]

Montgomery had a stronger affinity with Australians than any other senior British commander of the war. He was deeply and enduringly grateful for their contribution to the Eighth Army's victory in November.

After Alamein, Montgomery commanded the Eighth Army through Tunisia, Sicily and Italy before leaving in December 1943. He led the 21st Army Group in the invasion of Normandy and the campaign through north-western Europe and into Germany. Though controversial, tactless and self-serving, he was one of the war's most successful commanders.

General Montgomery wearing a slouch hat presented him by Australian troops. He later added badges from various Eighth Army units. (AWM 044866)

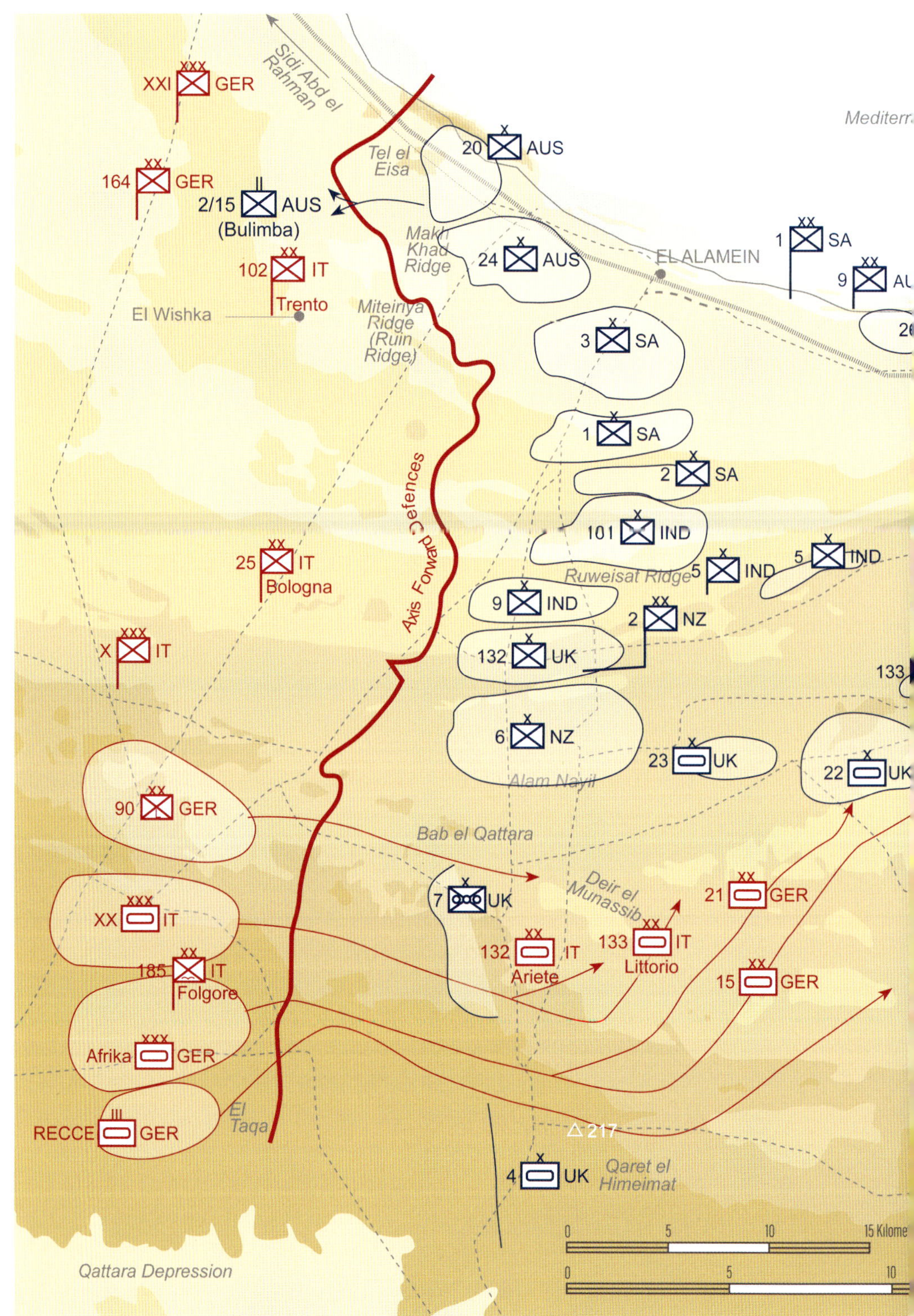

Mediterr
Sidi Abd el Rahman
XXI GER
164 GER
2/15 AUS
(Bulimba)
102 IT
Trento
El Wishka
Tel el Eisa
20 AUS
Makh Khad Ridge
24 AUS
EL ALAMEIN
1 SA
9 AU
Miteiriya Ridge (Ruin Ridge)
3 SA
1 SA
2 SA
101 IND
Ruweisat Ridge
5 IND
5 IND
Axis Forward Defences
25 IT
Bologna
9 IND
2 NZ
X IT
132 UK
133
6 NZ
Alam Nayil
23 UK
22 UK
90 GER
Bab el Qattara
Deir el Munassib
7 UK
XX IT
132 IT
Ariete
133 IT
Littorio
21 GER
185 IT
Folgore
15 GER
Afrika GER
RECCE GER
El Taqa
217
4 UK
Qaret el Himeimat
0 5 10 15 Kilome
0 5 10
Qattara Depression

Map 13: The Battle of Alam Halfa, 30–31 August 1942

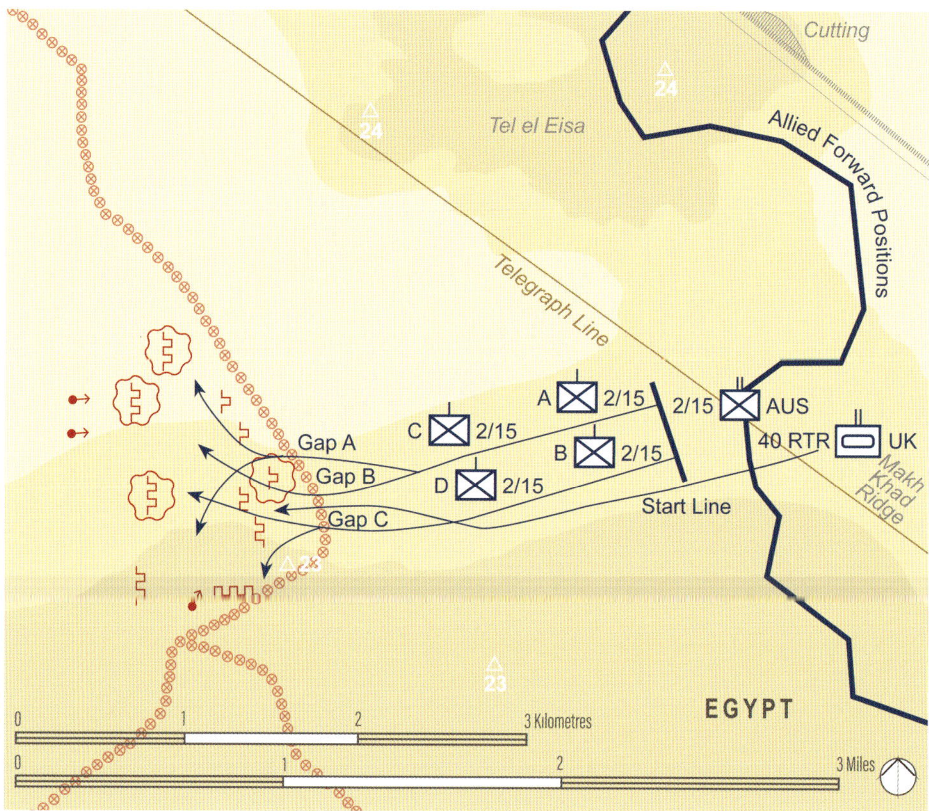

Separated from the others while on a covering party and wounded by a booby trap, over two days he crawled the 3 kilometres back to his lines. Lieutenant Adnams found him lying on his back, one arm through the barbed wire, badly wounded in the calf and foot, with his face sunburnt and swollen. Briefly opening his eyes, he muttered to Adnams, 'I came home on the star you told me to, Boss'. Adnams had clearly briefed his men on how to return to friendly lines. His patrol's experience illustrates the challenges of maintaining control in the dark, especially when leaders have to form detachments and these become embroiled in separate fights. Adnams and the battalion commanding officer were subsequently called to brigade headquarters, where they met Generals Morshead and Montgomery. 'Monty' questioned Adnams closely about the succession of minefields they had encountered. He found it hard to believe that the patrol had come through all these minefields and booby-traps. Adnams, exhausted and resenting doubt being cast on his story, said cheekily to the army commander, 'Well, you've got our bloody prisoners to ask, haven't you, sir!'[64]

(Above) Map 14: Operation Bulimba, 1 September 1942

Another outstanding patroller was Captain Bill Cobb of the 2/15th Battalion. Cobb had already won a Military Cross for his fine patrolling and leadership in Tobruk, where he had helped to establish his battalion's esprit de corps. At Alamein on 4–5 August 1942, he led a 13-strong fighting patrol, the battalion's first in this campaign. They were tasked, based on information Cobb had obtained on a reconnaissance patrol the previous night, with obtaining identification of the German unit facing them. Some 2700 metres from their front, and nearly 1500 metres north of Ring Contour 25, the patrol was challenged. They went to ground and waited twenty minutes amidst silence. Cobb realised that the enemy suspected their presence, but was determined to accomplish his task. When the bolt of a German machine gun was pulled back in a post just 15 metres away, he decided to attack. Cobb led the assault, throwing a No. 69 grenade which silenced the 'Spandau', but not before a burst wounded him in the leg and hit two other patrollers. The survivors pushed on, killing six enemy soldiers and taking a prisoner. Cobb now ordered a withdrawal and went to help the man in charge of the prisoner. Germans in nearby posts were firing on the party, and a short-range burst from a submachine gun killed the prisoner and wounded Cobb in the arm. Cobb shot the submachine gunner with his pistol and ignored other enemy fire to search the dead prisoner's body and cut off his shoulder straps. These and the man's paybook helped to identify the enemy unit. Cobb, a tall 25-year-old grazier, was awarded a bar to his Military Cross. He would be killed on the first night of the battle of El Alamein, mourned by a company who loved him for his courage and sympathetic leadership.

The man who took the prisoner on Cobb's patrol was Corporal Alick Else. As the patrol withdrew, Cobb blacked out due to his arm wound. Else took command and, after giving orders, personally took Cobb on his back and carried him for some distance. When Cobb regained consciousness and told Else he could stumble along, Else replied that he would carry Cobb even if he were 'bloody well dead'. Other men helped and eventually they found a stretcher, while Else made numerous direction changes to ensure that the party evaded enemy fire.

Alam Halfa and Operation Bulimba

On 30 August Rommel launched a major offensive – unknown to him it would be his last – designed to achieve a major breakthrough. This was to be a right hook around the British line. Using Ultra intercepts, Montgomery was ready for this attack, which his strong forces held at Alam Halfa ridge.

When the breakthrough failed, Rommel hoped to draw Montgomery into an attack but 'Monty', determined to avoid being drawn on to Rommel's anti-tank gun screen, stayed put. After six days, Rommel withdrew.

The only significant Australian action in the battle of Alam Halfa occurred on 1 September, when the 2/15th Battalion was sent with British tank support to capture West Point 23, a strongly defended position south-west of Tel el Eisa. This ambitious attack, officially called a 'diversion', was probably intended also to find out about the

Operation Bulimba (2/15th Battalion attack near Tel el Eisa, Egypt), September 1942, by Ivor Hele.
This magnificent painting of Operation Bulimba is on display at the Australian War Memorial. McLachlan is depicted swinging his Tommy gun as a club, while the figure firing the Bren gun on the right is based on Bambling.
(1965, oil on canvas, 153 x 275cm, AWM ART27559)

enemy defences, to test current methods of breaching minefields and to hone infantry–tank cooperation. It was codenamed Operation Bulimba after a Queensland beer.

Two companies led the attack that morning. The right-hand company was led by Captain Lance Bode, who had earned a Military Cross for leading a superbly successful raid in Tobruk and whom Morshead considered one of the best soldiers in the 9th Division.[65] After making some progress, this company became pinned down and Bode was killed. The left-hand company, following close behind the supporting artillery barrage, had more success. Captain Len Snell led the men with great dash, carrying a rifle and bayonet, and together they crossed the minefield and overcame a series of enemy posts before reaching the objective. Private Reg Bambling played an extraordinary part. His section was mopping up behind two others but as they went through the outer wire of German defences, the section commander was killed and just four men were left standing. Bambling took command and led them through the inner wire, where he could see an enemy post spitting fire at the forward troops who had unknowingly bypassed it. Firing his Bren from the hip and calling his men on, he charged this post, killing five Germans and capturing an officer and ten men. He detailed one of his men to take these prisoners to the rear, while Bambling and his two remaining men attacked another post about 50 metres away. Again he fired from the hip, but he went down when shot in the back and left shoulder. As he lay in the open, mortar fire lacerated his legs. When a British tank appeared, Bambling pointed out to its commander the enemy post and asked him to fire at it. The tank did so, killing and forcing the surrender of more enemy. Bambling was credited with ten enemy killed and thirty-five captured, and with silencing four machine guns and five submachine guns. The two brave men who had accompanied him, unnamed in the records, carried him out. Bambling's three wounds were serious, but he survived them and was awarded a DCM.

Corporal Horton McLachlan was also a section leader in Bulimba. As they attacked German posts on the southern boundary of the attack, his platoon commander, Lieutenant Dave Weir, was blinded by fragments from a grenade. 'Kill that German', he urged McLachlan, who obeyed by putting a bayonet through the enemy soldier. McLachlan paused briefly to take stock, then circled behind the crew of a German machine gun firing from the left. He bayoneted the two German gunners and then, as he moved back to his section, bayoneted another German who confronted him. He next swapped his rifle and bayonet for a Tommy gun from a wounded man and, after trying unsuccessfully to get more men to tackle two machine-gun posts on a ridge 200 metres up ahead and to the right, 'decided that I would have a go myself'. Using his submachine gun to keep their heads down, he saw two Germans dash from their weapon pit, where their machine gun had jammed, into the other pit. When he was just 20 metres away, all four occupants of the pit jumped out and ran for another dugout. He killed all four with a burst of fire. He then reached that dugout and killed its sole occupant. After moving on to yet another dugout and shooting its three occupants, he was out of ammunition and headed back over the ridge. As he crossed a partly covered bunker a German grabbed him by the leg. McLachlan kicked him into the dugout, and when

An infantry sergeant of the 9th Division in September poses confidently. The caption calls him one of 'Morshead's Men'. (PHOTOGRAPHER: FRANK HURLEY, AWM 151142)

A CORPS COMMAND FOR MORSHEAD?

Montgomery made various command changes to the Eighth Army in August, including three new corps commanders. Morshead was not one of them, even though, as Blamey pointed out, Morshead had more desert experience than any of the three appointees, and more success in all forms of warfare. Morshead asked directly why he did not receive the command of XXX Corps, which was instead given to Lieutenant General Oliver Leese. Montgomery explained that because Morshead was not a regular, professional soldier, he lacked the requisite training and experience. Blamey felt that the reason was an 'unconscious arrogance' which made the British command reluctant to allow Dominion officers to command British troops.[66] Morshead downplayed his disappointment but reported that it had been made clear to him that Dominion commanders were ineligible for corps command. His status as a citizen-soldier and his disagreements with Auchinleck and Ramsden may also have been factors. This is not to say that Montgomery did not regard Morshead highly. Before the October battle he advised Morshead that if Leese became a casualty he would take command of XXX Corps. These events illustrate the historical challenges that Australia, as a junior partner, has had in having its senior officers appointed to positions of influence in coalition forces. They also highlight the need for a strong national command presence of the type embodied by Blamey.

a helmeted German emerged, knocked his helmet off and clubbed him to death with his Tommy gun. One of his men passed him a grenade, which McLachlan threw into the post, killing all inside.[67] A gunshot wound would fracture McLachlan's wrist at Alamein in October, ending his frontline service. Ivor Hele portrayed McLachlan and Bambling in a remarkable painting of Operation Bulimba. These two men exemplified the way combat units sometimes rely on a small number of what the famous American combat officer Dick Winters calls 'killers' – men with an instinctive understanding of what is required in battle.[68] Sadly, despite these outstanding actions, the Bulimba raid was largely a failure, and started to go wrong from early on. The Commanding Officer, Lieutenant Colonel Bob Ogle, was badly wounded just as the unit reached its objective and his replacement, Major Colin Grace, discovered that communications with units further back were out. The commander of the tank squadron was killed and thereafter the tanks' contribution was feeble: the two rounds directed by Bambling reportedly comprised the only aimed tank fire directed at Germans in the battle. The British tanks received remarkable support from Australian engineers, including Lance Corporal Harold Baggaley. Once gaps had been made in the enemy minefield for tanks to pass through, Baggaley was ordered to remain at one and ensure the safety of tanks passing through. When other sappers in the area became casualties to enemy mortar, machine-gun and sniper fire, Baggaley's area of responsibility widened and for 2½ hours he was in charge of guiding the tanks and keeping them off unmarked minefields. Several times he walked in front of tanks to direct them. On one occasion, to prevent a tank from running on a mine, he ran in front of the vehicle and was knocked over. Hurt but not seriously injured, he did not dare leave the post for aid. When the order to withdraw came, he again assisted the tanks going through the minefields and was among the last to leave. He even had the presence of mind to grab a Vickers machine gun from a wrecked Bren carrier.

The Germans in this area were well supported by tanks, artillery and mortars, and were determined to fight. By the time Grace ordered a withdrawal, the 2/15th had suffered fifty-nine killed or died of wounds, two captured and 125 wounded. The unit took 140 German prisoners and estimated that they killed 150 enemy.

Operation Bulimba was allegedly valuable to Montgomery as a source of information on enemy defences around Tel el Eisa, but also as an exercise in infantry–tank cooperation.

(Opposite)
Lieutenant General Oliver Leese, GOC XXX Corps (third from left), has an informal conversation on 25 September 1942 with his divisional commanders (from left to right): Lieutenant General Morshead; Major General Douglas Wimberley, GOC 51st Highland Division; and Major General Dan Pienaar, GOC 1st South African Division.
(IWM E17427)

Morshead was busy as preparations began for his division to take a leading role in the great British offensive that was coming. In a 1944 letter to the Army's Director General of Public Relations, Morshead outlined the obstacles facing the division:

> *The terrain here was hard and undulating, the only vegetation being a low, prickly bush known as camel thorn. Opposing defence lines were frequently thousands of yards apart. It was impossible to advance during daylight without being seen. Defence lines consisted of heavily manned strongpoints, usually protected by barbed wire and carefully sited minefields. Some of the minefields extended several hundred yards in depth [this was an underestimate]. To reach an objective the infantry often had to move 2,000 to 3,000 yards [about 1800 to 2750 metres] over open country, cross the minefields through which sappers must quickly prepare gaps, and finally come to grips. During all that time the attacking force would be subjected to the concentrated fire power of a modern army.*[69]

The essence of his preparation, and the new preoccupation of the Eighth Army, was training. Montgomery recognised the high quality of his troops, but believed that the failure of the July attacks was due largely to a lack of training for the task of breaking through Rommel's lines. Montgomery emphasised the need for each formation to train in the type of operations ahead – night operations, and infantry cooperation with engineers and especially with tanks. Realism and rehearsals were vital. Morshead formed a divisional training team which coordinated 'full dress' rehearsals designed to give the troops vital skills in breaking into mined and defended areas, and in cooperating with tanks. Morshead needed no reminder of the importance of training. Alec Hill, who served on his staff at Alamein, said Morshead 'would not have seen himself as second even to Montgomery as a trainer'.[70]

As always, some men still recovering from the hardships of the front line resented intensive training, but it was sold shrewdly to the troops. Hard-bitten Lance Corporal Jack Craig, who had at first thought of training as 'bastardry', later decided that assault courses were more enjoyable than battalion and brigade 'stunts of endless marching'.[71] Leslie Watkins of the 2/13th compared it favourably with exercises in Syria, which he and many others had regarded as pointless. 'The boys entered into this training with spirit', he recalled, 'knowing that this time they were not just being buggered about'.[72]

The concept of reducing important tasks to 'battle drills' became a focus of training throughout the Eighth Army. Many new drills were based on recent experience. Cooperation between arms, central for so long to German tactical superiority, was increasingly

(Opposite)
Into action, by William Dargie.
A 1942 painting of three Australian infantrymen advancing into action in the Middle East.
This work was reproduced in the frontispiece of the 1942 Australian War Memorial publication 'Soldiering on', with the title *Advancing Infantry*.
(Oil on linen canvas, 146 x 123 x 8.1cm, AWM ART22232)

Dargie

recognised as the key to success. Sappers, for example, reflecting on 'Engineer Lessons from recent operations' argued that enemy action had rendered it impractical to lay mines in front of the foremost positions, and that the infantry needed to seize an 'outpost line' within which sappers and infantry could lay their protective fields. Engineers also needed to accompany armoured units to clear mines and to destroy damaged enemy tanks and vehicles. The Australian engineers began training six weeks before the opening of the battle, practising alongside infantry units – by battalions and brigades, in daylight and at night – on an area sown with unarmed mines. The value of this training would be exemplified at the height of the forthcoming battle when the engineer officer who had trained beforehand with the 2/48th signalled Hammer: 'By God I like fighting with the 48th'.[73]

Cooperation between infantry and armour was considered especially significant. Royal Tank Regiment units not only trained but also bivouacked with Australian infantry units. For example, the entire 2/17th Battalion saw a tank demonstration on 27 September and had a lecture from the 40 RTR commanding officer, who answered many questions.[74] The 40 RTR's war diary refers to many exercises carried out with Australian battalions in September and October, as well as 'a fixed drill … worked out between tanks and Inf. for dealing with a number of common contingencies'.[75] These processes led to improved cooperation and better relations between the two groups, as exemplified by the fact that when 40 RTR men were ordered to hide their black berets as part of a deception plan, the headgear that many produced were 'Australian bush hats'. Naturally, some exuberant Australians tested the boundaries. English-born Private John Butler of the 2/23rd Battalion recorded in mid-October an exercise involving fireworks, thrown by umpires from a jeep, to register where shells had hit. These shells 'killed' one of Butler's friends, Chappy, who miraculously managed to pick up the firework and throw it into the jeep. Its occupants included the presiding umpire, a British brigadier, who in his speech at the post-mortem, announced sourly, 'I do not appreciate the Australian sense of humour'. Butler added afterwards in his diary: 'well I do, and I've had an Iti hand grenade thrown at me!'[76]

The Australian battalion commanders were demanding and realistic trainers. Bob Ogle of the 2/15th was characterised as a 'great trainer', pushing his battalion every day in hard exercises. Noel Simpson 'tore into' the 2/17th on arrival in March 1942 and concentrated on readying them for mobile offensive operations of the type they had not experienced in Tobruk. He put great pressure not only on the other ranks but also on his company commanders to maintain the highest standards in all aspects of their roles. Heathcote 'Tack' Hammer was also exceptionally demanding of the 2/48th from the time he took over in January 1942. He routinely pushed his men to their physical limits, but also worked assiduously on a meaningful training schedule, including TEWTs for the officers, followed by company and battalion exercises and follow-up conferences. Like Simpson, he could also be sharply critical. However, his reputation had gone up in the July battles, when he had proved himself a fine battle commander. The battalion training culminated in valuable 'full dress rehearsals' conducted by a divisional training team in October.[77]

The inculcation of battle drills reached a point where, in the midst of the battle, an order for a battalion's operations on a particular night might include the phrase 'administration normal', and the troops knew the many details that phrase covered, including loads carried, arrangements for mines, food, ammunition, water, sandbags, and what to do on encountering mines and once an objective was occupied. Hammer reflected after the battle that reducing tasks to drills like this left the individual soldier 'free to think and use his initiative'.[78]

The plan for the October battle was Montgomery's but it evolved over weeks of discussions with corps and divisional staffs. The final plan did not follow the usual pattern of desert assaults. Each side had a firm flank on the coast – the Australians taking the traditional position of greatest danger and honour on the right of the line – and used the main coastal road as its chief source of supply. The usual plan of assault in the desert war was to employ armoured forces to outflank the inland end of the line and then threaten the enemy's supply lines. Montgomery's plan for the October battle was to employ infantry to make the main thrust, and on the coastal flank. They would smash open a lane in the enemy defences through which British tanks would 'debouch' and draw the German armour into a battle in which the Panzers would be worn down and eliminated.[79] An elaborate deception plan was created to convince the Axis that the main thrust would come in the south and at a later date than really intended. Elements of this 'Operation Bertram' included dummy vehicles, spurious radio traffic and the slow construction of a dummy pipeline in the south as well as tanks camouflaged as trucks in the north. German commanders later testified to the effectiveness of these measures designed to fool them as to the location and timing of the attack.

Eighth Army, late October 1942

XXX Corps (Lieutenant General Leese)

23rd Armoured Brigade Group (Brigadier Richards)
9th Australian Division (Lieutenant General Morshead)
51st Division (Major General Wimberley)
2nd New Zealand Division (Lieutenant General Freyberg)
1st South African Division (Major General Pienaar)
4th Indian Division (Major General Tuker)

XIII Corps (Lieutenant General Horrocks)

7th Armoured Division (Major General Harding)
44th Division (Major General Hughes)
50th Division (Major General Nichols)

X Corps (Lieutenant General Lumsden)

1st Armoured Division (Major General Briggs)
10th Armoured Division (Major General Gatehouse)
8th Armoured Division (Major General Gairdner)

Eighth Army's main blow would come from XXX Corps in the north. Its four divisions – 9th Australian, 51st Highland, 2nd New Zealand and 1st South African – would break through the Axis defences on a front about 10 kilometres wide and 6 kilometres deep. They would establish two corridors through which the armour could drive, reaching the enemy gun-line on the first night. The 9th Division's task, a formidable one, was to form a solid front on the northern flank, including the most heavily defended area near the coast road. While the Australians pushed west and created a corridor to the south of this road, they had to ensure that the Axis did not use the road for their own breakthrough attack. The Australians were bound to be heavily involved in both attacking and defending. XIII Corps would attack in the south. The 24th Brigade, the only Australian brigade not committed to the main assault, would make a diversionary attack along the coast.

Total strengths of the two sides are given in Figure 3. The German official history gives the 'fighting strength' of the two forces as 195,000 in the Eighth Army as opposed to 60,000 (including 28,100 Germans) in the *Panzerarmee*.[80]

In some areas, the Allies were now matching or superior to the Axis in quality as well as quantity. The Sherman and Grant tanks, which had bolstered the Eighth Army's tank strength, were generally a match for the German Mark IIIs and IVs. The artillery arrangements would be far more coordinated than at any other time in the desert campaigns. After Alam Halfa, Montgomery appointed his former artillery commander in the United Kingdom, Brigadier Sidney Kirkman, as his chief artillery officer (BRA) and ordered him to develop a fireplan for the coming offensive. Backed by Mongomery's authority, Kirkman reorganised the Eighth Army's artillery, with an emphasis on centralisation but also restoring authority and resources to his divisional artillery commanders. The latter had been sidelined in previous campaigns, though in the mid-July battles there had been some coordinated artillery efforts and the Australian and New Zealand divisions had always maintained their organisations untouched. The fireplan for XXX Corps involved 408 field guns and forty-eight medium guns. Thanks mainly to suggestions by New Zealand Brigadier Steve Weir, the effectiveness of defensive artillery fire was improved by the adoption of 'Stonks' – fire into predetermined rectangles of 1200 by 600 yards (c. 1100 by 550 metres) – while creeping barrages were reintroduced to guide the infantry during their advance and set the pace by making 'lifts' every two minutes. Communications were enhanced too. In short, the 'networked' artillery arrangements of the British would make the coordination of artillery more effective and allow the guns of an entire corps to be concentrated on a single target if required.[81]

Air support arrangements and techniques were also improved under Montgomery, who stated that cooperation with the Royal Air Force (RAF) was his highest priority.[82] He worked closely with Air Vice-Marshal 'Mary' Coningham. A centralised air command was created, and as aircraft were no longer tied to specific ground units, air power could be concentrated for maximum effect as the changing battle demanded.

STRENGTH OF OPPOSING ARMIES

ON 23 OCTOBER 1942

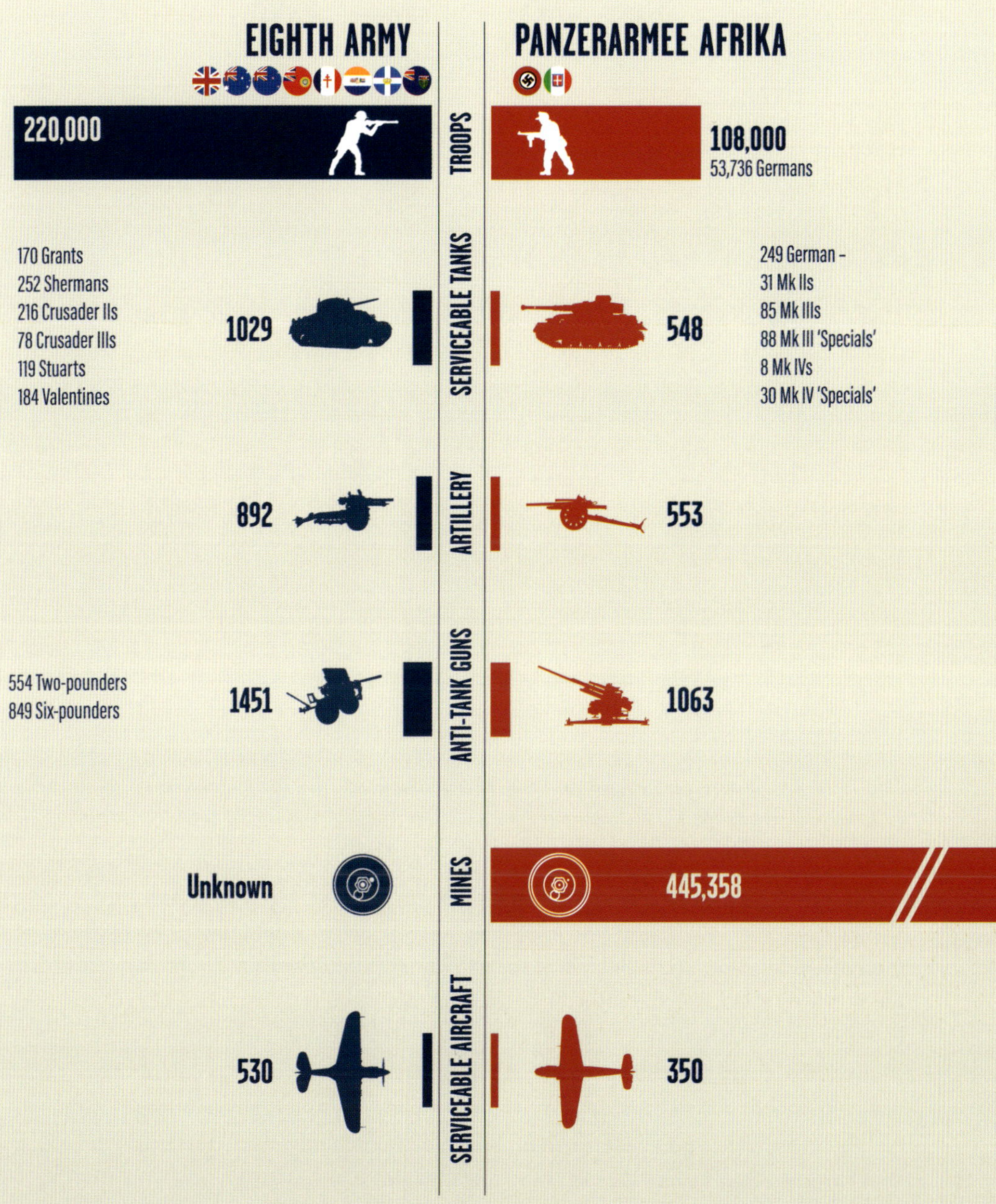

Figure 2: Strength of opposing armies on 23 October 1942 [83]

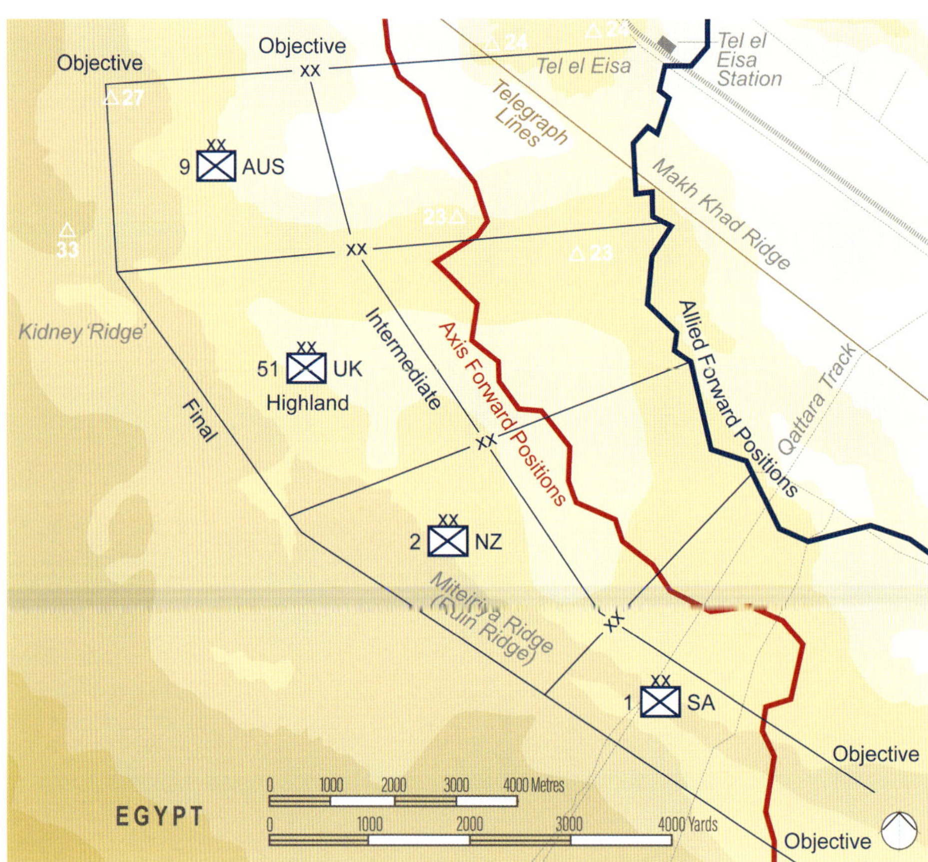

Map 15: XXX Corps' initial objectives for Operation Lightfoot, 23–24 October 1942

The Axis line comprised approximately seven divisions, five of them Italian. Rommel's armour was in small battle groups spread evenly behind the main line. His 90th Light Division was in reserve on the coast road. Rommel's plan depended on defence in depth – with infantry outposts and the main defence line to hold on long enough to allow the mobile reserve to deploy and counterattack. The main defence line was 1–2km behind the outposts and 1–2km in depth. The Axis artillery was deployed on the presumption that the northern flank was the most likely area for Montgomery's attack. Of forty-five gun batteries facing XXX Corps, thirty-three faced the 9th Division's front.[84]

Rommel envisaged that once the Allied *Schwerpunkt*, or main point of attack, was detected, mobile forces would gather to beat it back with pincer counterattacks, though fuel shortages were a potential problem. Enormous minefields ensured that the whole area could not be taken in one bound. Rommel, who had been an infantryman till 1940, was not ignorant of siege tactics and defences. He had arranged for an explosive carpet to be laid several kilometres wide, with half a million mines. Within them were 'Devil's gardens'

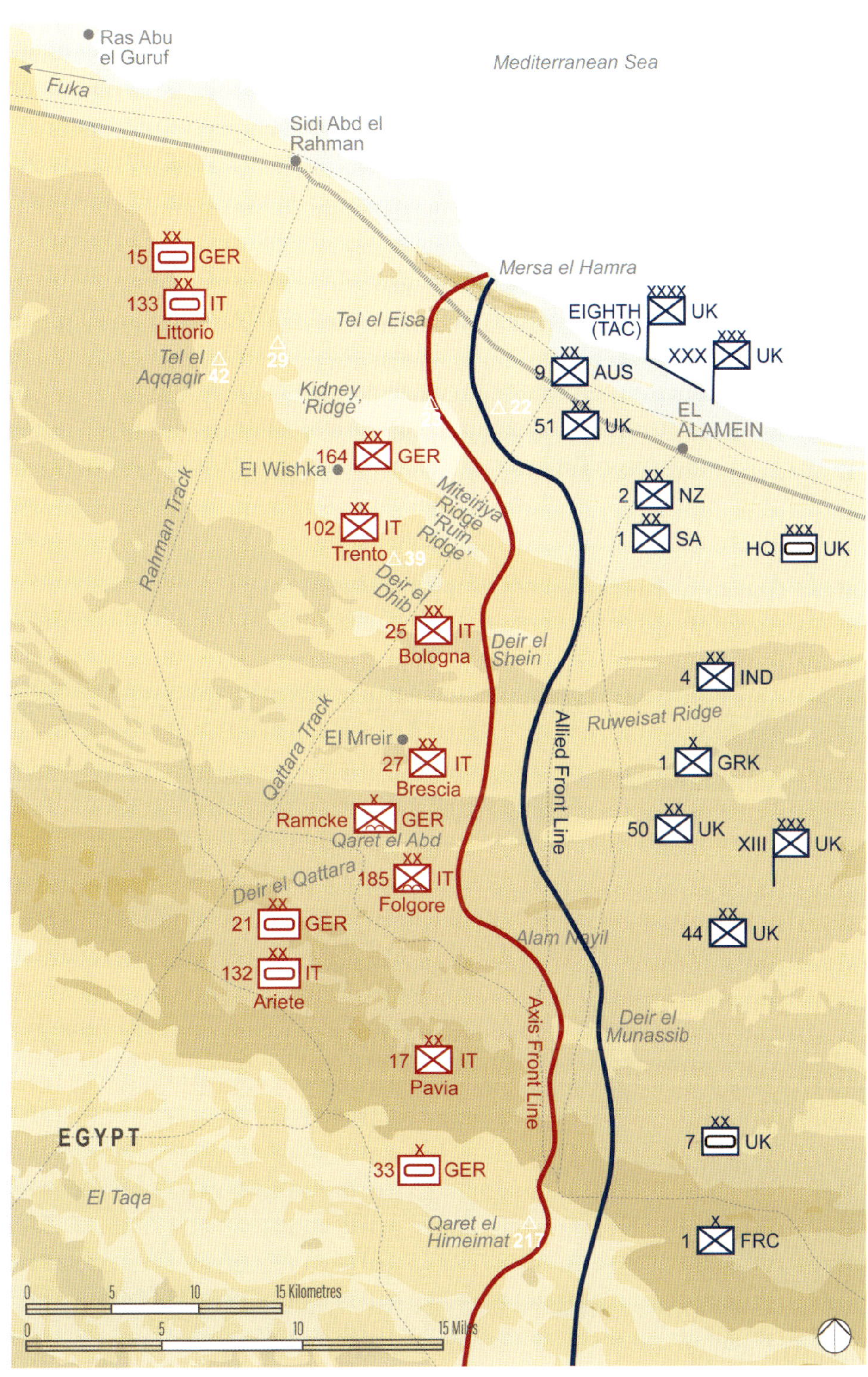

Map 16: Allied and Axis dispositions at El Alamein, 23 October 1942

of booby traps and anti-personnel mines, which Rommel believed could block a British advance. By late October, the Eighth Army faced more than 445,000 mines, all but several thousand of them anti-tank mines. The traditional method of dealing with them involved sappers slowly using hands and bayonets to locate and lift mines, and this remained the main method despite the arrival of some flail tanks (which used chains attached to rotating drums to explode and clear mines) and 500 electronic mine detectors. The 9th Division had only thirty-six of these detectors.

From the time of Tobruk, the Germans were used to positional defensive warfare, something also familiar to many of their officers from the First World War. Nevertheless, Axis forces were suffering from poor health due to fatigue, lack of supply and inadequate rations. They were at the end of an immensely long line of communications.

The British had not previously won a single clear-cut offensive victory against the German–Italian *Panzerarmee*. The implication of the lack of opportunity for manoeuvre in the Alamein position and the strength of the enemy defences was that if Montgomery was to win, he would need to grind the enemy down. A battle of attrition would be needed, but

Lieutenant General Morshead and Brigadier Windeyer talk at the sandbagged headquarters of the 20th Brigade. (AWM P01614.011)

one in which he could use his superior firepower to reduce his opponent's ability to inflict harm.[85] He was realist enough to recognise the need for what he termed a 'dogfight'.

Montgomery was planning to destroy his foe not with manoeuvre, but with 'methodical progress', 'part by part', slowly and surely. A 'break-in' by infantry would be followed by an armoured 'breakthrough', then a 'crumbling' stage as the enemy infantry were worn away. There was no detailed exploitation plan.[86]

In England in March 1941, Montgomery had argued that 'the Germans do not move at night' and that 'we have got to cultivate the art of moving by night'. He made a conscious decision in Egypt to conduct his main attacks at night, and the Eighth Army devoted a great deal of time to training for nocturnal operations, though arguably if they had devoted more time to honing their doctrine for daylight attacks, that may have brought victory too. For the initial attack, guide parties would direct units on three axes per battalion, while drills were developed to enable units to know how far they had to go, how far they had gone at any one time, and the direction they were supposed to be going. Tapes and stakes with rearward shining lights would be placed, and report and traffic-control centres established to keep forward headquarters informed. On the first night, a section of the 4th Light Anti-Aircraft Regiment would fire their guns periodically along the axis of advance of the leading Australian battalions, while searchlights would aid the artillery in timing and direction. Apart from Very lights used for signalling, the Australians made little use of flares, unlike the Axis forces.[87]

On the eve of the battle, the men of the Eighth Army heard a 'Personal Message from the Army Commander'. Montgomery told his army that they were about to embark upon 'one of the decisive battles of history … the turning point of the war' and one in which they would 'hit the enemy for "six" right out of North Africa'.[88] He spoke to his commanding officers separately on 10 October, telling them that 'as are the leaders so are their commands', and urging them to be 'enthusiastic, confident, determined, efficient' so as to inspire their men to be the same. Company and battery commanders were informed about the plan on 17 October, and at Montgomery's insistence 21 and 22 October were spent raising the morale of the troops to 'the highest pitch'. Final orders were also issued to the troops on those days.[89]

Morshead distributed his own instructions to prepare his division for the battle. In an address to his battalion commanders issued on 10 October, he delivered his vision of how his formation would be involved. 'This battle will be a real rough house', he began, 'it will be a killing match'. Morshead wanted his battalion commanders to impose their will on their men, demonstrating enthusiasm, confidence, determination and efficiency. He sought to avenge the loss of Tobruk, stressing that he wanted no Australians to surrender unwounded. 'There have been far too many unwounded prisoners taken', he warned. 'The modern term "in the bag" is too excusable'. Morshead wanted his men to be 'good staunch Australian[s] and not emulate the Italians'. He urged the officers who would lead his men into battle two weeks hence to 'work, think, train, prepare [and] enthuse'. He concluded:

'We must regard ourselves as having been born for this battle'.[90] At divisional headquarters an accurate large-scale model of the ground was used to brief first commanding officers and later company commanders and junior leaders.

The 2/13th Battalion history notes that its CO, Lieutenant Colonel Bob Turner, went around to each company in turn, giving informative and encouraging talks to which the men listened intently. The text he gave them for the battle ahead came from Shakespeare's *Macbeth*: 'Be bloody, bold and resolute!'[91] The men's recorded reactions to this reference were unenthusiastic, and the great sacrifices the 2/13th men would soon make owed more to other motives, such as loyalty to their mates and to their battalion and its sub-units.

Charles Weir of the 2/24th was more prosaic but nevertheless well summed up the reasons the Australians could be confident, when he told his battalion: 'We have the strength, we have the support, we have the experience, and, above all, we have the determination to succeed'.[92]

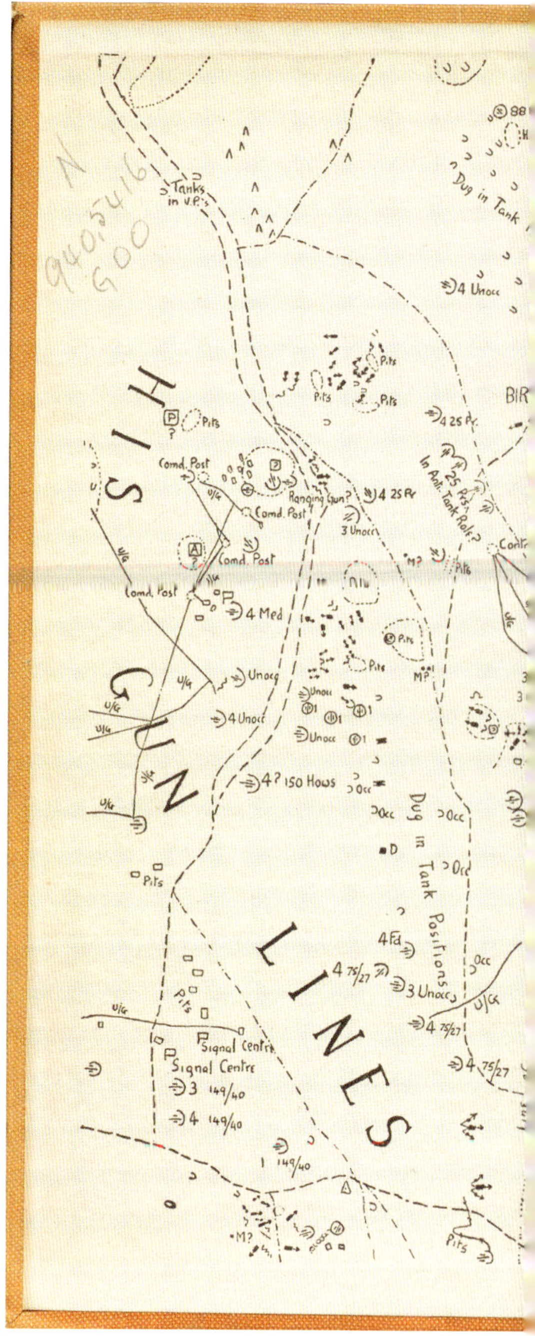

In a letter to his mother, Warrant Officer 'Cobber' Craig of the 2/13th described the scene in his company in the hours before the attack. He could see groups of men sitting around, cleaning and loading rifles and machine guns, and filling magazines. Runners made their way around the lines, delivering last-minute orders to platoon and company commanders. Craig's company commander, Captain Ross Sanderson, went with Craig around the platoons, to have a few words with the men he would soon lead into battle. 'He spoke beautifully', Craig recalled, and then shook hands with each of his platoon commanders and wished them luck. Back at his company headquarters Sanderson 'shed a few tears', saying to Craig, 'Cobber, we have a grand lot of boys here, I wonder how many of these faces we will see this time tomorrow?'[93]

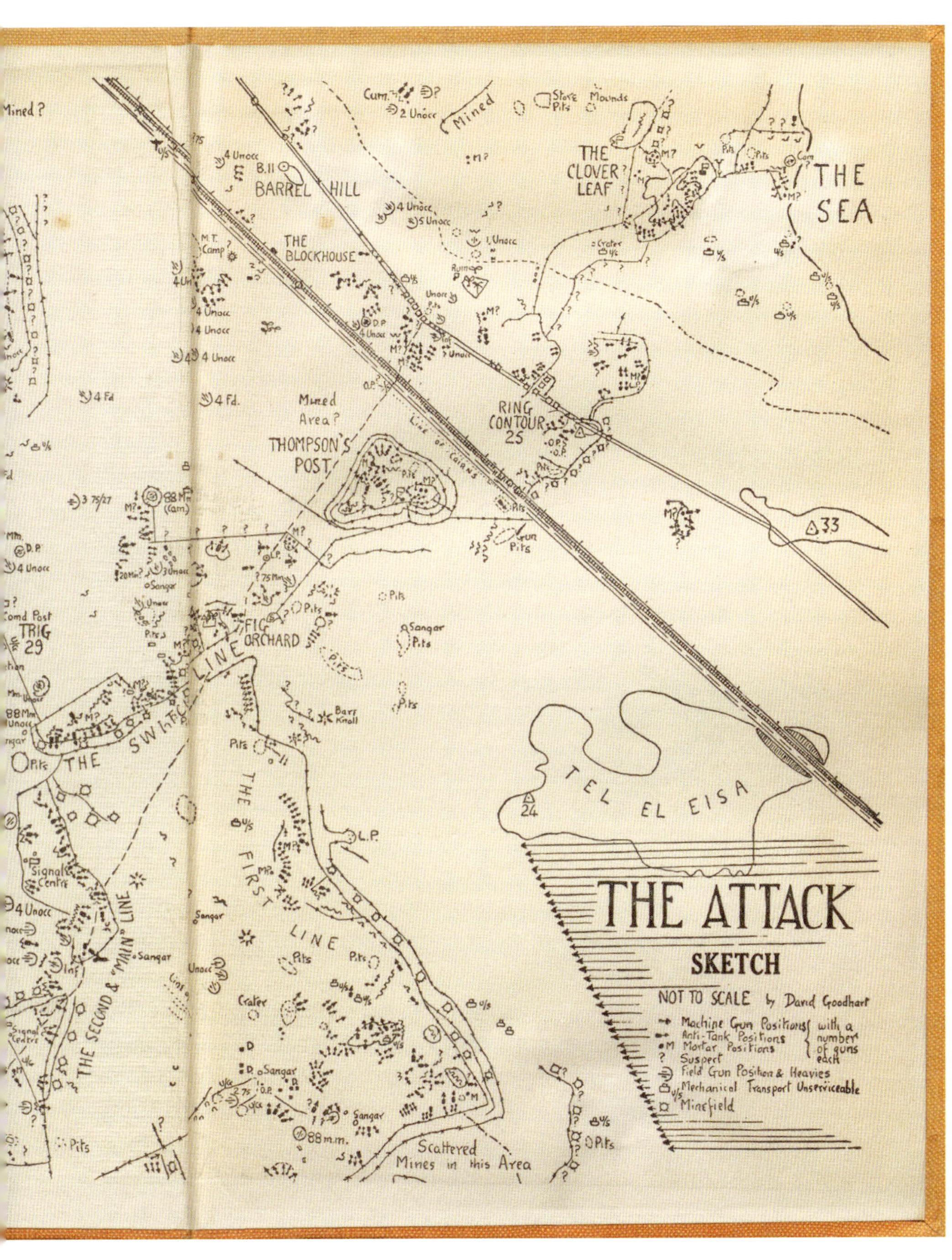

Map 17: Sketch map of Axis defences in the Australian sector, 23 October 1942. (From David Goodhart, *We of the Turning Tide*, endpapers)

The artillery regiments put in prodigious effort preparing for the battle, their tasks including producing detailed gun programs, digging a gun line further forward than ever and camouflaging it, and laying deep telephone cables.

The 9th Australian Division included just eleven of the Eighth Army's ninety-four infantry battalions. Battalion war establishment was thirty-six officers and 812 other ranks, while actual strength on the eve ranged from thirty officers and 621 others (2/28th) to thirty-six and 740 (2/13th).[94] The 9th Division constituted the army's only full-strength and experienced formation. It had 4000 reinforcements waiting in Egypt. The Indians, New Zealanders and South Africans were under-strength, and the Highlanders were new to desert operations. A captured German intelligence summary dated 10 October rated the 9th Division 'the best British troops on the Alamein front'.[95] That judgement was about to be tested.

Australians of the 2/3rd Pioneer Battalion watch a tank and infantry cooperation demonstration in September 1942. (IMAGE COURTESY OF TED CARTER).

CHAPTER 5

THE GREAT BATTLE BEGINS

23–25 OCTOBER 1942

THE OPENING BOMBARDMENT fired by 880 guns at 9.40pm on 23 October is the most famous part of the Battle of El Alamein and one of the defining moments of the entire war. Those guns fired counter-battery bombardment at known enemy gun positions for fifteen minutes, joined by Allied aircraft. This was the largest bombardment seen up to that point in the desert war, and indeed the biggest seen by British Commonwealth forces since 1918. It made a huge impression on eyewitnesses, including the 2/13th's 'Cobber' Craig, who later wrote, 'The sky rocked ... it was like the onset of an earthquake accompanied by a vicious lightning storm'. He called the noise 'deafening'. Private Fairbrother of the 2/28th reported the concussion stopping his watch. One of the Australian gunners, Joseph Stokes, was elated by the spectacle: 'For this we had striven and sweated ... our lives took on new meaning and assumed heroic proportions'. The bombardment's scale and technical efficiency were calculated to boost the morale of the attackers and diminish that of the defenders on the receiving end of the seemingly unlimited resources it suggested. After the bombardment ceased, there was a pause for five minutes, during which two searchlights pointed skyward. At 10.00pm they swung inward to form a pointed arch. At the same moment the guns resumed their bombardment, but with even greater intensity and this time as a barrage ahead of the troops, who now began their advance. A continuous stream of tracer shells from 40mm anti-aircraft guns pointed them in the right direction. About 900 artillery rounds per minute were falling on the enemy facing XXX Corps.[96]

(Top to bottom)

A photograph of the opening bombardment from the collection of Brigadier Alan Ramsay, CRA of the 9th Division.
(IMAGE COURTESY OF ALAN SANDBACH)

The opening barrage as it looked from the wagon lines of the 24th Battery, 2/12th Field Regiment.
(IMAGE COURTESY OF MICK DOOLEY)

Walking steadily through the dark and dust haze, the infantry soon encountered the eastern edge of the German minefields and outpost line. 'Operation Lightfoot' was the codename for the great battle, and it referred to the need to negotiate minefields. The sappers' work was vital on that first night. Typifying their bravery was Sapper Tom Broadhurst of the 2/3rd Field Company. The 28-year-old tanner was often in trouble with authority, especially for going AWL, but the citation for his Military Medal said his courage and worth had 'long been outstanding'. On this night he was assigned to a company of the 2/17th Battalion to deal with anti-personnel mines. Though under fire, he continuously moved across the company's front, disarming anti-personnel mines and booby traps, warning the infantry of dangers and earning great praise from the company commander. Later in the battle he acted as a runner, taking messages between his engineer company and the infantry, and also guided two Matilda 'Scorpion' flail tanks through the minefield. Though wounded, he remained on duty.

Typifying the bravery of the sapper officers was Lieutenant Arthur Stevenson of the 2/13th Field Company. The 28-year-old former civil engineer was attached to the 2/15th Battalion to clear minefields and generally assist the infantry. He had already reconnoitred extensive anti-tank and anti-personnel minefields when word came that one of the forward

companies needed ammunition urgently. Stevenson volunteered to take the ammunition vehicle and did so after himself making a gap wide enough. Later that first night, he helped to capture a dug-in tank and its German crew, and then destroyed the tank. Largely due to Stevenson's work, the battalion lost not a single vehicle to mines in the entire Alamein battle. On the first night, the Australian engineers had to deal with half a dozen types of mines from four countries as well as home-made booby traps. They suffered the second heaviest casualties of the sappers of any division, with thirty killed and wounded on 23–24 October.

(Above) The Royal Engineers Clearing the Mine Fields at the Start of the Battle of El Alamein, 23 October 1942, by Terence Cuneo. A dramatic painting that also shows the mechanics of mine-clearing: one man carries a detector, followed by a prodder, while a white tape marks the lane. (IMAGE COURTESY OF THE ESTATE OF TERENCE CUNEO)

(Opposite) A 25-pounder gun firing during the famous night artillery barrage of 23 October. (IWM E18469)

OBSTACLE CLEARING AT ALAMEIN

El Alamein represented the largest obstacle clearance and breaching effort in Australian military history. The main impediment to the Eighth Army's initial advance was the half a million anti-tank and anti-personnel mines laid by Rommel's army in belts lying parallel to the front but also in diagonal and flanking directions. Although with help and care the infantry could move through most minefields, their successful consolidation on newly won ground depended on the ability of vehicles to bring their support weapons forward rapidly. Thus, the success of the 9th Division, and indeed the whole Eighth Army in the battle, required the speedy opening of mine-free routes.

Disarming the mines was challenging. The Teller anti-tank mine, the main German type, came in two versions, one of which could not be disarmed without being destroyed where it lay. Even those which could be disarmed by removing an igniter might be fitted with anti-handling devices and thus be hard to 'delouse'. Chief among the anti-personnel mines was the 'S' mine (*Schrapnellmine*) which, after being triggered via a trip wire or a three-pronged pressure fuse, leapt from the ground and detonated at waist height. Inserting a nail or similar metal piece into the safety pin hole could neutralise it, but it too could have an anti-handling device fitted. Many of the mines encountered were captured British ones.

The Australian field companies allotted to the leading brigades on the first night had to make and mark gaps in the minefield, but also provide detachments to breach wire obstacles with Bangalore torpedoes, widen the minefield gaps, and help the infantry lay anti-tank mines during consolidation. The tasks were so demanding that sub-sections of the 24th Field Park Company and the 2/3rd Pioneer Battalion were given supporting tasks. Barton Maughan described the Eighth Army's mine-clearing method in the official history:

> *First, the field had to be detected; then its home and far boundaries were established and marked, and a centre line for the lane to be cleared was also marked. Next the outer edges of the lane were marked and the field was cleared of 'S' mines. Finally the anti-tank mines were lifted and the cleared gap was marked with lights and signs.*

Five reinforced sections, each 87-strong, undertook this work on the first night. In each section, a five-man reconnaissance party followed the leading infantry, reeling out a tape as they went and placing stakes with rearward shining coloured lights (colours depending on location within the field) at the home and far edges.

In between they stooped and used the backs of their hands to brush the ground for trip wires. Two men, tied to each other to keep them the required eight feet apart, pinned parallel tapes to the ground either side of the centre line to designate the boundaries of the lane to be cleared.

Spaced further back came other working parties who, in an operation requiring dexterity and courage, cleared the anti-personnel mines within the lane, which was then cleared of anti-tank mines. Those operating the few electronic detectors had to stand upright while sweeping in a circular motion, but generally the detection was done by men crawling the entire length of the gap, sweeping carefully with their hands within touching distance of their neighbours.

On the first night the sappers assisting the 26th Brigade, on the right of the advance, passed through the final minefield at 3.40am, only thirty minutes behind schedule: a fine effort given that the engineers had encountered and breached five separate minefields, sown with German, British, Egyptian, Italian and French mines as well as various booby traps. The sappers assisting the 20th Brigade, on the left, made slower progress, for they encountered a maze of minefields six times deeper than anticipated, and laid with no apparent system. Here too, there were many varieties of mines, including aerial bombs attached to tripwires, and anti-personnel mines fitted with anti-lifting devices.

Sappers of the Highland Division defuse 'S' mines, a job also done by Australians of the neighbouring 9th Division. (IWM E18936)

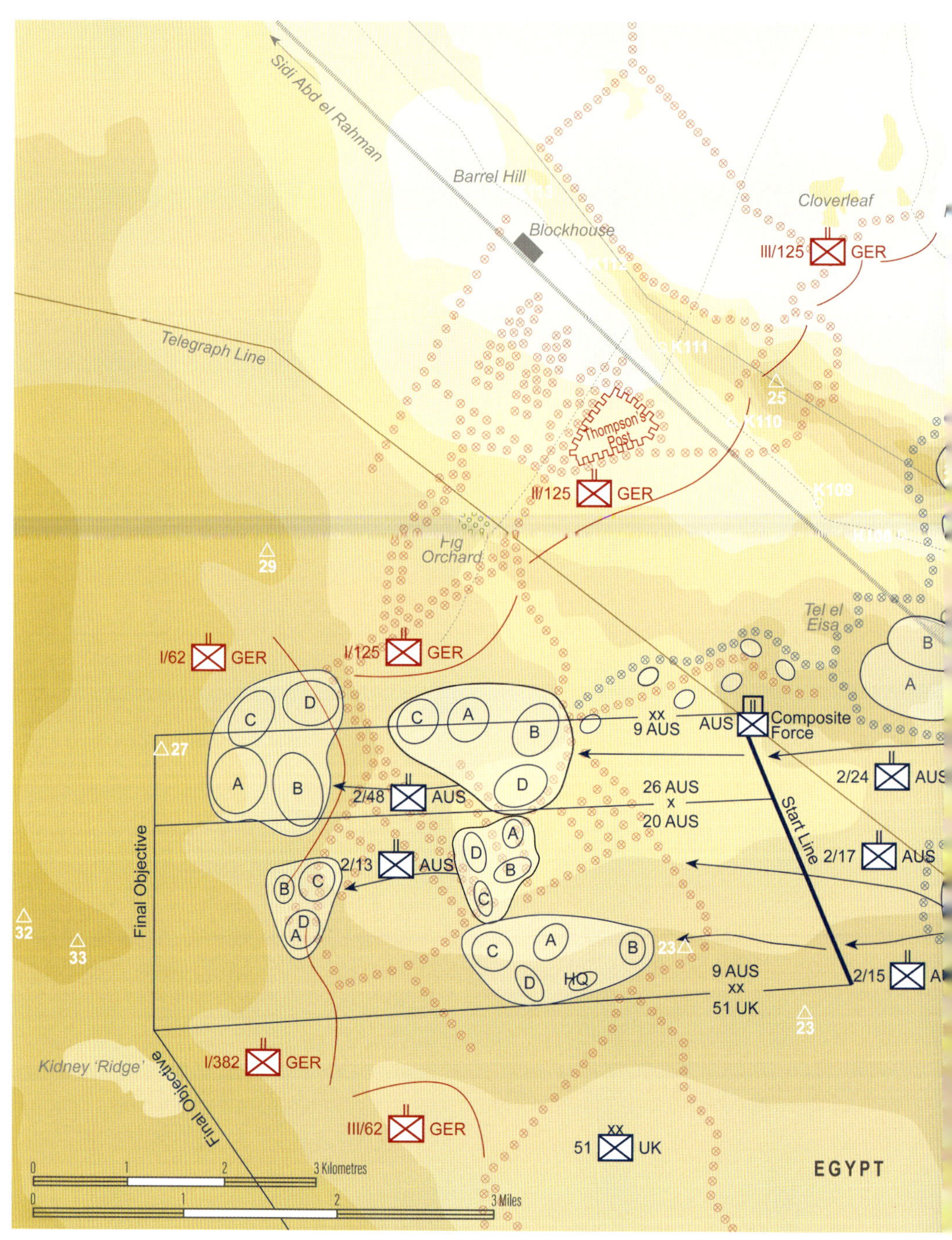

Map 18: Australian dispositions at dawn on 24 October 1942

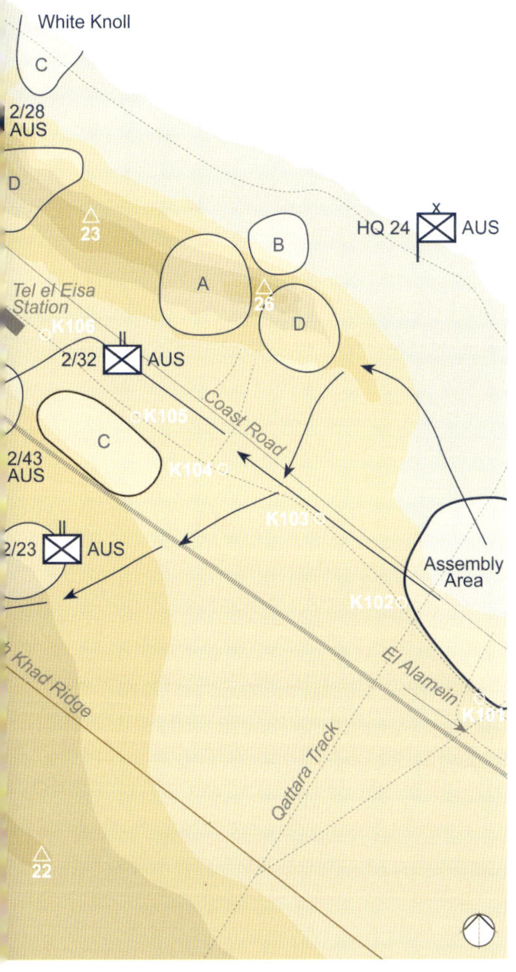

The engineers proved their worth time and again in succeeding days. They used wireless communications on an unprecedented scale and with great success. For example, after a German minefield map was found on the eve of the key assault on Trig 29 on 25–26 October, the engineers were informed and able to achieve a much shorter and quicker clearance. In the course of the battle, the engineers suffered over 100 casualties, including one-quarter of the strength of the 2/7th Field Company.[97]

As this suggests, there were plenty of defenders still in the fight. On the 9th Division front, three Australian battalions led the advance through the minefields and against dug-in enemy infantry: the 2/24th from the 26th Brigade, and the 2/15th and 2/17th from the 20th Brigade. Two battalions, the 2/48th and 2/13th, were scheduled to conduct a forward passage of lines through them, and advance to second objectives about 5 kilometres beyond the start-line. Battalion commanders, who were given scope to configure their attacks as they chose, placed two or three companies in the first wave.

On the right of the main Australian advance was the 2/24th Battalion. It made good progress against Italian posts, but mortar and machine-gun fire inflicted casualties, including the two leading company commanders. Lieutenant Tony Greatorex took over one company. It was the 37-year-old farmer's first battle, but he confidently organised the troops on their first objective. A few days later, while still acting company commander, Greatorex was wounded when an enemy machine gun opened up from the flank and inflicted many casualties. Greatorex personally led a successful section attack on the post, which was found to be a derelict tank. He was later wounded a

CONSOLIDATION AND RE-ORGANISATION

On the first night, and the succeeding ones, the Australians undertook what had until Montgomery's arrival been called 'consolidation', but at his insistence was now called 're-organising'. It was imperative to have a well-rehearsed effective drill for beating off the German counterattacks that invariably followed when the Australians captured ground. Indeed 'reorg' remains crucial today. Lieutenant Colonel Hammer wrote detailed notes on the topic after the battle. He first set out the typical situation as a battalion began to re-organise. It was dark, the unit had just advanced 7,000–10,000 yards (about 6,400–9,150 metres), shelling was coming from all sides and perhaps from one's own forces, ranks were thinned by recent heavy fighting (including commanders), the fog of war (dust, smoke, wire, mines and booby traps) was up, men were tired from physical effort and battle, the captured ground was unknown and there was limited time before daylight. He emphasised the need to make accurate calculations about the newly occupied ground, using a map where possible to select the reorganisation position. Company commanders were to pace out distances between platoons, and platoon commanders to do the same with sections. The selected ground had to provide a daylight field of fire. Defence in depth was important, as was avoiding huddling. Each company should receive orders regarding the supporting weapons operating in their area, and account for features on the ground such as tracks and fences. Once the layout was determined, a 'dig-in period' began, with single slit trenches sited for all-round defence. Every man was to have a set task, be it pick, shovel, sandbags, sentry, patrol or runner, and all were to be told of the location of other sub-units. Lucas lamps were used to communicate with supporting weapons, including where possible anti-tank guns, medium machine guns and mortars. A Echelon vehicles and carriers were to bring up more anti-tank mines, wire, sandbags, corrugated iron headcover, ammunition, food and water. A 'super-guide', a man of initiative, was allotted to keep battalion headquarters informed (it in turn was in contact with brigade HQ) and speed up the process of re-organisation. Hawkins anti-tank mines should be laid one per yard, for a total of 3000–4000. The men should now be ready for the 'always-to-be-expected dawn counter attack and the inevitable daylight counter attacks'. A golden rule was 'unselfishness', with commanders from platoon up to battalion not just doing their own job but also all they could to help units on either side of them. Every individual should be 'kept in the picture'.[98]

(Opposite) Consolidating: Egypt 1942 (detail), by British war artist Jack Chaddock. This artwork well exemplifies the dangers, difficulties and haste involved in consolidation at Alamein. Chaddock served in the 51st Highland Division. (IWM ART LD 3399)

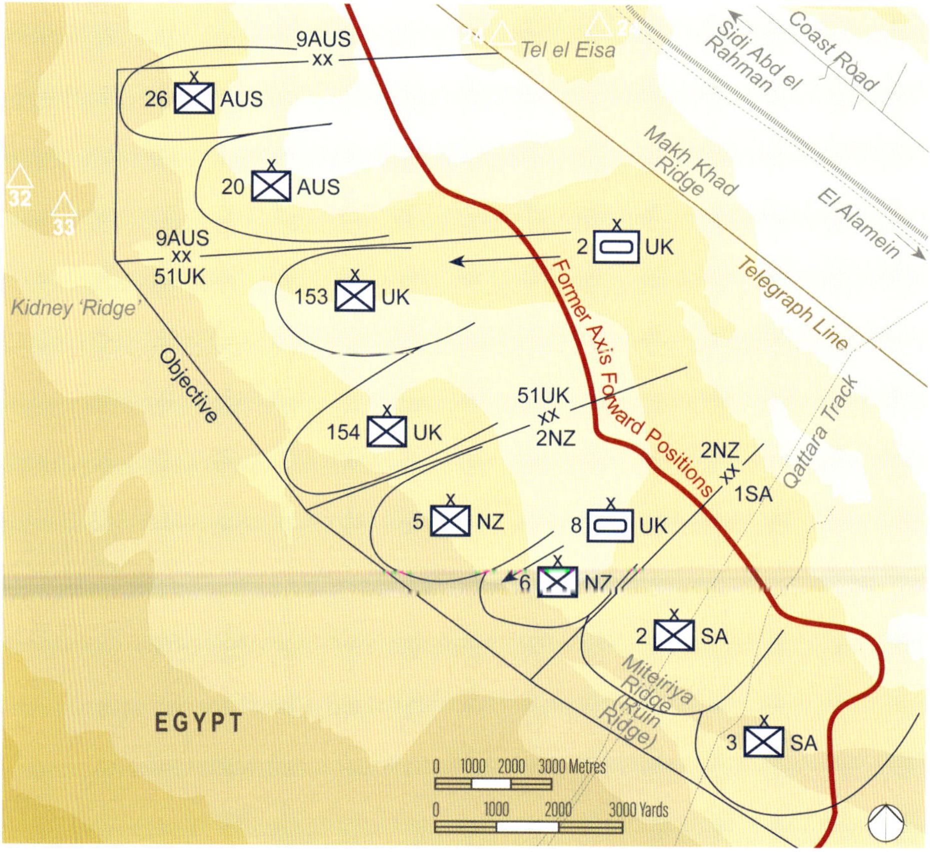

9AUS
XX
Tel el Eisa
Sidi Abd el Rahman
Coast Road
26 AUS
20 AUS
Makh Khad Ridge
El Alamein
32
33
9AUS
XX
51UK
2 UK
Telegraph Line
Kidney 'Ridge'
153 UK
Former Axis Forward Positions
Objective
Qattara Track
51UK
XX
2NZ
154 UK
2NZ
XX
1SA
5 NZ
8 UK
6 NZ
2 SA
Miteiriya Ridge (Ruin Ridge)
EGYPT
3 SA
0 1000 2000 3000 Metres
0 1000 2000 3000 Yards

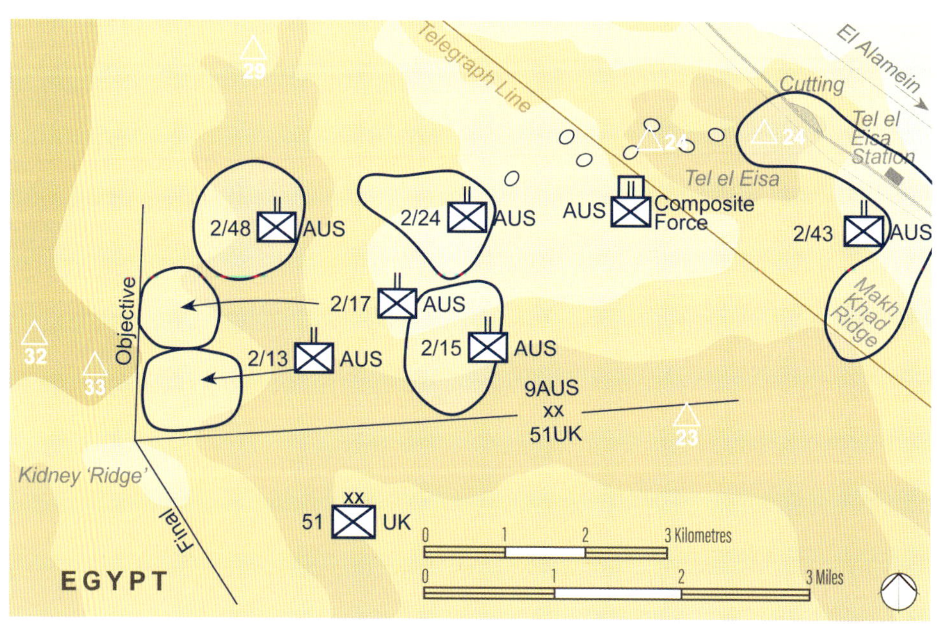
Telegraph Line
El Alamein
29
Cutting
24
Tel el Eisa Station
Tel el Eisa
2/48 AUS
2/24 AUS
AUS Composite Force
2/43 AUS
Objective
2/17 AUS
Makh Khad Ridge
32
2/13 AUS
2/15 AUS
33
9AUS
XX
51UK
23
Kidney 'Ridge'
Final
51 UK
EGYPT
0 1 2 3 Kilometres
0 1 2 3 Miles

second time while reconnoitring forward to locate the source of more machine-gun and anti-tank fire.

Men like Greatorex ensured that the first enemy posts and remaining wire obstacles were overcome, and within two hours the first objectives had been taken. The 2/48th achieved the night's final objective, 3500 metres from the brigade start-line. The 2/13th had a much broader front to cover: two companies had to advance across a front more than 2 kilometres wide. They had trained to attack with tank support, but when the enemy minefields proved to be not 230 metres deep as expected, but over 1400 metres deep, gaps could not be opened in time for the tanks, so the infantry went in alone. Their opponents were determined Germans. The first two companies made good progress, but when the second group of two passed through at 3.00am they encountered fierce resistance. Captain Ross Sanderson, who had dreaded losses on the eve of battle, went forward to accept the surrender of some Germans and was shot dead. Lieutenant Edward Norrie had already been seriously wounded but took command and led the men on into the attack. When he too was killed, Lieutenant Charles O'Connor ignored his own wounds and took up the baton, calling for volunteers to attack a nearby post. He led twelve men in the attack, which overcame the post in hand-to-hand fighting but saw O'Connor wounded again, this time mortally. By now the company had only one officer remaining, Lieutenant Fred Treweeke, who would be killed four days later. On the battalion's left flank, Sergeant Roy Easter was commanding a platoon. Following his company commander's orders, he attached them to the Gordon Highlanders of the 51st Highland Division in an advance for more than 700 metres, personally destroying two German machine guns and their crews.

The 24th Brigade was also involved, launching diversionary raids to the right of the main advance. Under 'Plan Bertram', dummy figures 70–275 metres apart were also illuminated to draw German fire and create alarm along the line.[99]

By the end of the first night, none of the four XXX Corps divisions had fully reached its final objectives, the precondition (together with clearing mine-free passages) of the intended armoured breakthrough. Nevertheless, each was close and had created large penetrations. The 9th Division captured 127 Germans and 264 Italians during the attack.

Montgomery's plans for the initial stage of the battle had not succeeded. The attack in the north had 'broken in', but the tanks had not passed through and beyond the enemy defences. The attack south of XXX Corps had failed too. One tentative feature of the original plan that remained a possibility was to cut off the enemy between the sea and the northern flank of XXX Corps.

(Opposite, top to bottom)
Map 19: XXX Corps dispositions, dawn, 24 October 1942
Map 20: The attack continues, 24–25 October 1942

During daylight on 24 October, the Australians did not advance, while artillery dispersed several Axis attempts to form up for tank and infantry counterattacks. To complete the capture of his objectives, Lieutenant Colonel Turner of the 2/13th rashly planned to attack in daylight, but brigade headquarters did not approve of this potentially costly plan. Turner's thinking remains a mystery, as he was killed by a shell blast that afternoon.

That night, the 20th Brigade completed the advance to the previous night's objective. Sergeant Easter of the 2/13th proved his worth for a second successive night. Tall and laconic, an outstanding patroller, he now took out a patrol to gather information on enemy dispositions. Discovering a group of enemy between his patrol and the battalion lines, he attacked and inflicted at least eight casualties for no loss to themselves. Easter's report persuaded the CO to attack without artillery support, so as to achieve surprise. Their attack was a complete success.

October 24 set a pattern for the days ahead: enemy counterattacks in daylight, followed by Australian advances at night. The Germans had been caught by surprise on 23–24 October, not least because Rommel was in Germany recovering from illness and his replacement, General Georg Stumme, suffered a fatal heart attack in the Australian sector on 24 October. However, by the time the initial objectives in the north had been taken, late on that day, the Axis forces had formed a new defensive line. Although corridors were now open for the British armour, which made some forward progress, it was unable to hold the ground beyond in daylight or to break the German anti-tank cordon.

'Black Sunday': 25 October

The following day, 25 October, was very taxing for the Australians as Axis counterattacks, shelling and sniping inflicted heavy casualties. Lance Corporal Cyril Mears of the 2/17th wrote in his diary, 'Jerry has been shelling all day ... We just have to lie in shallow holes, wondering who is next to go'. The 2/17th alone suffered twelve killed and seventy-three wounded on this 'Black Sunday', as the battalion called it. One private recorded being told by an exhausted stretcher-bearer that they had carried over a hundred casualties that day. That required going above ground, as did the work of the signallers, one of whom wrote: 'George and I shudder each time we leave our just below ground level shelter'. They sought the cover of rocks, damaged trucks and guns.[100]

About forty tanks (probably exclusively Italian) attacked across the 20th Brigade front, but Australian anti-tank guns halted them at close range. The 2-pounder guns of the 2/13th Battalion accounted for at least seven. Private Leslie Watkins was one of the 2/13th gunners. He was 'excited and itching to have a go'. Exhibiting excellent fire discipline, they held their fire as the tanks approached: ' ... 500 yards, 400 yards, 300 yards. Still we waited'. At a hundred yards, as if on command, the guns fired. 'As fast as the gun was loaded', Watkins remembered, 'I fired. As soon as I put two shells into a tank, I would shift target'. How many tanks he hit, Watkins could not say, but he recalled being 'drunk with excitement ... just blasting away at targets'.[101] Sergeant Allen Bentley was commanding

THE 6-POUNDER ANTI-TANK GUN

Though the 6-pounder was designed in 1938, once the war began it was long considered impractical to change production and training routines and replace the 2-pounder. It had a lower profile than the 2-pounder, and a more conventional split trail carriage. The first 6-pounders were not employed in action until April 1942. The 6-pounder anti-tank guns were 'really first-class weapons for their task' at Alamein, as they could knock out any Axis armoured vehicle on the battlefield.[102] The only Australian unit to employ them in the battle was the 2/3rd Anti-Tank Regiment, which began receiving them in July. Two of the regiment's 6-pounders together destroyed at least seven German tanks in defending the foremost positions of Tel el Eisa ridge on 13 and 14 July. Both guns were destroyed and the crews suffered heavy casualties from close-range fire. More than 100 members of the unit were killed or wounded in the July fighting. The unit had sixty-four of these guns by the time of the October battle, when they proved crucial, particularly on 31 October – 1 November.

DATA FOR MK II

CALIBRE
57mm

WEIGHT
1143kg

PROJECTILE
6 pounds (2.72kg) AP

EFFECTIVE RANGE
1510m

CREW
6

MUZZLE VELOCITY
821m/sec

RATE OF FIRE
15rpm

Australian gunners of 2/3rd Anti-Tank Regiment man a dug-in 6-pounder gun at Alamein.
(IMAGE COURTESY OF MURRAY WELTON)

DANGEROUS DRIVING

DRIVERS AT ALAMEIN

The men in the rifle companies sustained the highest casualties, but the battle of El Alamein was a traumatic ordeal for the entire 9th Division. Vehicle drivers are one example. Bren carrier drivers did valuable work, for example carrying ammunition, wounded and active troops, but their vehicles were vulnerable targets. Truck drivers were at risk too, as they brought forward troops and supplies.

A gunner reported seeing drivers take it upon themselves to drive behind the front on 25 October, calling out, 'Casualties?' Several trucks were hit. On 26 October, as the 2/48th Battalion seized the vital Trig 29, the battalion's trucks assembled nearby, ready to bring forward anti-tank mines to be laid across the newly won ground. A stray shell hit one truck loaded with mines, which in turn set off explosions among at least four other mine-laden trucks. None of the drivers in the trucks could be saved, though to the onlookers' astonishment, stretcher-bearers tried to rescue them, rushing in among the flaming wrecks and the screaming, writhing bodies. An entire ambulance crew was also killed as they drove to the area, which was now attracting intense enemy shelling.[103]

Two members of a 2/32nd Battalion Bren carrier crew in the Alamein area. The carrier had a 3-man crew, with the driver at the front to the commander's right. The hull on the commander's side jutted forward, with provision for a weapon – here an anti-tank rifle. (PHOTOGRAPHER: F LITTLEJOHN, AWM P02522.007)

the 2/13th's anti-tank platoon, which on previous days had suffered numerous casualties, including its officer. The sub-unit was so short of men that Bentley helped man a gun. He waited until the leading tank was very close (between 40–200 metres according to different sources) before opening fire and knocking it out with his first shot. Bentley had qualified at an anti-tank course just three months earlier. His gun accounted for five or six tanks before he was wounded in the chest and head. He was only evacuated when he collapsed and became unconscious. Like Bentley, earlier casualties to this platoon forced Private John Taylor to a more senior role than would be normal, and as the enemy tanks approached, he commanded a gun crew. They destroyed two tanks. Though still under fire, Taylor then took sticky grenades and went out to destroy the abandoned tanks. The following day he and another man crawled out to two enemy tanks disabled on a minefield, destroying them though pinned in no-man's-land for five hours.

Lieutenant Fred Wallder commanded a troop of 6-pounders of the 2/3rd Anti-Tank Regiment that accounted for nine tanks in the 25 October attack. His success was credited largely to his 'careful siting' of the guns.[104] Manning these guns was of course dangerous, and the enemy would destroy thirty-six of the regiment's guns during the battle.

The field artillery was also playing a vital defensive role. A platoon commander later wrote a great tribute to the Australian forward observation officer attached to the 2/17th and located just 40 metres away on this Black Sunday. Enemy shells had fallen on the area all day, said the infantry officer, killing and wounding men, destroying vehicles and even entering the trenches. Nevertheless, the artillery officer, Lieutenant Tim Rodriguez, had stood in the open behind his Bren carrier throughout, undeterred by shells bursting around him as he observed enemy fire and directed the friendly artillery's response. At one point shrapnel penetrated his shirt, damaged his wallet and binoculars and struck his carrier.[105] The 2/17th Battalion history mentions disapprovingly that the temporary brigadier, Brigadier Hugh Wrigley, visited the unit that day and strongly criticised Rodriguez for his 'indiscipline in concentrating two vehicles and inviting enemy fire' – the flat open terrain meant the only way to protect vehicles was to disperse them – as well as having a go at Battalion headquarters for not being dug in well enough and for having dead still lying around.[106] Wrigley had a point on both matters, but 're-organising' in a timely manner in such a hot spot was challenging.

The day was also stressful for the 26th Brigade, further north. 'Terrific battle from dawn', wrote Frank Legg, the Regimental Sergeant Major of the 2/48th Battalion. 'Breakfast at 10 – too dangerous for bog. All movement draws the crabs'. The war diary praised the 'magnificent and gallant' work of the stretcher-bearers, who were generally 'the only people above the surface of the ground which was continuously swept with fire'. One of them, Private Ernest Moore, carried a Red Cross flag as his only protection when he went to the aid of a mortally wounded comrade. Moore died amidst intense small arms fire.[107]

Sergeant Bill Kibby also braved this fire at least five times, crossing open ground to mend signal wires damaged by the shelling. This was typical of his leadership since the start of the battle. He had not only taken personal risks, but also directed his platoon's fire and encouraged his men. On the 23rd he had been courageous and aggressive in the attack; now he showed skill and bravery leading the defence.[108]

On the evening of 25 October, Rommel arrived at the front. He immediately ordered that the British be thrown out of captured territory, but this meant the Afrika Korps leaving their prepared positions and coming into the open. That was exactly what Montgomery wanted as a means of destroying the German armour. Rommel's spirits appear to have been low. He was not at his best in positional fighting. His problems were about to get worse, but although the Eighth Army had made some territorial gains, Montgomery had achieved neither a decisive breakthrough nor so weakened the *Panzerarmee* that it could not fight back fiercely.

CHAPTER 6

TURNING POINT

25–29 OCTOBER

MONTGOMERY'S PLAN OF SENDING his tanks beyond the enemy defences had not eventuated, but the possibility of attacking north in the hope of cutting off enemy forces on the coast – foreshadowed in pre-battle planning – now came into focus. Thus, HQ 9th Division was not surprised to receive orders from XXX Corps on 25 October to proceed with this attack on the night of 25–26 October. Morshead chose the 26th Brigade to launch the attack. Now began what General Montgomery called the 'crumbling' phase of the battle, in which the Axis forces were ground down by Allied infantry attacks and their own counterattacks. The Australians were central to enforcing and bearing the cost of this policy.

The seizure of Trig 29

The attack's chief objective was Trig 29, a flattened spur that one Australian likened to a large sand dune. Although only 6 metres higher than the surrounding desert, it dominated the area of the Australians' initial attack and the ground which sloped down northwards to the railway. Its value for observation across the flank of the initial assault had been recognised in the planning for Lightfoot, and it would have been one of the first-day objectives had it been considered achievable. Instead, it was designated the first 'exploitation' task. The Afrika Korps war diary recognised an attack in this area as its 'greatest danger', presumably because of the observation it gave over the surrounding area and its potential as a launchpad for attacks further north and west.[109]

Just before dark, the 2/48th's Lieutenant Colonel Hammer gathered his senior officers to tell them of the plan. As they listened, squatting around a rudimentary dugout, an enemy shell exploded just 10 metres away. No one was hurt, but while Hammer continued unperturbed, his officers took notes 'in strictly recumbent postures'.[110]

Australian patrols and observation of enemy movement suggested that the area of the planned 26th Brigade attack was being reinforced, but also that the ground between the 2/48th Battalion and Trig 29 was not mined. A stroke of good fortune helped the Australians to fill the considerable gaps in their knowledge of enemy dispositions and movements. At dusk on 25 October, a German reconnaissance party came towards the 2/48th Battalion lines. As they stood, hands on hips, Vickers gunners attached to the 2/48th Battalion opened fire from less than 100 metres away.[111]

Among those captured were the acting commander of the 125th Panzergrenadier Regiment, who was mortally wounded, and the acting commander of that regiment's 2nd Battalion. They were carrying maps and sketches detailing the enemy dispositions, the proposed reinforcement of the area, and minefields. The young battalion commander was unwounded, and seemed very frightened. He talked freely to his 2/48th Battalion interrogators, including a German-speaking member of the intelligence staff, and confirmed that the track northwards to Trig 29 was not mined.[112] The 2/24th Battalion, which was to execute the attack with the 2/48th, had also found a map among captured documents that enabled them to avoid a minefield that had been in their path in the original plan.[113]

The view west from Trig 29, as it looked in 2012. (IMAGE COURTESY OF PETER STANLEY)

The 2/48th Battalion was ordered to move northwards astride the track to Trig 29, which it would capture. Determined to seize the position in a swift and devastating surprise attack, Hammer arranged for a highly mobile company to make the final assault, its two leading platoons travelling on ten Bren carriers. Following them would be four carriers towing 37mm anti-tank guns, and then a troop of towed 6-pounder guns, with the reserve platoon riding on *portées.*

After this attack had begun, the 2/24th Battalion would form up in an area cleared earlier by the 2/48th. It would then attack north-eastwards along the 'switch line' – a term for the Axis defences set up behind the main line as protection against a sudden breakthrough to the coast from the east. The 2/24th's ultimate objective was the Fig Orchard, a readily recognised feature at the junction of the switch line and the enemy's front wire. Supporting the attack would be the divisional artillery's three field regiments, three additional field regiments and two medium regiments, a total of some 250 guns. This was an extraordinary number for one objective. They would fire timed concentrations, moving ahead of both attacks. Wellington bombers would also drop 115 tons of bombs on the battle area.[114]

Just after midnight, as the 2/48th rifle companies crossed the long white tape that represented their start-line, behind them an artillery shell struck one of the battalion trucks. The vehicle was loaded with mines, and the explosion set off a chain reaction among four other mine-laden trucks. The concussion was such that the driver of a truck 65 metres away was thrown from his vehicle. Ten men were killed, and two thousand mines and much valuable equipment was lost.

Meanwhile, the assault on Trig 29 began. The 2/48th's two leading companies secured their intermediate objective, 1000 metres from the start-line, on time. Then the carrier-borne company passed through, driving four abreast at 24 kilometres per hour. They covered the 1100 metres of desert in just nine minutes, arriving on the spur one minute after the artillery concentration lifted. The carrier-borne company's arrival almost at the top of the dust and smoke-shrouded Trig 29 completely surprised its numerous German defenders. They fought back though, and there followed a short, fierce hand-to-hand battle, in which the Australians used bayonets and 'killed with great determination'. Corporal Kingsley 'King' Albrecht was leading one section when his platoon was halted by heavy machine-gun and cannon fire apparently coming from a strong post. Albrecht charged towards the post with his rifle and bayonet, only to discover that the 'post' was in fact a dug-in Panzer III. Rather than seek cover, he continued forward and used a No. 73 anti-tank grenade against the tank. This rendered the crew unconscious before they were killed with hand grenades. Albrecht received a head wound from shell fragments but continued to lead his platoon, though covered with blood. This fighting, the hardest ever experienced by some of the Australians, captured the spur. More than 100 Germans of the 125th Panzergrenadier Regiment were captured and nearly as many killed.[115]

The supporting company following the carriers ran into heavy automatic and mortar fire from a series of posts to the west of the ridge as they approached. Lieutenant Taggart and four others in his platoon were killed as they attacked a series of posts here, and soon only seven members were still unhurt. Two of them, 40-year-old Private Percy Gratwick and section commander Corporal Bart Lindsey, summoned the courage to stand and charge the posts. Gratwick, in the lead, destroyed one post with a grenade, bayoneted a submachine gunner firing at him, then ran into another post and killed an entire mortar crew before being shot down. He was awarded a posthumous Victoria Cross. Lindsey, who received no award, would lose an eye in the fighting that night or the next day.

Gratwick's action unnerved the Germans in the area, and his company commander, Captain Bob Shillaker, grabbed the opportunity to secure vital ground west of Trig 29. Shillaker, just 23, had also been outstanding at Tel el Eisa in July. Two Italian battalions and a company of German tanks sent to Trig 29 that night could not prevent its capture. The Germans reported seeing thirty British tanks on Trig 29. Perhaps they mistook the diminutive Bren carriers for tanks. By daylight the weary men of the 2/48th Battalion were established in shallow trenches on Trig 29 behind 2000 mines. The innovative idea of using the carriers to seize Trig 29 had been vindicated.

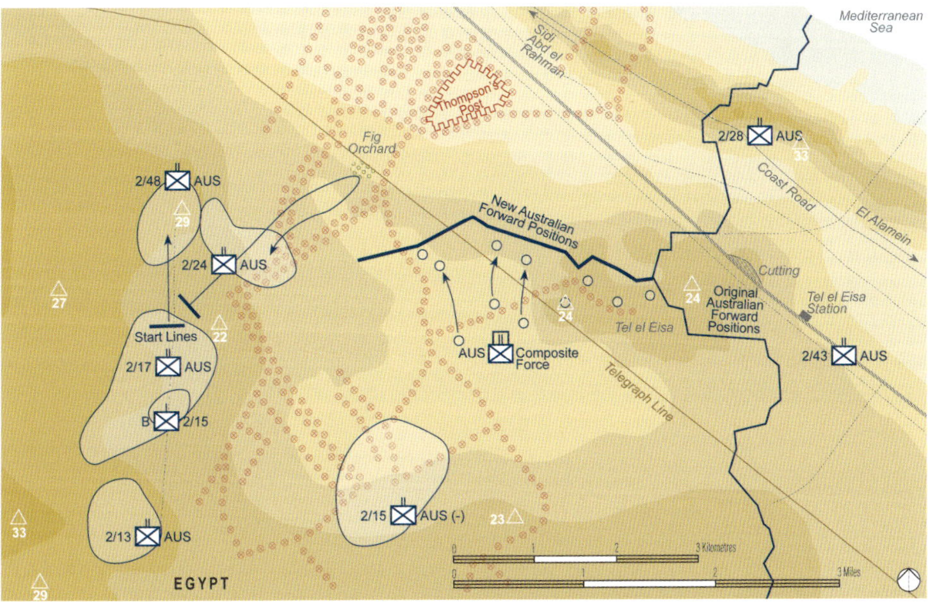

Map 21: The 'crumbling' begins – 26th Brigade attacks, 25–26 October 1942

Attack by 2/24th Battalion, El Alamein at night, 25–26 October 1942, by William Dargie.
Dargie's portrayal of C Company of the 2/24th Battalion under fire while preparing to advance from its start-line on the night of 25–26 October. (1973, oil on canvas, 3130 x 1890 x 111mm, AWM ART27821)

The 2/48th's successful action that night was enormously significant, not only for the vital ground captured but also for its impact on Rommel. It initiated in his mind the idea that Montgomery intended to make his main breakthrough on the extreme right of the Eighth Army line. As Ronald Lewin says in his authoritative account of the Afrika Korps, 'the underlying theme of Alamein, often overlooked by analysts, is the unremitting pressure exercised by 9 Australian Division and the frequent attempts made by Rommel to conform by shifting his weight to the north'.[116]

Forty minutes after the 2/48th Battalion attack began, the already depleted 2/24th Battalion advanced north-east against the strongest enemy defences encountered by the 26th Brigade at El Alamein. They achieved their intermediate objective. Sergeant George Berry, commanding a platoon, rushed and subdued two enemy posts by himself before his platoon followed him through intense fire. Once the company reached its objective, a cunningly sited enemy post proved an obstacle. A three-platoon assault was planned and Berry was first into the post, where in the words of his DCM citation 'he carried out terrible execution with the bayonet' until a gunshot wound broke his arm. As the battalion fought around and beyond the Fig Orchard, its final objective, the CO, Lieutenant Colonel Weir, decided to withdraw to the intermediate objective, probably because the unit had sustained so many casualties that it could not hold more. During this withdrawal, six men were killed or wounded by a single S 'Jumping Jack' mine. The battalion still managed to link up with 2/48th Battalion to form a continuous defensible line.[117]

Rommel was horrified at the loss of Trig 29, which the Germans called 'Hill 28', and from 26 October launched repeated efforts to recapture it.[118] If one includes abortive efforts to form up for attacks, there were twenty-five separate organised attempts to recapture the hill. Most were broken up by the tremendous artillery support available to Trig 29's defenders: the forward observation officers could call on as many as 360 guns to smash attempts to regain the height, vindicating the recentralisation of artillery control implemented by Montgomery and Kirkland before the battle. There was artillery action of some kind in progress day and night throughout the battle of El Alamein, but Trig 29 came under such attention that it became the most shelled location on the entire battlefield. As the result of lessons learnt in the July fighting, virtually all infantrymen had overhead cover – sheets of corrugated iron were included in the reorganisation stores – which reduced casualties. One of the forward observation officers there was Lieutenant Bob Menzies of the 2/7th Field Regiment. Since the first day of the battle, Menzies had been working on the forward slopes of Trig 33, where his predecessor had been killed by enemy fire. Now on Trig 29, Menzies established an observation post again in an area offering little cover among defences already devastated by shell fire – from that dangerous but vital ground he could see up to 4500 metres in all directions. For 48 hours he directed fire that broke up many Axis counterattacks and though relieved for one night he then returned to the job on 28 October.

The Germans and Italians sent against Trig 29 did come close to recapturing it. Indeed, on one occasion, a German commander reported that his men had captured the hill, only to find that they were still several hundred metres short. The height was held till 27 October by the 2/48th Battalion, and then from 28 October by the 2/17th Battalion. Both battalions suffered heavily.

Planning the next attack

Montgomery's senior staff officer, Freddie De Guingand, wrote on 26 October, 'If we go on as we are, sooner or later the enemy will have to employ 21 Panzer Division in the Northern sector'. When that happened, Montgomery would have the option of releasing his armour to break through in the south. Until then the 9th Division had days of hard fighting ahead.

Montgomery knew that he had to conserve his infantry, especially in XXX Corps. The South Africans had started understrength and had few reinforcements, so could not be committed to any major attacks. The New Zealanders had one major attack left in them and they were ordered into reserve. The 51st Highland Division had taken heavy losses in the initial attacks. The 9th Division had already suffered heavy losses too, but Montgomery knew that the 9th alone – with 4000 reinforcements in Egypt – could make up for losses, where other divisions could not. This cruel accounting, where the loss of individuals did not matter, was an inescapable calculus for an army commander. On 25 October, Montgomery had directed Morshead to 'Attack North' once Trig 29 had been taken. An attack was planned for the night of 27–28 October, but on the 26th, when Montgomery ordered XXX Corps to take a short rest from major operations, it was agreed that the corps would complete 'mopping up' and the 9th Division attack would be postponed to the night of 28–29 October.[119]

On 27 and 28 October, Rommel's forces continued to try to force the Australians off Trig 29. A veteran Australian machine gunner on the hill remarked of one attack: 'I was in France in 1918 but I didn't see as many Germans as all those bastards comin' this way!' The most determined attack faced an estimated 248 rounds of artillery fire per minute for the first five minutes before falling back. 'If Jerry is not bomb happy, he is not human', wrote one Australian infantryman.[120]

The Axis artillery fire was taking a toll too. Signalman Bob Anson wrote in his diary under 28 October, 'Trig 29. The worst spot I have been anywhere in this war'. He listed eleven comrades killed at or near the hill and concluded: 'Soon be none of us left'. Little wonder that his battalion's war diary described the efforts of the signallers on Trig 29 as 'superhuman'. Private Vic Walshe of the 2/17th Battalion Intelligence Section saw horrifying evidence of the enemy artillery's effectiveness when he went forward looking for two artillery signallers who had lost contact. The young men presented a 'bloody mess ... hanging grotesquely from the beams' of their dugout. Shocked, Walshe had to go back and tell the artillery FOO of his discovery, only to be asked to return and confirm it. He brought back the FOO's binoculars as proof.[121]

Map 22: The 'fateful' attacks of 28–29 October 1942

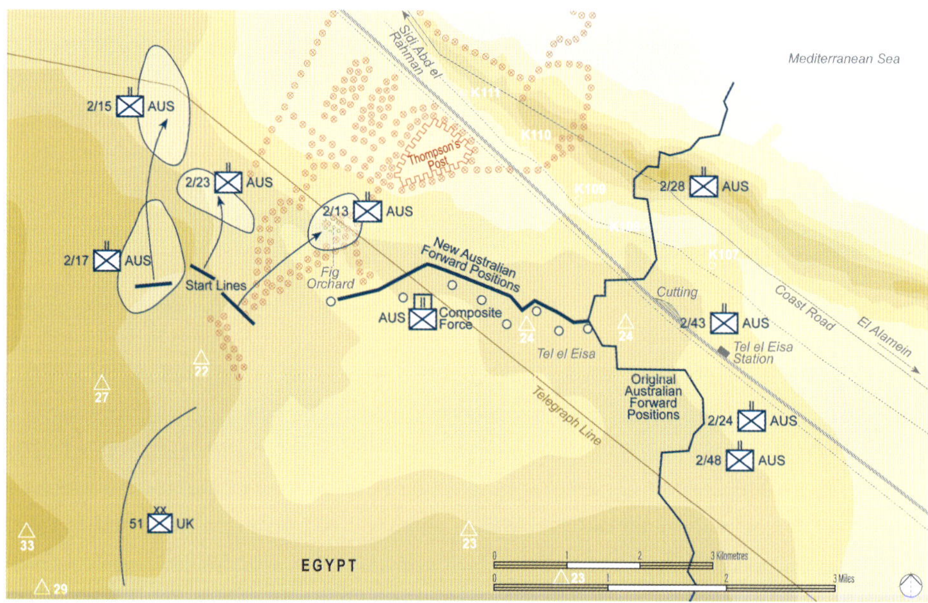

Resuming the offensive on the 'fateful' 28–29 October

Early on 28 October, Morshead presented the final plan for that night's attack to his commanders. The plan was to maintain pressure on the enemy and open the area south of the coast road for supply and casualty evacuation. It involved both the 20th and 26th Brigades, with a vague reference to the 24th Brigade exploiting once the plan succeeded. The 20th Brigade was to hold Trig 29 with the 2/17th Battalion, while the 2/15th advanced northwards from there and the 2/13th advanced to the north-east. The advances of the 2/13th and 2/15th Battalions would secure the flanks for the 26th Brigade attack, which had three stages. First, the 2/23rd Battalion and the 46th Royal Tank Regiment would capture and hold segments of the main road near Kilo 113. This would protect the second-stage attack, to be made eastwards along the main road by the 2/48th Battalion. Attacking the enemy from behind, it would capture his forward defences on the road, which would then be open. In the third stage, the 2/24th Battalion would follow the 2/48th and take Thompson's Post from the north, thus completing the capture of the area south of the main road. If these advances succeeded, the 24th Brigade and British armour could exploit westwards.[122]

Morshead's plan, which he discussed with Leese and Montgomery, was highly ambitious, and in hindsight had so many difficult objectives that it seems unlikely to have succeeded. After nearly a week of fighting, the 53-year-old Morshead and his headquarters were exhausted, and it is understandable that they made mistakes. Morshead recorded that Montgomery approved of his tactics but doubted that the British armour would be able to offer the support the Australian was hoping for.[123]

So, on the night of 28–29 October, the 9th Division resumed the offensive. The 20th Brigade had been relieved by a brigade of the Highland Division, and at 10.00pm on 28 October, the 2/13th and 2/15th Battalions launched attacks north-east and north respectively from Trig 29. Both achieved their goals, though at a cost. The 2/13th Battalion found itself in the 'Fig Orchard', from which the 2/24th had earlier been evicted. This area was riddled with booby traps and mines, and filled with the stench of death. The strain of this location on men already pushed to the limit was tremendous.

The 2/15th gathered for the attack in a restricted forming-up place near Trig 29 and came under heavy shelling. The commanding officer, Lieutenant Colonel Keith Magno, refused an offer of shelter from this bombardment, insisting on being with his men as they crossed the start-line. He was advancing with the forward troops when word came back that he had been wounded. His carrier driver went forward and found Magno lying in a shallow depression. He had lost an arm and received severe head and stomach wounds. He was conscious, calm and still concerned about his men as, under 'incredibly heavy' machine-gun fire, he was taken to a British aid post. He died two days later. Major Bruce Strange took over the battalion, despite an arm wound.[124] Strange would remain in command until the night of 1–2 November and receive a DSO for his 'utmost vigour, aggressive spirit and initiative' in this period.[125]

The bombardment supporting the 2/15th's and 2/13th's attacks stunned the enemy. The 90th Light Division's war diary described the barrage that suddenly lit up the horizon in the northern sector as 'reminiscent of Great War days'. To the staff at the 20 Brigade Headquarters, the 2/15th's advance 'proceeded entirely according to plan'. Its final objective, 3000 yards (about 2740 metres) from the start-line, was reached at 11.52pm. No minefields had been encountered, 'its casualties were very lt [light] and it proceeded to dig-in without serious difficulty'.[126]

To participants in the attack, the official account would have sounded simplistic and bloodless. Private Eric Lambert, who was at the 'sharp end' of this assault and was a skilled writer, wrote his own version that reveals the confusion of close-quarters night fighting. His diary entry for that day began, 'A fateful date for us all'. He gave a powerful account of the emotions and confusions experienced by ordinary Australians in this and many similar actions:

> *Almost as soon as our own barrage began the Hun replied & he was right among us. Capt Jubb was badly hit. How I came thru' it God only knows; men on either side of me were falling & I became convinced I bore a charmed life & no longer bothered to go to ground. Ahead of us loomed a ridge; machine guns pelted it from both sides. The bullets as they came past me were like comets. We doubled over & into soft white sand, each moment a hideous clamour of shell burst, black smoke a mad flash revealed low bushes & white sand, the black shadows of men falling; cries, supplications, laughs, & the din.*
>
> *Passing thru' the post taken by the Coy in front all its defenders lay dead in trenches,*

except one whom I sent careering fearfully back with his arms up. Past here death and blood came thick among us ... for a moment chaos & disorganisation reigned, but the line reformed, the shells cut among us like scythes. Brennan came running back, his arm pouring blood, seeking a stretcher-bearer. His dirty wide eyed face passed mine & was gone; Beard, hit by the same shell, lay bleeding to death. Men wandered everywhere bleeding, hoarse, distracted. 1000 yds past that post Mahoney stopped us. We began to dig like things possessed expecting the counterattack. [127]

A laconic diarist described the same attack with one word: 'Dreadful'. While Lambert's account reveals fear, horror, violence and uncertainty that are absent from official accounts, he and his comrades shared the commanders' satisfaction with the battalion's work that night: 'The cold moonlight poured down on a scene of elation', he wrote. However, he was concerned less with tactical achievements than with the fruits of battle: 'Loot was everywhere', he gloated. Yet Lambert was also aware of the price paid for these prizes. Far from believing casualties to be 'very light', he concluded that the action had almost halved his platoon's strength. The 2/15th Battalion suffered forty-five casualties and buried eighty-nine Italians killed in the assault; there were about 130 prisoners, mostly Italians. The battalion consolidated its new positions, which thrust out into the enemy's lines, by digging in and laying anti-tank mines.[128]

2/13th in the Fig Orchard

The 2/13th Battalion that attacked north-east from Trig 29 was a shadow of the force that had started on 23 October. The average strength of the rifle companies was just thirty-five. Their men were exhausted after four days and five nights of intense action. B Company, one of the two forward companies in the attack, now had to cover a frontage of 200 metres, and advance some 2300 metres. Commanding the company was Lieutenant Malcolm Vincent, as the previous commander, Lieutenant Fred Treweeke, had been killed by airburst while deciphering for Vincent his almost illegible notes on the CO's orders for the night. When Vincent met the CO, Lieutenant Colonel George Colvin, he received little further information before the latter was called away. Enemy fire landed on the forming-up place, and once the advance commenced, the supporting barrage seemed inconsistent in timing.

The battalion struck the edge of an extensive minefield, liberally laced with booby traps, some 1400 metres from its start-line. Nevertheless, within seventy-five minutes of the beginning of the advance, sappers had cleared a 320-metre gap, and the battalion reached its first objective at the same time as the 2/15th. Just after midnight, the 2/13th attained its final objective. Both forward companies' objectives contained many booby traps and mines. 'Cobber' Craig of A Company wrote, 'He had them set up in their doovers [dugouts] in discarded packs on the ground, in water bottles, in every imaginable place. You only had to screw the top off a water bottle and bang up you went. We lost many of our boys that night on these filthy traps'.[129]

Major Bruce Strange (left) and his driver in the desert. Strange would receive the DSO for his courage and initiative at Alamein. Later he would be a psychological casualty of war: he committed suicide in his tent in Queensland in 1944. He was just 31 years old and suffering from depression attributed to malaria and his war service. (AWM P04602.001)

As the two reserve companies came forward, they found themselves under fire from enemy machine-gun posts which had inevitably been passed unseen by the widely spread advancing forward 'companies'. While mopping up began, battalion headquarters established itself in former German positions just forward of the Fig Orchard, which the 2/24th had briefly held on the 26th. Here, the 2/13th also found many 'S' mines and booby-traps, which were soon causing casualties. A platoon of the 2/2nd Machine Gun Battalion that came forward with the 2/13th dug in about 500 metres east of the Fig Orchard. Hurriedly removing gear from their trucks, they put all their stores in a heap. As men gathered round to collect the gear, mines and booby-traps buried just below the surface exploded, inflicting some ten casualties. Sappers worked bravely and desperately under fire to clear the area.

To help them through their sixth night of battle, B Company of the 2/13th was issued 'Pep B tabs' – amphetamine pills. The medical officer observed the tablets' effects clinically, recording the men's comments as 'very favourable': 'felt like continuing the attack', said one; 'had no desire to try and get some sleep after digging in', said another. A third was able to write nonchalantly the next morning that they had reached their objectives easily and had not been shelled much, though he added that his platoon had neither officers nor sergeants, and was under the command of a lance corporal.[130]

For all the horrors they endured, the 2/13th and 2/15th had achieved their goals of the night of 28–29 October.

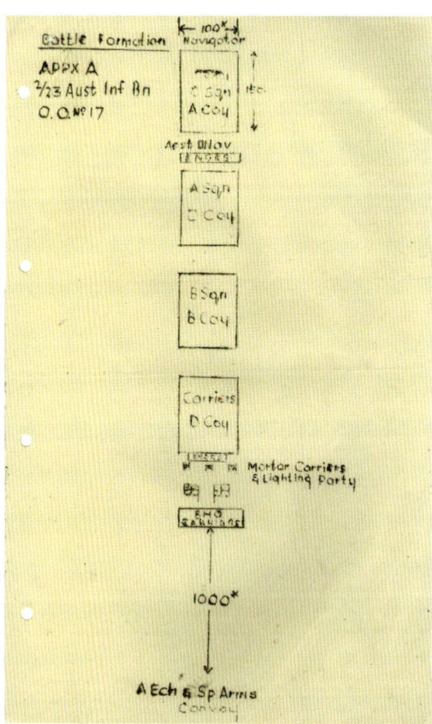

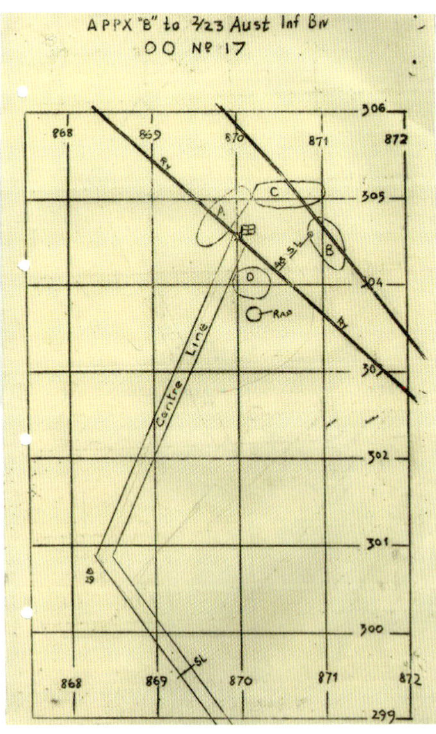

Ride of the 2/23rd

The third Australian battalion that attacked that night was the 2/23rd Battalion, which was ordered to drive between the ground just won by the 2/13th and 2/15th and to secure a foothold on the main road. In entering the battle for the first time, the battalion was fresh and would be supported by Valentine tanks of the 46th Battalion, Royal Tank Regiment (RTR). The two units had been training together for a week, and Lieutenant Colonel Bernard Evans of the 2/23rd and Lieutenant Colonel Clarke of the 46 RTR had made detailed arrangements. Clarke was popular among the Australians, who called him 'Wirewhiskers'.[131] All three battalions of the 26th Brigade had been allotted tasks for this night, but the 2/24th and 2/48th could advance only if the 2/23rd and the tanks succeeded in reaching the railway line, and exploited from there to secure a forming-up place on the main road from which its sister battalions could attack.

The 2/23rd's plan involved mounting as many men as possible on Bren carriers. The remaining troops would ride on the tanks. Evans's idea was to advance more rapidly than on foot and to maintain closer touch with the tanks, in order to obtain greater surprise. There were reportedly few defences between Trig 29 and the railway, but it was known that the enemy was altering his dispositions to meet the threat to his coastal flank.

The tank force struck trouble even before it left its own defence lines. The unusually dark night and the dust obstructed visual communication among the tanks, and at least five struck 'friendly' mines before they had reached the start-line. Two specially formed Australian and British navigating teams could not help, for they attracted so much enemy fire that all members were quickly hit or scattered. According to one diarist, the start-line had been mistakenly placed on a fully occupied German headquarters. Close-range enemy machine-gun and anti-tank fire troubled the attackers from the time they moved off the start-line at 11.30pm.

The assembly area and start-line had been reconnoitred twice by the Intelligence Section and BHQ personnel of the 2/23rd – the second time in borrowed Bren carriers on the afternoon of the attack – but not by the tank commanders. The early stages of the attack suggest a degree of undue haste and carelessness in the preparations.[132]

After the initial explosions, several tanks moved to the flanks and incurred further casualties on their own mines. 'It was bloody chaos', observed one Australian eyewitness. 'You couldn't see for dust and there were dead and wounded everywhere'. Infantrymen who tried to communicate with the tank crews to help guide them had little success, for most of the commanders were buttoned-up inside.[133]

(Opposite, left to right)
Figure 4: The battle formation of the 2/23rd Battalion and 46 RTR for the attack on the night of 28 October 1942, as shown in the orders for the operation. One squadron of tanks was attached to each of the three leading infantry companies. (FROM AWM52, 8/3/23/30)

Figure 5: Diagram from the 2/23rd Battalion's orders for the night of 28 October showing the intended centre line of the assault, running north-east from the vicinity of Trig 29. Also shown are the battalion's intended defensive positions astride the coastal road and railway, so sited to provide a secure start-line for another attack by the 2/48th Battalion. (FROM AWM52, 8/3/23/30)

Lieutenant Merv Horan of the 2/12th Field Regiment calls 'Fire!' near Tel el Eisa. His regiment fired approximately 180,000 rounds during the battle, a remarkable average of more than 7,000 rounds per gun. (IMAGE COURTESY OF MALCOLM DOOLEY)

Several mine-clearing tanks cleared mines, but in the process so damaged the metal superstructures supporting the drums that they could not drive forward, instead becoming obstacles to the following tanks. As the latter tried to avoid the blockage, more were lost on mines and to anti-tank guns. Burning tanks, ricocheting armour-piercing shells and enemy flares soon lit up a chaotic scene. To add to the Australians' confusion, Lieutenant Colonel Clarke of the 46 RTR lost contact both with his own brigade HQ and the 2/23rd Battalion, because he had gone forward to investigate the mine situation. He was also twice wounded.[134]

The enemy fire forced the infantry to dismount, and the 2/23rd's attack turned into a series of local actions, controlled by surviving platoon commanders. On the left flank, A Company lost all its tanks but made some progress. After machine-gun fire killed Lieutenant Jack Ottley as he led his platoon forward on the extreme left, Sergeant John Young continued with his section, guided by the light of burning tanks. The light gleamed on the long barrel of an 88mm gun, screened behind sandbags. Firing bursts from his submachine gun, Young led an attack on the post, from which overcoated figures quickly emerged with their hands up. Corporal Bill Bosanko's section found itself amid German positions when its supporting Valentine was destroyed. He and his men subdued two enemy posts, the defenders of one of which tried unsuccessfully to avoid capture by shouting, 'Don't fire, we are Aussies'. The Germans surrendered and volunteered to carry back a mortally wounded Australian.[135]

Early in the attack, A Company's sergeant major, Warrant Officer Ken Joyce, was behind the turret of one of the foremost tanks when it exploded. He felt as if he were blown ten feet in the air. He came down dazed, but still holding his Bren gun. All officers of the company were soon killed or wounded by the machine-gun and mortar fire, and Joyce took over, with the help of sergeants who became platoon commanders. Joyce led a successful attack on a gun position, then advanced some 300 metres and took a series of German trenches. He counted seventy-five men with whom to push on to the main objective, a ridge some 500 metres ahead, from which two machine-gun posts were constantly firing. He contacted battalion headquarters and arranged for Vickers machine guns to neutralise the enemy machine guns. His force was just 100 metres from one of the posts when the moon appeared from behind clouds and they came under fire again. A nearby soldier was felled and three rounds hit Joyce's haversack. When the moon clouded over again, Joyce approached the pit from the flank and killed its occupants with grenades. The other machine gun was subdued, and once the Australians reached the top of the ridge, the defenders surrendered. Joyce sent forty prisoners back, while fewer than forty of his original party dug in and held their ground.

The surviving tanks began moving again at 12.55am, but six 50mm anti-tank guns soon engaged and sent them scattering in disorder. Because the 2/23rd's infantry companies had been paired with individual tank squadrons, they too were split up in the confusion.[136]

The tank-riders probably suffered the most. For example, Sergeant Jim Slight's section was on a tank that went well forward before hitting a mine, which killed the whole tank crew and wounded all but two of his section. Slight jumped off the tank before it exploded, bayoneted three Germans in a dugout, and then regained the tank, only to be thrown into the air by the explosion. An anti-tank shell blew away his left ankle, and a comrade lost both feet. The two uninjured survivors joined a small party of Australians who engaged in fighting so close that the enemy were able to capture a Bren gun. Three Australians were wounded trying to recapture the gun.[137]

When one of the lead Valentines in the centre received a direct hit, Privates Ralph Reichman and Cecil Hanlon were the only riders able to walk away. They were joined by a survivor from another company, who barely escaped death or capture when he mistook a German in a nearby trench for an acquaintance. All three Australians climbed onto another tank, which was soon struck in the turret by an anti-tank shell. Rather than run, the Australians bravely tried to help the wounded British tank commander out of the vehicle, and had lifted him on to the turret when a shell hit him again and threw Reichman off the Valentine. Reichman was wounded in the leg and as Hanlon dressed it, yet another shell struck the tank and tore its front open. The driver jumped clear, as his tank careered on down a slope. Reichman struggled back and told Colonel Evans that the enemy was well dug-in and fighting hard.[138]

At some point after 1.00am, Evans realised that there was no possibility of continuing the attack in conjunction with the tanks and that many of his men were defending rather than attacking. Fortunately, some of the German positions they now occupied were well suited to defence. A sergeant at battalion headquarters heard Evans 'telling the tank comdr what he thought of his bloody tanks etc., and it gave all and sundry who was in earshot great pleasure to know that he was of the same opinion as ourselves, buggar [sic] the tanks the lads said, and they had reason to go crook'. The Australians, including Evans, were willing to sheet home the blame for what had gone wrong to the tanks, when in fact riding in on them, which had cost lives, had been Evans's idea. Moreover, blaming the tanks for not performing well at night while going through minefield gaps that deprived them of their manoeuvrability was harsh.

At about 3.00am, Evans was so angry he threw his helmet on the ground and said 'Well boys; this looks like the end of the 2/23rd Battalion!' Yet rather than give up, he led sixty to seventy men – all he could gather – into an attack that captured the main enemy position, including the six 50mm guns mentioned earlier and 160 prisoners, almost all of them Germans.

Private John Butler of the 2/23rd wrote in his diary that Bernard Evans 'proved himself this night a leader of men', carrying out the battalion motto: 'If you cannot find a way, make a way'. He also recounted an incident where Evans told a tank driver to move forward and clean up Axis posts. The driver asked whether that was his colonel's order. 'Damn your Colonel, I'm your Colonel, now follow me', was Evans's reported reply, and he followed it up by jumping into his jeep, waving his revolver and successfully charging the enemy position. Sergeant Fred Carleton said of Evans, 'Bernie never relaxed his efforts, he kept the

A German 50mm anti-tank gun and two dead members of its detachment at Alamein.
(STATE LIBRARY OF SOUTH AUSTRALIA SRG435/2/463)

spirit of all and sundry up by his dymatic [sic] personality'.[139]

At 4.00am Evans reported by wireless that his force of sixty to seventy men was now digging in on ridges about 1000 yards (914 metres) from the front line. He had insufficient troops to continue the attack and was not in communication with any responsible officer of the 46 RTR. That night, the 2/23rd had suffered 207 casualties, including sixteen officers. In most respects the attack had been disastrous, though the individual infantrymen had shown great courage and initiative and Morshead praised the battalion for its determination. Butler was astonished by their high morale in the aftermath of the battle, recording that 'after going through the worst kind of hell their high spirit remained with them and they could be seen in the moonlight standing in groups – smoking of all things – and chatting away as though they were in their home town main street or bush walks, heedless of snipers, anti-tank bullets, mortars, machine guns and shell fire'.[140]

The attack had been catastrophic for the tank crews, too. Joyce talked angrily next morning to tank men, but mellowed when he heard that they now had only fourteen of the forty tanks which had started the attack. The 46RTR war diary says the number was in fact just seven runners. Not only Clarke, but all his squadron leaders were wounded in the fighting. Another 2/23rd man who had criticised the tank men also softened after looking inside one of the tanks destroyed by a mine. He 'marvelled at those crews who are stuck inside them, they have my admiration, we say a lot about them but after all when one considers the limit of the vision etc, they do a damn good job'.[141] He could have added the difficulty of fighting a tank in the dark. Morshead's elaborate and overly demanding plan of attacking from a base created by the 2/23rd's attack was now dropped. Instead, the 2/23rd was ordered to consolidate and establish contact with the 2/13th and 2/15th Battalions, on either side of it. The 2/24th and 2/48th were ordered to return to their lying-up areas.[142]

INFANTRY–ARMOUR COOPERATION

The fighting at Alamein between July and November 1942 was probably the largest-scale example of infantry–armour cooperation in Australian military history. Of course, the tanks were usually operated by British crews, not least because the Australians' only armoured unit was its cavalry regiment. Although the record of cooperation between Australian infantry and British tanks in the First Libyan campaign of 1941 was excellent, at Alamein disasters outnumbered successes. Poor coordination was an issue in Australian attacks of 22 July, 27–28 July, 1 September, 28–29 October, and even on the first night of the attack, 23 October, when hoped-for tank support did not materialise. In July, problems had included persistent ignorance about the limits of armour, and scratch pairings – where the first time an Australian battalion worked with an armoured unit was in an actual attack.

Between the July and October battles, though, time was given to honing infantry and armour cooperation, with British tank crews even bivouacking with the Australians. Minefields scuppered plans on 22 July, 23 October and 28–29 October. Perhaps most importantly, once the firing started and the tanks had their hatches down, it was very difficult for them to communicate with the infantry, who had to bang on the side of the tank to get the crew's attention, unless the tank commander was risking his life by poking his head out of the turret. Not until 1943 would phones be fitted on the back of Allied tanks for infantry communication. Even in the battle's last days, Morshead's hard experiences with tanks made him sceptical about their ability to arrive on time and make a difference, and Montgomery had warned him of the same problem when the Australian plan for 28–29 October was discussed. Employing tanks in the dark in a mine-strewn desert in an era without night vision devices, reliable communications or GPS was inherently problematic.

A Valentine tank in the Tel el Eisa area during preparation for the October battle.
(PHOTOGRAPHER: FRANK HURLEY, AWM 013462)

Although the operation was a disaster, with the plan to capture a stretch of the road unfulfilled, it put Rommel in a state of great anxiety. He spent the night on the coast road, from where he and his staff could see and hear signs of battle. At 3.00am, while the 2/23rd was struggling, Rommel was reflecting that it seemed likely that his forces could not take much more of these heavy attacks. He ordered the Afrika Korps to prepare a counterattack for the following morning with all eighty-one available tanks, if the enemy broke through.[143] He sent an instruction to all commanders: 'The present battle is a life and death struggle. I therefore demand that every officer and man gives his all …'[144]

Montgomery was also anticipating the climax of the battle. For days, he had been planning eventually to send the tanks through the salient that the 9th Division had created, on the northern coastal sector. His staff, who were following the 'Ultra' intelligence reports arriving from Bletchley Park, realised that the Australian attack in the north had, as hoped, drawn German units, and especially German armour, northwards. They sought to persuade Montgomery to switch the *Schwerpunkt* of the proposed armoured attack to the mainly Italian formations south of the railway line. At first, Montgomery was disinclined to accept the logical conclusion of his own tactics and of the Ultra intercepts. The news that the 90th Light Division had moved north of the railway finally swayed him. At 11.00am on 29 October he decided on the breakout – codenamed Supercharge – that would determine the battle's outcome.[145]

29 October

Rommel's counterattacks on 29 October fell mainly on the 20th Brigade's battalions, including the temporarily attached 2/23rd. The 2/13th had occupied the Fig Orchard the night before, and because the 2/23rd had not reached its objective, the 2/13th's left flank was dangerously open. Though heavy flanking fire struck them, they tried to 'mop up' their area. An eleven-man patrol from C Company set out to subdue one troublesome post, but a mortar bomb landed among them, killing or wounding all but their officer. C Company now comprised just twenty-two men. Nevertheless, it was ordered to send out another patrol, to eliminate a mortar post. Ten men crossed a minefield and, using grenades, forced the surrender of four Germans manning machine guns. They then rushed the mortar post and, after a melee which included a fistfight between an Australian and a bigger German opponent, captured it. The Australians returned through heavy fire with the recalcitrant Germans, the machine guns and the mortar. The 2/13th remained virtually isolated, and communications spasmodic.

Soon, the 2/13th was rendered leaderless for the second time in the battle. Battalion headquarters, located in a captured command post and thus easy for the enemy gunners to locate, received a direct hit at about 9.00am. It killed the new adjutant and severely wounded the CO, Lieutenant Colonel Colvin. Colvin and another wounded officer were carried 1500 metres under fire to the aid post. The second in command, Major Charles

Daintree, could not be contacted: days later it emerged that he had been badly wounded by an airburst shell and evacuated. Lieutenant Barton Maughan – later official historian of Alamein – kept the headquarters going, until in the afternoon Major Joe Kelly, a former 2/13th adjutant now working on divisional headquarters, was sent forward to take charge. Kelly's arrival gave a much-needed boost to the morale of the battalion, which now counted just 100 men in its four rifle companies. Kelly reinforced them with men from Headquarters Company and 'B' Echelon: drivers, clerks and storemen.

Artillery fell on the unit all day, directed from Ring Contour 25, north of Thompson's Post. Every movement in the open drew fire, not only from artillery but also machine guns and snipers. On the 29th and the two days after, several 2/13th patrols sought to investigate Thompson's Post. Conflicting reports returned, probably because the so-called 'post' was in fact many posts in an area that was nearly 1000 metres square, extremely difficult and dangerous to approach, and overlooked by Ring Contour 25. Every 2/13th patrol had to be accompanied by sappers, so acute was the danger from 'S' mines and booby traps, especially at night. These inflicted casualties in all companies. Added to the constant danger was the smell of numerous German corpses. The battalion historian talks of 'the Orchard of dreadful memory'.[146]

On 29 October the 2/15th Battalion was also dangerously exposed in a salient jutting well into the enemy's northern positions. In the morning, some Italian and German troops, the latter in vehicles, were captured when they stumbled into the Australian lines. Tank and artillery fire hit the battalion all morning, but when five Panzer IIIs approached and opened fire, they were driven off after an anti-tank gun destroyed one.

An enemy ambulance flying a Red Cross flag and loaded with wounded was captured when it approached the battalion's defences: the Australians considered this justified as two of its personnel were seen to be wearing binoculars.[147]

In the early afternoon, enemy tanks and infantry opened fire from 300 metres. Anti-tank and artillery fire halted the attackers, who left behind a burning Panzer III, but the Australian anti-tank gunners lost several men and five guns. Another fierce attack, launched at 5.00pm by about two battalions of German infantry, supported by tanks and self-propelled guns, was thrown back by machine-gun and artillery fire. According to a prisoner, the attackers intended to recapture all of the Australian northern positions down to Trig 29. Instead, at last light the enemy infantry could be seen digging in 350–1500 metres away from the Australian defences. There followed a 'nerve-tearing night of stands-to & hourly expectations of an attack'.[148] That night, four infantry assaults on the battalion line were repulsed, and enemy wounded could be heard afterwards.

On 29 October, the 2/17th at Trig 29 were again subjected to heavy shelling and machine-gunning. Corporal Cyril Mears, whose company had advanced the night before to link the 2/17th with the 2/15th Battalion, wrote, 'we do not know who is who, the enemy is confused but fighting hard'. The results of enemy confusion and the previous night's fighting were all around him: 'Dead lye unburied everywhere, the stench is almost unbearable'.[149]

'DECISIVE FACTOR': EIGHTH ARMY ARTILLERY

For the entire twelve days and nights of the battle, Australian artillery was active, and most of that action was heavy. German reports repeatedly mentioned the strength of British artillery, which in the October battle was clearly the British force's greatest asset. Abundantly supplied, centrally directed and rapidly available, it gave the infantry a decisive advantage over their enemy. Little wonder that a subsequent official British report stated: 'Artillery correctly handled is a battle winning factor ... It dominated the Alamein battle'. The mass of XXX Corps heavy and medium artillery was concentrated on the Australian front. The enemy artillery fought back throughout, and even as late as 1 November an Australian could write: 'His Arty is better than ours – he knows how to use it'.

Nevertheless, Axis artillery support was rendered increasingly ineffective. Flash spotting and sound ranging stations as well as aerial reconnaissance identified their batteries, which were then shelled or bombed. Their ammunition supplies were disrupted and vulnerable communications made their fire unreliable and inaccurate. German general Wilhelm von Thoma estimated that by the end of the first week one Axis shell was fired to every ten Allied. In the course of the battle, Commonwealth batteries' 834 25-pounders fired a total of just on a million rounds, an average of 102 rounds per gun each day. The medium regiments' 4.5-inch and 5.4-inch guns fired 133 and 157 rounds per day per gun. The effect was to give the infantry a curtain of steel available virtually on call, provided the forward observation parties could see the target and communicate with their guns. Brigadier Kirkman's centralisation of artillery control was vital here. Critical, too, was the use of wireless, allowing the forward observation officers to switch targets and concentrate guns in an unprecedented way. Defensive fire tasks were simplified and speeded up by dividing the enemy's ground into small areas, each with a codename, such as Melbourne, Broome, Galway and Fremantle. Several regiments could promptly bring down their fire on that area, as one gunner recalled: 'That code-word – nothing else – rippling through the phones from Infantry H.Q. to Brigade, from Brigade to Regiment, command-posts, guns – brings down appallingly concentrated fire on top of the bewildered Germans'.[150]

In the gun positions, the gunners of the field regiments, clad mostly in just shorts and boots, sweated over many long and crucial firing programs. Blackened with cordite, shrouded in dust, amid ear-splitting and continuous noise and countless empty ammunition boxes and rolling 'empties', they dragged heavy ammunition boxes into place and gun trails into position. Stukas, counter-battery fire and premature explosions were a threat.[151]

Empties. One of the numerous dumps of ammunition boxes filled with empty shell cases seen along the desert artillery front. In the opening barrage of the battle for Egypt, 800 guns went into action and 500,000 rounds were shot off, at Tel el Eisa. (PHOTOGRAPHER: FRANK HURLEY, AWM 014162).

For all the lessons that the battle gave Australians on the mass use of artillery, their applicability as the Australians' war moved to the jungle were limited. Never again would Australian troops be able to call on the concentrated fire of 360 guns from fifteen regiments. The official historian noted how the following year, in New Guinea, Morshead had 'come back from a war in which divisions fought as divisions, and artillery barrages on the maximum scale were used, to one in which it is news that there is one Jap [light AA] gun in a certain area'.[152] At the same time, the experience in that 1943–44 New Guinea campaign told the Australians that they needed more artillery support, and the more generous support offered in the final campaigns proved invaluable.

A 2/17th man described a 'shell-happy' comrade, wandering about, 'muttering and writing hieroglyphics in his notebook; single ideas obsess him, and he worries himself to death'. Those with all their faculties still together wore clothes heavy with dirt and stink, much of their gear lost or ruined, and uncertain as to how the battle was proceeding. However, small things could lift morale: a period without enemy shelling, a mug of water, a lucky escape. At some point in the day, or in the 'Beast' of a night, Corporal Mears wrote, 'looking around at the boys they looked all in, no wash for seven days, how much longer can it last'.[153]

On the morning of the 29th, the 2/23rd was placed temporarily under command of the 20th Brigade, and ordered to stay put. The enemy sniped and shelled the battalion's positions from three directions: 'We laid low all day', reported John Butler. In mid-morning, the

Italian trenches captured at Alamein by the 20th Brigade. At far left in the trench lies a dead Italian, his head drooping forward. (AWM P01614.015)

(Opposite) Officers chatting after a parade at main headquarters, 9th Australian Division, at which officers and men of the division who had been awarded decorations for gallantry in the recent operations were presented with the ribbon of their decoration by Lieutenant General Sir Leslie Morshead, General-Officer-Commanding AIF (M.E.). (PHOTOGRAPHER: E E SMITH, AWM 024975)

German II/125th Regiment, which had borne the brunt of the night's attacks, radioed their divisional headquarters: 'We cannot hold our positions any longer'. Yet they continued to fight hard. Only on the night of the 29th could the 2/23rd move forward into the gap between the 2/13th and 2/15th Battalions. This gave greater security to those exposed battalions, and facilitated the forthcoming operations of the 26th Brigade, which would attack north through the 2/15th on 30–31 October. By 8.45pm the 2/23rd had advanced 1000 metres, made contact with the 2/13th and 2/15th, and in Morshead's words, was in 'text book posn'. This seems an odd term for a decimated unit occupying ground not originally allotted to it, but Morshead congratulated Evans on 'a magnificent fight' and its subsequent reorganisation.[154]

In the late afternoon of the 29th, Morshead outlined the plan of forthcoming operations at a conference at the 9th Division headquarters. That morning, Montgomery had received intelligence the German forces had been pulled north and were no longer 'corsetting' the Italians. This was partly because Rommel feared that a great breakthrough attack would be made in the north, probably north-west towards the coast road, and possibly on the night of the 29th. A German official report added that virtually the entire Afrika Korps had of necessity been fed into the northern front because of the huge losses taken by the German 164th Light and Italian Trento Divisions.[155]

25-POUNDER QUICK FIRING (QF) MK II ON CARRIAGE 25-PDR MK I

The 25-pounder was a gun/howitzer, combining the strengths of both types of ordnance. Its carriage included a circular firing platform that enabled the gun to be traversed easily and quickly, by just one man. This proved especially valuable in the early desert battles, when the 25-pounders were pressed into service as anti-tank guns whenever the 2-pounders were outranged. This tended to lead to the guns being dispersed and used in 'penny packets'. By the time of Alamein, though, the Eighth Army, including the three field regiments of the 9th Australian Division, was using 25-pounders in a concentrated manner that fully exploited this classic weapon's range, durability and hitting power.

CALIBRE
87.6mm

WEIGHT
Approx 1800kg

PROJECTILE
25 pounds (11.34kg)

AMMUNITION
HE, Smoke, AP and Illumination

MAXIMUM RANGE
12,252m

CREW
6

MUZZLE VELOCITY
532m/sec

An iconic image of an Australian 25-pounder gun in action on 10 July – baptism of fire for two of the 9th Division's three field regiments. From that day, the 9th Division artillery did outstanding work at Alamein. Soon after this photograph was taken, the gun was hit: its gunshield was holed, the range cone damaged and both tyres deflated, but the crew kept firing. (AWM 024513)

CHAPTER 7

CLIMAX

30 OCTOBER – 2 NOVEMBER

NOW THAT MONTGOMERY had decided to launch 'Supercharge' at the junction between the German and Italian forces, the Australians needed to maintain the pressure on the Germans in the north. Eighth Army Headquarters regarded the attack planned for the evening of 30 October as a 'feint' – that is, it was intended to draw a reaction rather than reach an objective. It was significant that six Scorpion flail tanks, half of the Eighth Army's remaining vehicles, were allocated to the feint.[156] Over the next few days, the 9th Division's efforts to ensure that Rommel remained convinced of a dire threat to his positions in the coastal sector and reacted accordingly resulted in some of the most demanding, costly and important fighting undertaken by Australian soldiers in the Second World War.

'We should certainly have been failed!' – the plan

Morshead gave his commanders the detailed plan and allocation of tasks on the morning of 30 October. It was a modified version of the attack postponed on the night of 28–29 October. The concept of attacking eastwards along the main road was retained, but whereas previously the 2/48th Battalion was to do this alone, now the 2/24th would assist it. Moreover, the northward thrust on the western flank, originally aimed at reaching the road and stopping, was now to be directed all the way to the coast, so that the German forces to the east of the new Australian front line would be trapped.[157]

It is difficult to understand why Morshead chose both of these options. Had he concentrated on the advance to the coast, this would have been demanding but achievable, and would have maintained great pressure on the enemy. The advance along the main road, on the other hand, was bound to stretch to breaking point the resources of the depleted battalions allotted to it. Moreover, if, as Maughan says, one original purpose of this attack was to open up a possible avenue for Montgomery's breakthrough along the axis of the coast road, that justification was no longer relevant since the development of Supercharge, aimed further south. The other original purpose of the coast road attack, to allow easier supply and ambulance traffic to the forward brigades, does not seem worth risking the annihilation of two battalions to achieve.

The 26th Brigade was given these twin tasks, and was to advance from the firm base held by the 20th Brigade, including the 2/23rd Battalion. To undertake a role similar to that of the 2/23rd under the original plan, the 2/32nd Battalion was attached to the 26th Brigade. So too was the previously unblooded 2/3rd Pioneer Battalion, which was assigned the unenviable job of advancing north from the road to the sea. Although the 40th Battalion, Royal Tank Regiment, was to be in support, the attack was to be made without tanks. Morshead explained to Blamey, 'As result of two experiences in present operations' – one of which was clearly 28–29 October – 'we are NOT using tanks in the attack'.[158]

The plan had four phases. In Phase One, the 2/32nd Battalion was to enter the battle by advancing from the existing front line and capturing an area astride the main road in the vicinity of hill B11, known from its navigation beacon as 'Barrel Hill'. It was to secure the area against attacks, which were likely to come from the north, north-west and west.

From this secure base, the 2/24th, on the right, and 2/48th would attack eastwards astride the main road, thus launching Phase Two. This attack would be pursued eastwards, clearing enemy defences on both sides of the road – to a depth of 1100 metres – till the battalions reached the rear of the enemy's front line, 3000 or more metres away opposite the 24th Brigade. Then Phase Three would begin, with the 2/24th exploiting south to capture Thompson's Post, and the 2/48th capturing the Cloverleaf feature and reaching the coast.

In Phase Four, the 2/3rd Pioneer Battalion, fighting its first-ever battle, would attack northwards from the vicinity of Barrel Hill, reach the coast and then reorganise, facing east and west to prevent enemy forces from escaping or reinforcing the area. The pioneers and the 2/32nd would have anti-tank and medium machine-gun support. Artillery support was available in the form of 360 guns.[159]

This plan was complicated and unrealistic. It relied upon each phase running successfully to time and ignored the precedent of previous days, in which the German forces had shown a continuing ability to frustrate Australian plans. The greatest challenges were to the 2/3rd Pioneers, an incomplete unit with limited training as infantry and lacking the full range of supporting weapons of an infantry battalion; and to the understrength 2/24th and 2/48th Battalions, the combat power of which was depleted by the order for them to attack on divergent axes in the second stage of their advance. Brigadier 'Rickie' Richards, commander of the British 23rd Armoured Brigade, joked to 'Bomba' Wells, the GSO1 of the 9th Division, with whom he had studied at Camberley staff college, 'If we had put in this solution to the problem at Camberley, we should certainly have been failed!'[160] Probably with good reason. Wells should surely have said something to Morshead, questioning the wisdom of this plan. Between 25 and 29 October the Australians had, at great sacrifice, made a huge contribution to the development of the battle. They had captured high ground at Trig 29 that Rommel was desperate to regain, and by their actions in the north had persuaded him that the Australians were the bearers of Montgomery's *Schwerpunkt*. The Australians' contribution and sacrifice were about to become still greater.

30 October, day: sandstorm and preparation

The 2/48th Battalion, which was to move up that night and take a key role in the operations ahead, had enjoyed a comparatively good night's rest behind the lines. The sound of thirty Stukas 'parading' nearby woke them. After an hour of peace, sunshine and breakfast, a dust storm arose, and though it ensured relative peace on the 20th Brigade front, it was a nuisance on a day when other Australians had much preparation to do. Late in the afternoon, the 2/48th received news that the attack would occur that night. After a quick meal and hurried attention to final details, all were aboard the trucks at 6.45pm, moving forward for the fourth time in eight days towards the enemy lines.

David Goodhart, a gunner who saw 2/24th and 2/48th men around Tel el Eisa at this time, writes that the infantry were remarkably confident; that rather than talking of 'attacking' areas or using the conditional 'if' when discussing outcomes of the night's attack,

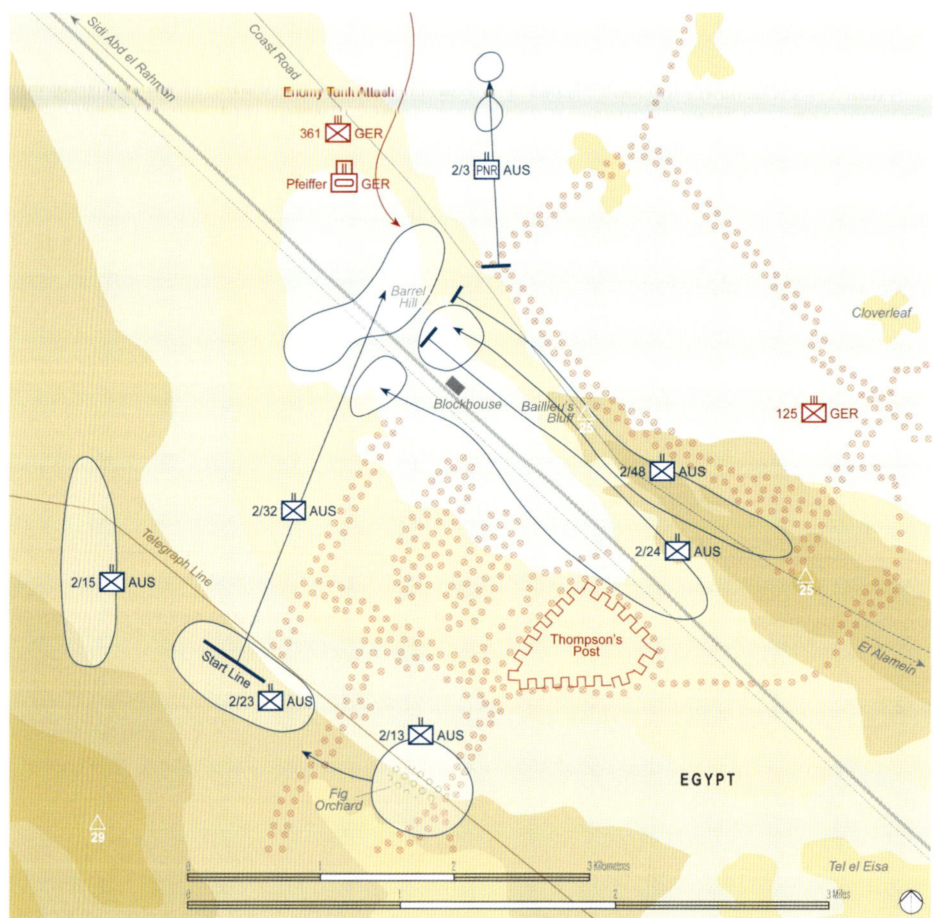

Map 23. Maintaining the pressure, 30–31 October 1942

they said we are going so many thousand yards tonight, or we are going along the main road. Goodhart says that the infantrymen made these statements not boastfully, but calmly and with 'gentle single-mindedness' and awareness that they or their mates may be killed.[161]

Yet there must surely have been soldiers who faced the experience with considerable anxiety. At some point on this day, Private Jack Abraham of the 2/48th wrote in his diary. The entry does not entirely make sense, but delivers something of the worry that must have gone with many on that move forward: 'attack on again tonight suppose to make right to the coast [b]ad [b]ad show very few of Coy left'. This last point gave every reason for concern, as even the normally confident 2/48th Battalion war diary mused: 'The task is a tremendous one … tonight the bn will be engaged in its most difficult task since the offensive was launched with the total strength of four rifle coys only 213'.[162] Abraham was one of the vast majority of this group who were to be victims of a great carnage. The 2/24th entered the action in a similar predicament: even after transferring all available men from Headquarters Company, their rifle companies totalled only 206 men, of whom just five were officers.

They would not lack aerial and artillery support. During one forty-minute period in the afternoon, three light bomber formations dropped 269 250-pound bombs on a single enemy strongpoint, as preparation for the night attack. On 28 October Rommel portrayed his situation as 'extremely critical', describing his men as 'suffering severely from the British air force'. He urgently sought Luftwaffe support to counter bombers and fighters operating 'day and night in almost ceaseless attacks'.[163]

The view south from the Blockhouse in 1997. The 2/32nd advanced over this ground on the night of 30 October 1942. (AUTHOR'S COLLECTION)

Phase One: the 2/32nd advance towards Barrel Hill

The 2/32nd Battalion that led the new northward attack was fresh but understrength. Even at the opening of the battle, it was 250 men short. One company's strength was just sixty-five; Corporal Jack Castle wrote of having just four men in his section.[164] The battalion was supported by the Rhodesian 289th Anti-Tank Battery and two platoons of the 2/2nd Machine Gun Battalion.

The 2/32nd advance had two stages. First, from a start-line between the 2/15th and 2/23rd Battalions, it had to cross the railway line and then advance about 2500 metres to secure Axis positions to the immediate north. In the second stage, it had to go less than 400 metres further, but this involved much: securing the feature 'B11', or Barrel Hill, clearing up positions north of the road, and then reorganising so that the following battalions could begin Phase Two.

The advance began at 10.10pm, ten minutes after the accompanying barrage began. A and B companies were followed by C and D, and the enemy fired on the Australians from between 550 and 1300 metres into the advance. Flares gave away the enemy presence on this dark night. Fire from an enemy post near a burning tank killed one platoon commander, and a desperate situation was only resolved when artillery fire caused the post to surrender. Two machine-gun posts opened fire on A Company from the right. Sergeant Duncan MacDonald organised a party comprising himself and three others to attack these posts. Two of his men went down wounded as they got close. One dropped a Bren, which MacDonald picked up and used to continue the attack with Private Alex Davidson. MacDonald fired on both posts while advancing, and then he and Davidson each charged a post. MacDonald killed all four occupants of one, while Davidson captured the other, bayonetting one man and taking six Germans prisoner. While MacDonald went to look for an escort, Davidson turned the captured machine gun on groups of enemy troops visible by the light of flares.[165]

By the time the battalion reached the railway, it had for few losses overcome considerable but irresolute opposition, and captured at least 175 prisoners, mostly Germans, as well as two field guns and much equipment. The battalion did not, and possibly could not, clear up enemy posts that were outside its narrow 550-metre frontage. These posts later harassed the 2/32nd's supporting traffic and had to be destroyed by following battalions. On reaching the railway, the 2/32nd paused briefly before continuing towards its subsequent objectives.[166]

The fighting now became much harder. C Company was pinned down by machine-gun, anti-tank and shellfire coming from the front, left and right. Two platoons subdued the sources of anti-tank and machine-gun fire, taking numerous prisoners, but the company was shelled for most of the night. By about 4.00am, it was just 22-strong. Not surprisingly, it did not achieve fully its objective of advancing westwards once north of the railway.

B Company suffered heavy casualties, but reached Barrel Hill and reorganised around it. After the fifteen minutes' pause at the railway, A Company sent a patrol across the line to capture the so-called 'Blockhouse', a six-room railway gangers' accommodation block which the Germans were using as an aid post. After the rest of the company came forward,

the patrol resumed its advance to the main road, so a start-line could be laid for Phase Two of the night's operations – the 2/24th and 2/48th Battalions' advance. The patrol met no opposition, and after the two battalions passed through, it returned to the Blockhouse.

By then, many wounded 2/32nd men were in the building, which was now under the command of the battalion medical officer, Captain Bill Campbell. Three captured German medical officers and nine orderlies assisted him in looking after the wounded of both sides. A section of the 2/11th Field Ambulance later settled there too, so 'a kind of international medical post' operated in this very exposed location for the next few days.[167]

There was confusion among the 2/32nd's forward companies. Several failed to follow the usual procedure of arranging the laying of telephone lines, all of which consequently had to be laid in daylight. Moreover, one of C Company's platoons went 'missing' till the following afternoon.[168] After the troops had moved beyond the railway line, the 2/32nd CO, Lieutenant Colonel John Balfe, and his wireless operator were on the track when a group of about six Germans approached, apparently to surrender. Then one German fired a pistol he had concealed in his overcoat, wounding Balfe in the arm. Balfe emptied his own pistol into the enemy and escaped over the railway line.

The Blockhouse, photographed in 1942 from the north.
(IMAGE COURTESY OF PETER BANNIGAN)

The railway embankment presented a potential obstacle to the whole operation. If supplies were to reach the men north of the railway, the 2/32nd's vehicles would have to cross. The height of the embankment at the railway was unknown before the advance – suggesting a lapse in reconnaissance or intelligence – but the 2/3rd Field Company was given the task of advancing with the 2/32nd Battalion and cutting the rails, removing the sleepers and breaching the embankment to continue the mine-free tracks into the northern part of the battlefield. On reaching the embankment, however, the engineers found it to be 12-feet high and they could find no possible detour. A mine had halted their bulldozer, so some fifty men used shovels to create a crossing. Guncotton charges brought for blowing the rails failed, so ammonal from sticky bombs was moulded to fit the rail section. This worked, but not until 3.45am, after three hours' work by the engineers, did the 2/32nd's vehicles move over. The 2/32nd headquarters set up at the gap, which proved to be a most dangerous location.

As the engineers toiled at the embankment, enemy forces moved down the railway line from the west and established posts from which they could fire at the obvious defile presented by the gap. Their machine guns raked the gap and railway from a range of 250 metres. The number of machine guns increased, and were supplemented by artillery, which was only withdrawn at first light.

The 2/32nd headquarters received much of this fire. Lieutenant Colonel Balfe was wounded again, this time in the shoulder, and had to be evacuated. The RSM and an officer were mortally wounded. Luckily, none of the vehicles traversing the gap caught fire and offered illumination for the enemy machine gunners. The gap was kept open.[169]

Major Bob Joshua took charge of the 2/32nd and, despite a thigh wound from a sniper, moved two companies to their prearranged positions south of the line. The 26th Brigade report later criticised the battalion for not pushing out far enough, and thus creating a secure base forming-up place for Phase Two, and for not mopping up all opposition within their captured area. Nevertheless the 2/32nd had, broadly speaking, achieved its goals.

The battalion's onslaught had seemed fierce to the enemy. The headquarters of the 90th Light Division received a message that after the Australians crossed the railway near the Hut (as the Germans called the Blockhouse), they engaged the Germans there in 'terrific infantry fighting'. An Italian officer in a nearby artillery unit wrote in his diary of 'hand-to-hand' fighting, in which Australians 'roaring drunk on whisky' were fighting like madmen on the other side of the railway. He asserted that the wounded had 'horrifying tales to tell'. The notion of the Australians being drunk was almost certainly fallacious, as was a German belief that twenty-five to thirty tanks supported this assault on 30–31 October. Their reported ferocity, however, was probably genuine.[170]

Jack Castle, whose company was in the Blockhouse area, wrote of the men's surprise that, contrary to what they had been told, the enemy positions were occupied. He estimated that his company suffered 25 per cent casualties, and concluded that the 2/32nd was 'surrounded except for small narrow strip back to our lines'.[171] This was a natural concern to men who knew they were perilously close to the hub of the enemy defences. When the 2/32nd had finished moving that night, two companies were north of the railway and covering the road from reverse slope positions on B11, while the other two rifle companies were south of the railway, prepared for any attack from the west.

Morale-boosting support was around them in the form of powerful Australian and Rhodesian 6-pounder anti-tank guns, located on B11 and on both sides of the railway.

Phases Two and Three: the 2/24th and 2/48th on the road east

In Phase Two, the 2/24th on the right and 2/48th on the left were to capture the main enemy defences on the coast road, east of the base established by the 2/32nd Battalion. The start-line for the attack was 230 metres west of the Blockhouse, and extended north from the railway to B11. Reaching and departing from this line was a story in itself for the 2/24th and 2/48th Battalions.

The 2/48th and 2/24th set off for the Phase Two start-line just twenty and thirty minutes after the 2/32nd, whose path they followed. Congestion on the tracks and minor mopping up caused delays. On reaching the railway, the 2/48th found the situation 'far from stabilised'.

Looking east along the railway line to the Blockhouse in 1997. From about 100 metres further west, the Germans fired machine guns and artillery along this line on the night of 30–31 October.
(AUTHOR'S COLLECTION)

There was much enemy fire north of the railway line, and the battalion encountered resistance 'at every step' as they made their way towards the start-line. Against a background of constant noise from friendly artillery, and the barely faltering light of enemy flares, Lieutenant Colonel Hammer sent a company and a platoon to eliminate some enemy posts.[172]

After their return, the battalion was moved some 200 metres forward of the start-line, into a depression which gave better cover from enemy fire still coming from the west. However, they were now hit by 'friendly' fire. Consequently, the RSM, Frank Legg, wrote, 'We were shelled by our own 25 prs. I was wounded – shrap in neck – and 3 landed in D Coy'. Indeed, one fell in the midst of the company but failed to explode. Legg noted some slight panic among the men, and the battalion history concedes that the men 'grew tense under the strain of waiting'.[173]

When the 2/24th men arrived at the start-line, they assumed that their absent sister battalion had already started the attack, and so began their own advance on the right of the road. Eventually Lieutenant Colonel Weir received a message to halt his battalion until the 2/48th arrived.

A dilemma now arose. The artillery program had begun on time at 1.00am, and the advance was now fifteen minutes, or nearly 1000 metres, behind the barrage. This was a worrying gap, considering the depleted state of the battalions and the strong defences they were expected to capture. The Germans in those defences would now have time to prepare for the Australian assault after the barrage had passed. The artillery barrage could be refired, but this required forty-five minutes from the time of the request.

Rather than wait under fire for that long, and given that his battalion had already advanced some distance, Hammer decided to try to catch up with the barrage. He informed Lieutenant Colonel Weir, and after the battalions re-established contact some 500 metres from the start-line, the advance to the first objective began in earnest.

Thompson's Post: 2/24th Battalion's attack

The 2/24th Battalion advanced with two companies forward. Within 800 metres of the start-line, C Company, on the right, had caught up to the artillery barrage and had to halt for a few minutes to wait for it to lift. This was one of few occasions in Phase Two when either battalion had effective artillery support. This shelling was coming from the east, in front of the battalion, so the danger zone in front of the artillery concentrations was wider than usual. Long-range enemy machine-gun fire from the left cost one sergeant an eye, but C Company reached its objective with few casualties and little fighting.

It was a different story for B Company, leading the advance on the left. Just 450 metres from the start-line, German machine gunners opened fire at close range. The company lost its radio communications when its two signallers and their wireless were hit. Sergeant Len Dingwall had commanded a platoon since its officer had been wounded on the first night of the battle. He had led them in capturing two posts on the night of 25–26 October. Now he led his platoon in taking three machine-gun positions. Then the survivors of his and two other platoons attacked a strongpost based on an anti-aircraft gun, apparently an '88'. Taking these positions against point-blank fire came at a cost: B Company's strength was now about nineteen. They were eventually halted some 200 metres from their goal, but platoons from the following A Company and the 2/48th arrived and carried the company on to their objective.[174]

C and B Companies had now reached the first, intermediate objective of Phase Two. D and A Companies had the task of carrying through to the final objective of Thompson's Post. They were under continuous enemy artillery and mortar fire on the way forward. When they passed through at the intermediate objectives, the stiffest resistance continued to come from the left, against A Company. Its commander and two NCOs were wounded on the way to the first objective, so Lieutenant Frank Nelson led as the company ploughed into fierce fighting. An enemy post located under and around a truck was captured after a well-aimed Australian grenade set the vehicle alight. Nelson was wounded and Acting Company Sergeant Major 'Tex' Alleyne took over. His men eliminated one enemy post with grenades, but as Alleyne and several others negotiated wire in chasing its fleeing defenders, another nearby post opened fire. Several men were hit, and Alleyne was killed trying to rescue one of them. Some 650 metres short of the final objective, A Company was completely halted.

D Company's commander, Lieutenant Eric McLeod, then ordered his men to assist A Company by attacking from the south-west. They entered an anti-tank minefield, where machine guns and anti-tank guns stopped their advance with close-range fire. McLeod took a Bren gun and rushed forward, firing from the hip, but was killed. Warrant Officer Class 2 Fred Cameron rushed to McLeod's aid but was himself wounded. So too was Corporal Jimmy Anderson, but not before he used a Bren to kill all the occupants of an enemy post. He crawled back to Cameron, who now withdrew the eight able-bodied men of the company some 100 metres to the railway line. There they dug in and were ordered to cover the area between the railway and the road.

A Company had captured a further post, but now comprised just nine men. Their commander, Sergeant KT 'Katie' Lewis, ordered them to dig in where they were. Like D Company, the other companies were ordered into positions south of the railway line. Between them, the four rifle companies now numbered seventy-four men.[175]

The wounded Cameron was sent back to the Regimental Aid Post (RAP) for treatment and to tell Headquarters 26th Brigade what had transpired.[176] Brigade sent a discomforting reply to Weir – 20th Brigade had passed on information that one of its patrols had entered Thompson's Post, the object of Phase Three, after dark on 30 October and found it unoccupied. Weir was ordered to verify the report.

Weir personally led a sixteen-man patrol through the wire and minefield. Nearly 400 metres into the post, enemy fire killed one Australian as he threw grenades at its source. The patrol then withdrew 'precipitately', as Weir put it, though when one of them was wounded, a stretcher-bearer, Private John O'Brien, turned back and carried him out.

Thompson's Post was certainly occupied. When Weir returned to his battalion, he received significant news of the progress of the 2/48th Battalion, whose part in the Phase Two attack we must now examine.

'Into the very muzzles': the 2/48th Battalion's attack

As the 2/48th Battalion advanced on its first objective, its frontage was 400 yards (366 metres), expanding to 800 yards (732 metres) by the time it reached the main road. It encountered little resistance before reaching a bend. Then 'every inch of the way had to be fought for', wrote the battalion's diarist, and there were still some 2400 metres to go to the final objective. Fire came from in front, and from the enemy facing the 2/24th on the right.

After crossing the main road, C Company on the left was slowed by a series of ridges and by heavy fire from what was identified as anti-tank guns, mortars and machine guns. Against this fierce opposition, the 2/48th did not reach its first objective until 3.00am. It fell well behind the artillery program, which it appears the infantry had no means of adjusting without a lengthy delay.[177] The Phase Three goal of advancing to the coast behind

(Left to right)
A 20mm German anti-aircraft gun captured by the 2/24th in the fierce fighting of 30–31 October.
(IMAGE COURTESY OF WES BENTLEY, PETER BANNIGAN AND DAVID PEARSON)

An 88mm gun captured on the night of 30–31 October 1942, probably by the 2/24th. This particular gun is now on display at the Australian Army Tank Museum at Puckapunyal. (IMAGE COURTESY OF MURRAY HAMILTON)

the prepared barrage was no longer practical.

The forward companies were so undermanned that they could not eliminate all the posts in their way. Men fell, killed or wounded by fire from the rear, and only with heavy fighting could the reserve companies advance. One of them, A Company, found itself moving into a gap which developed between the two forward companies. Most of its officers became casualties. After the first objective was reached, this depleted company ran into tremendous mortar and machine-gun fire. The company commander, Captain Bob Shillaker, was then severely wounded. When the last remaining officer, Lieutenant Bev Hamilton, was killed, Sergeant 'Diver' Derrick took over as company commander and carried on throughout the night, despite being wounded.

Hammer decided that lack of time and men now meant that the best he could achieve was to reach, rather than capture, the enemy's front line crossing the road.

Captain Bryant amalgamated his C Company with the forty-five men of A Company. As their composite company advanced to the left, Jack Ralla 'felt an awful burning pain in my left leg, and a hot searing pain shot up into my stomach'. Standing on his good leg, he tried to use his rifle as a crutch, only to find that the woodwork had been shot away. He sank to the ground, his left leg at right angles to his body and blood gushing from a wound in his groin. Bren gunner Private Mick Riley's platoon commander recalled, 'The company was pinned down by fire from several machine-guns, and Mick said "show me one of these guns Sir and I'll clean it up with my bren"'. Firing as he reached the crest of a ridge, Riley was hit in the head and killed instantly.[178]

Meanwhile B Company led the initial advance on the right, close to the road. Lieutenant Syd Caple was killed bravely assaulting one post. In a bayonet charge on another, Lieutenant Ken Allen was hit and three of his men killed or mortally wounded. Allen's section captured the post and took fifteen prisoners. The company commander, Major Geoffrey Edmunds, was badly wounded while leading a six-man assault on enemy posts.

Sergeant 'Snowy' Ranford, who had taken charge of his platoon when the officer was hit, directed the capture of two stubborn positions. An 88mm gun in the second one fired at the platoon, who destroyed it and fourteen men who were manning it and other weapons. In this assault, Ranford was wounded and his platoon reduced to seven men. When wounded again, in front of yet another enemy position, Ranford had to be evacuated. The wounded Lieutenant Allen was ultimately the only officer on his feet in B Company, which consisted of just five men; after taking the initial objective, Allen and his men supported D Company as it continued advancing on the right.

These two dwindling bands met ever-strengthening resistance, but fought forward another 450 metres. They had cleared the enemy from the last ridge to the west of Ring Contour 25, their Phase Two objective, when the attack lost momentum through lack of manpower. The assault was about 500 metres short when an enemy minefield, heavy protective wire and machine guns blocked the 'pitifully thin line'.[179]

In the battalion's desperate attempts to break through, some of its bravest men were killed, offering sad evidence of the fact that bravery alone is not enough to win battles. Corporal 'Spud' Hinson, who had earned a DCM at Tel el Eisa, was one, dying as he charged forward among the enemy posts. Sergeant Lindsay Goode, MM, also died. Some survivors were not much luckier. Private Jack Abraham, whose pre-battle doubts we read earlier, wrote his next diary entry at the 2/8th Field Ambulance, where he lay suffering from serious gunshot wounds to the abdomen, head (his left ear was nearly severed), leg and arm. 'May pull through', he wrote, and noted, 'Ended up in a bad way'.[180] Abraham owed much to the stretcher-bearers, who that night had a mammoth task. Most of their battalion became casualties, but they missed not a single man in their search for the wounded over the 3650-metre approach to the start-line, and the 3300-metre attack towards Ring Contour 25.[181]

The headquarters personnel of D Company were all killed or wounded, so the company lost touch with the rest of the battalion and advanced along the foot of the ridge, to the north of the other companies. Amazingly, it fought its way right into the enemy defences on the final objective. One wartime account describes the men 'walking into the very muzzles of machine-guns, sometimes the last survivor of a section bayonetting the gunners who had destroyed his comrades'.[182] Sixteen D Company men were killed in the assault on the objective, the German front line.

Just 50 metres from this objective, the company received intense fire from two mounds connected by a saddle. The Australians went to ground, but were still in the open. At least seven men died here, including the company's 'brilliant young commander', Captain Peter Robbins.[183] Among Robbins's papers was a recommendation, penned before going into action that night, that Sergeant Bill Kibby receive the DCM for his bravery on 25 October. It was Kibby who now took charge of the company, which was scattered and pinned down, and probably numbered no more than twelve men.

Kibby coordinated a two-pronged attack on the mounds. The left-hand mound was captured. Kibby led the attack on the right-hand one. Within 20 metres of the post, fire forced his group to ground. He jumped up and charged, throwing grenades in a lone attack that destroyed the enemy post. Then machine-gun fire killed him. His courage here and earlier in the battle was later recognised by the award of the Victoria Cross. There were only three eyewitnesses to tell his tale. The company now comprised six men, who withdrew south of the road. They could not find the rest of the battalion.

Battalion headquarters was south of the railway. At one stage it was nearly 400 metres ahead of the leading companies, and under fire near the final objective. Hammer ordered Warrant Officer Legg to take a party in a flanking movement to deal with a machine gun. Legg commented, 'Took 7 – lost 5 & then shot up from rear'.[184] The assault was unsuccessful, but despite the continuing heavy enemy mortar and machine-gun fire, headquarters remained where it was, and soon Hammer ordered the battalion to dig in nearby. He had tried unsuccessfully to contact the 2/24th, which had also withdrawn south of the railway. Indeed, with all signal sets destroyed and lines cut, he had no communications with anyone.

Hammer had again to make an unenviable choice. His unit was located about halfway between its first and second objectives. He had just forty-one men, some of whom were wounded.[185] Heavy machine-gun and mortar fire was hitting them from three sides. One source talks of the blast 'hurling the spades from their hands every few seconds'.[186] D Company was out of touch, somewhere to the left, and the 2/24th was not on the right where Hammer hoped it would be.

Hammer decided that he must abandon all hope of achieving his part of Phase Three, and instead try to reorganise in closer touch with 2/32nd Battalion to the west.[187] That way, if the 2/3rd Pioneer Battalion could achieve the objectives of Phase Four, 2/32nd and 2/48th would provide a base strong enough to ensure the enemy was cut off. At 5.30am he put this plan into operation, with the companies moving west in a defensive diamond formation. Barely an hour of darkness remained, during which they had to negotiate 3 kilometres of territory. Many dead Germans lay strewn in grotesque positions around the landscape, but the only live Germans seen were a dozen hiding in a strong dugout. Fortunately for both groups, these men chose to surrender at bayonet point rather than open fire.

Meanwhile, Hammer had set off alone to contact the 2/24th. He passed command to the adjutant, Captain Bill Reid, who had sustained three wounds that night. On the way, Hammer received a machine-gun bullet wound in the cheek, but left a message for Lieutenant Colonel Weir before returning to his battalion with two prisoners. By dawn the 2/48th had taken up position east of Barrel Hill. During the night it had suffered forty-seven killed, 148 wounded and four missing. Only four of the eighteen officers who began the attack were now alive and unwounded.

When Weir returned to the 2/24th Battalion after his foray into Thompson's Post, the significant news he received was of Hammer's intention to move back. Weir now had several options, none of them pleasant. He could use his tiny band to assault Thompson's Post, for which he would probably not have time to recall the artillery program which had been cancelled after 20th Brigade's report; he could stay where he was, in an isolated position which would undoubtedly attract intense fire at dawn; or he could move back to join the 2/32nd and 2/48th at their firm base. He chose the latter option. Safe though this choice seemed, it had terrible consequences.

Reorganised as two companies, the 2/24th marched in open order south of the railway, across ground that had been traversed earlier that night by one section of the battalion. There was no opposition, but 900 metres into the march two 1000-pound aerial bombs, attached to trip wires, were detonated. Twelve men were killed and sixteen wounded.

Weir was among the wounded, all of whom were bandaged by the indefatigable Private O'Brien. The casualties were carried to the Blockhouse while the remainder of the battalion marched on. Captain Harty, the last rifle company officer still standing, took command

Some of the German defensive positions at Ring Contour 25, photographed soon after the battle. (AWM 129001)

and led the 'sad handful' that comprised the battalion to Major Joshua of the 2/32nd, who allocated them an area south of the railway. To dig in, there were just fifty-four men of the 206 who had started the night's attack: forty-two had been killed, 116 were wounded (some of whom were still on duty), and two were missing.

Private Lionel Jeffcott of the Carrier Platoon courageously took a truck out to rescue the battalion wounded, some of them from a kilometre away. An unidentified Bren carrier driver did the same, until his vehicle was wrecked by a direct hit. Stretcher-bearers of the 2/24th, like those of their sister unit, reportedly missed not one wounded man out in the field on that grim night.

After carrying Colonel Weir to the Blockhouse, Sergeant Ewen French and several other 2/24th men sat outside the building and shared their rations with some Germans there. French thought it was silly to be fighting 'coves' just like themselves.[188] The 2/24th and 2/48th Battalions had again proved that their men were extraordinary 'coves'. With fewer than 400 men, and virtually no artillery support, they had together cut a passage more than 3 kilometres long and up to a kilometre wide in the enemy's defences, which were among their strongest on the battlefield. The 2/48th Battalion War Diary talks of the men's 'great determination' that night. It says, too, that even when the battalion had been reduced to forty-one men, 'the same offensive spirit was displayed as when they first went into action eager and fresh on the 23 Oct 42'. This may seem hard to believe. Some evidence lies in the casualties inflicted. The 2/48th captured about 200 Germans and destroyed an 88mm gun.[189] The 2/24th took sixty-two prisoners, including forty-eight Germans, and a veritable arsenal: an 88mm gun, two 50mm guns, two 20mm guns, two mortars, seven howitzers and twelve 'Spandaus'. These statistics do suggest the presence of a special 'offensive spirit'. Yet while these achievements reflected extraordinary courage and determination in the Australians, they made little or no difference to the outcome of the Battle of El Alamein. Two superb battalions had been virtually destroyed in the 'crumbling' process, and for no appreciable gain. This action in which their offensive spirit was so badly wasted also exemplified the sheer difficulty of carrying out complex night attacks.

Phase Four: The Pioneers' drive to the sea

In the late afternoon of 30 October, Lieutenant Colonel Alfred Gallasch returned to his unit, the 2/3rd Pioneer Battalion, with bad news. The anti-tank guns and machine guns originally allocated to the Pioneers were no longer available. This seems extraordinary, given that it was well known that the Germans invariably counterattacked to regain lost ground: how were the Pioneers to defend any ground they captured? In addition, Morshead had now given orders that, if the operations of the earlier phases of the attack went wrong, the 2/3rd Pioneers could act as a reserve to any one of the battalions involved. Only if the battalion were not required to support these battalions would it carry out the role originally assigned as Phase Four. As the Pioneers' history says, the new plan had more 'ifs' in it than a porcupine has quills.[190] One of the battalion's companies was attached to the 26th Brigade's Composite Force, which also included a company of the 2/2nd Machine Gun Battalion, a squadron of the divisional cavalry and anti-tank units, and was tasked with holding the gap between the 26th and 24th Brigades. Not only were the pioneers thus understrength, but this demanding advance would be their first infantry action.

The Pioneers set off in their trucks to Point 29 knowing that they would have no support but not knowing exactly which tasks would fall to them. From the rear of the vehicles, they could see only occasional gun flashes. As they approached their debussing point, mortar and artillery shells seemed to be landing closer, and small-arms fire could be heard tearing canvas or pinging off metal frames. A tracer bullet mortally wounded one passenger. The men were mightily relieved when, at about 11.00pm, they emerged into open air at their debussing point, even though they were now even more exposed.

The battalion next marched about 3600 metres to the railway. Several times, Australians escorting sullen-looking Germans loomed out of the dark. One group warned the Pioneers of a German post up ahead. Some 300 metres into the advance, enemy machine-gun fire targeted the Pioneers. Individuals saw tracers pass through the space between them and the soldiers marching in front of them. Most of the fire was knee-high, and Lieutenant Richard Malfroy, one of several who fell shouting, 'I'm hit', had his legs shattered.[191]

Two Pioneer platoons attacked the enemy machine gunners, one from the front and one from the flank. In the frontal assault, Private Allan Kerr, fighting alongside his brother, fell dead across a German machine gun he had put out of action. Corporal Wally Silversides charged the post, but lunged fruitlessly at a German and slipped. After recovering his footing, he landed a knockout punch. Lance Corporal Ted Mulley led a section which subdued one machine-gun post. Mulley was wounded in the right shoulder, but continued in the advance, against the Regimental Medical Officer's recommendation.[192]

The two platoons met during this fight, and might have shot at each other if not for their unmistakably Australian language. Major George Rosevear heard his platoon yelling wildly as they attacked. He proudly recorded the prizes brought in: '50 prisoners, 6 spandaus, numerous pistols and souvenirs and no casualties'. He expressed a common feeling about the battalion's first real action when he said he 'felt like purring'.[193]

Shortly after midnight, the battalion arrived south of the railway. There, they waited for more than three hours to be called into action. The enemy fire which troubled the 2/32nd from the west also plagued the 2/3rd Pioneers. Rosevear recorded being subjected to mortar, anti-tank, sniper and 20mm fire. A 20mm shell struck one of his NCOs in the groin: he died in 'great agony'.[194]

(Opposite) Infantryman, 9th Division, El Alamein, July–November 1942, by William Dargie.
The 2/24th's Captain Ted Harty was a company commander throughout the October battle. Indeed, by the end of 31 October he was the only rifle company commander still standing, and assumed command of the battalion. His battalion history calls the moustachioed Harty 'outstanding ... debonair and determined' and laments the fact that he received no award. The artist, William Dargie, entered this portrait in the 1943 Archibald Prize.
(1943, oil on canvas on plywood, 106.8 x 63.6cm; AWM ART26087)

The 2/3rd Pioneer aid post, sited in a hole in the railway embankment, was called upon to undertake an extraordinary operation. The chaplain, Eric Seatree, saw an ambulance driver, named McDonald, hit by enemy fire as he left his truck to help wounded men. Ignoring enemy machine guns, Seatree rushed to McDonald, applied a dressing and carried him on his back to the aid post. It was too dangerous to move him to the Blockhouse, so the medical officer, Captain Bob Day, performed the operation on a groundsheet spread over ammunition boxes in the dark. Despite the dust, grit and enemy fire, Day and his two assistants saved McDonald's seriously damaged leg, and probably his life.

Chaplain Seatree was awarded a Military Cross for his work at Alamein. On one occasion, he went out amid heavy artillery and mortar fire, scouring an area 200 metres south of the railway for casualties. On another, when shells were seen to explode among Australians 200 metres away, Seatree took a stretcher and helped bring in a wounded infantryman.

At 4.30am came the end of the Pioneers' anxious wondering as to which part of the 'If' plan would fall to them. The 26th Brigade sent the signal 'Broome', meaning that they were to carry out their original operation: the attack to the coast. Men assumed happily that the Phase Two and Three attacks must have succeeded. Of course, these attacks had not succeeded, and originally the Pioneers' attack was only to proceed if the earlier ones did. The 26th Brigade now ignored its own orders, for within about five minutes and with dawn not far off, the Pioneers were advancing.[195]

C Company, in the lead, had to go 1400 metres to its objective; then D Company would pass through, and advance a further 1300 metres to its objective, on the coast. Both had artillery support, though when brigade headquarters discovered that the advance had started ten minutes late, it ordered the refiring of the barrage. C Company passed through 'wondering' men of the 2/32nd and across the start-line that ran east from B11. They were met by enemy fire, but the operation started brilliantly. Far from being pinned down, they reached their objective on or even ahead of schedule, and took about eighty prisoners. As they dug in, D Company arrived and then, without pausing the regulation fifteen minutes, pushed on towards the sea.[196]

Up ahead, the supporting artillery was reassuringly pounding the enemy positions. However, as the Pioneers approached the barrage a problem arose. The bombardment was not lifting. Some 200 metres behind the barrage and 1100 metres short of their objective, the company had to halt. Even there, some of this 'friendly fire' landed among them. Daylight was beginning to illuminate the scene: one in which 'communications were right out', so the company, or indeed the battalion, had no means of communicating with the artillery or brigade. They could not find the forward observer or his truck, which they later discovered had been blown up. The company commander, Captain Joe Stevens, ordered the men to dig in where they were, 200 metres forward of the first objective. Ominously, anti-tank rifle fire knocked over sandbags as the Pioneers placed them around their new positions.[197]

Major Rosevear's B Company had captured sixty prisoners and was now also north of the road, in front of Barrel Hill. The battalion was so exposed that it was certain to be embroiled in a firefight once day broke. Only two trucks drove through the railway gap to provide ammunition before dawn. Even then, the foremost companies received little or none. The battalion now had no supporting arms, not even its own medium machine guns and anti-tank guns, and an average of about a dozen rounds of ammunition per man. It was a small force, almost surrounded, spread out over nearly a mile, with a very narrow frontage, and dependent on a tenuous connection with the rest of the division across Barrel Hill.

Morshead and the 30–31 October fighting

Morshead's plans for the night of 30–31 October had gone awry. The 9th Division report later argued that the German troops in the coastal sector had offered especially tough resistance and that they had done so because of the 24th Brigade's deception plan on the first night of the battle. According to this argument, the deception had worked so well that the enemy in the coastal sector believed they had defeated an attack equal to that which had succeeded further south. This had raised the garrison's morale to such an extent that, on 30–31 October, 'the enemy fought with a resolution which was not experienced elsewhere'.[198]

The German official sources, while acknowledging the courageous efforts of the 125th Panzergrenadier Regiment throughout the battle, do not support the notion that these

Some of twenty-six German prisoners taken by 12 Platoon, 2/3rd Pioneer Battalion, by dawn on 31 Oct 1942. (IMAGE COURTESY OF TED CARTER)

Germans fought with more determination than others.[199] Maughan generously considers the explanation 'plausible', but also deems it 'not a sound exculpation' for the 'strange' underestimate Morshead and his staff made of the enemy's defences and morale. He notes, too, that there was plentiful evidence elsewhere on the Alamein battlefield that the Germans could be expected to fight hard.[200]

That night, the Australians captured more Germans – 421 – than on any other during the battle, but the Germans on the coast still fought bravely, as Morshead acknowledged in his report on the action to Blamey. On other points, he was not so accurate. He reported that on the night of 30–31 October, '24 and 48 Bns captured first and second objectives according to plan and with normal losses'. He admitted that the battalions withdrew, but said this was because of the heavy casualties they took on the second objective. This report was inaccurate. Neither battalion had captured its second objective – though one weakened company of 2/48th Battalion had briefly reached its goal – and the losses were not 'normal', but crippling.[201]

Morshead's misleading report concealed the fact that his orders for the 2/24th and 2/48th attacks had demanded too much, and had resulted in failure and the decimation of two of his best battalions. Adding to the impression that Morshead was obscuring the repercussions of his planning was his disingenuous comment on the efforts of the 2/3rd Pioneers that night. He told Blamey that in this action, the Pioneers 'gained posn designed to cut enemy off'.[202] Again, as shown above, the plan was in fact not achieved: the Pioneers were unable to reach their objective on the coast.

A gap of 1100 metres lay between the Pioneers' foremost, pinned down, men and the coast. Moreover, as Maughan says, the salient they held was a 'brittle wedge'.[203] Maintaining or enlarging this wedge would have taken a miracle. Far from cutting off the Axis forces, by the end of the night of 30–31 October the Pioneers were in a position of extreme danger. Their advance had been thwarted by bad luck and bad management of the artillery support, but the flawed 'If' plan was always likely to give rise to catastrophe, as was the allocation to an understrength battalion of a task better suited to a brigade.

Alec Hill, a military historian and member of the 9th Division's staff, wrote of Morshead, 'In the light of the near destruction of two battalions of 26th Brigade and the near disaster to the Pioneers, one may reasonably ask whether Morshead asked too much of the troops employed'.[204] The answer to this question is 'yes'.

It was likely from the outset that the operation would not achieve its objectives, for Morshead was ordering two battalions that had already taken huge losses to capture ground which he knew was heavily defended. Providing artillery support for that advance towards the guns was difficult, and proved almost useless. Morshead also expected the 2/3rd Pioneer Battalion, an untested unit with only three of its four companies and no anti-tank or machine-gun support, to achieve one of the most difficult tasks assigned to any battalion in the whole battle.[205]

The 26th Brigade report blamed the Pioneers' failure on the lateness of the attack and the battalion's inexperience. Yet this was to ignore that the attack was ordered to continue even though its original trigger had not been met. It implied that with 'light casualties' it should have at least taken its objective. However, it was the divisional commander's responsibility that they were sent in so late, and without adequate support. Some blame is due also to the brigade commander, David Whitehead, even though he was carrying out orders given at a conference on 29 October. As the brigade report concedes, even if the Pioneers had taken their final objective, the absence of 'reorganisation stores' and anti-tank guns would have jeopardised their chances of holding on to what they had. That was especially so, given that had the Pioneers succeeded they would have faced ferocious attacks from the well-armed German units west of the pocket.[206]

Several points can be made in Morshead's defence.[207] As mentioned, he and his headquarters were exhausted. His was the unenviable task of maintaining pressure on the German forces to allow Supercharge to have the maximum chance of success further south. To do this, Morshead had few forces to call upon: by dawn on 31 October all but two of his battalions were in action. However, his use of the Pioneers instead of the 2/28th or 2/43rd Infantry Battalions is difficult to understand. Moreover, if he had sent not just the 2/3rd Pioneers but also the 2/24th and 2/48th Battalions to the coast, in a concentrated assault, the results would surely have been better. Instead, this night's attack is reminiscent of First World War battles in which Australian units made extraordinarily brave and bloody attempts to execute flawed plans. Exhausted commanders should ideally husband their forces and concentrate their combat power against clear and achievable objectives.

Despite all its failings, the attack ordered by Morshead achieved one major success. It had a powerful psychological effect on the Germans. They believed that the Pioneers had, in fact, cut off the Axis forces. The war diary of the 90th Light Division, which was responsible for that sector, noted that on the morning of 31 October it was apparent that the enemy's night attack had 'cut off' the 125th Panzergrenadier Regiment. That same morning, Rommel told Afrika Korps commanders that enemy troops were reported to have reached the coast. He later asserted that 'the enemy had forced their way through to the coast and cut off the 125th Infantry Regiment'. Their contact with troops further west was reduced and threatened but, in fact, the Germans east of the Pioneers were not physically surrounded. Yet the belief that they were 'cut off' clearly played on Rommel's mind. A key component of the German approach to the battle for the next two days was the conviction that all means should be used to save the 125th Panzergrenadier Regiment. In rescuing that unit, Rommel wanted also to destroy the Australian salient that was now in the way.[208]

A wartime account of the 2/48th Battalion's efforts said the fighting on the night of 30–31 October was largely responsible for Rommel's eventual defeat in the battle.[209] The attacks had been unnecessarily costly and resulted in a less than ideal posture for defence at dawn, but they had maintained the pressure on Rommel in the north. Moreover, although the Germans were soon to restore contact with the 'cut off' troops, the Australian attacks probably encouraged the Germans to withdraw from the area east of the 2/3rd Pioneer advance. These operations were the last and most desperate Australian attacks of the battle. The Australians' offensive potential was spent. From now until someone else in the Eighth Army achieved a breakthrough, the Australians would have to defend, trying to hold their recently won ground against everything the Germans could throw at them.

'If you want us, come and get us': 31 October, day

At dawn on 31 October, as the 26th Brigade prepared for the counterattacks that were sure to come that day, the southernmost of its battalions was the 2/24th, now reorganised south of the railway. Its rifle companies comprised one officer and eighty-four men.[210] The 2/48th had only two officers and seventy-two men in its rifle companies, which were about 275 metres east of Barrel Hill.[211] The 2/32nd Battalion was holding a line running from Barrel Hill, then south of the railway in the direction of the 2/15th Battalion. The 2/32nd's attack had been the only one which had put it into a position approximating that envisaged in the plan. Also in the vicinity were the B2 Platoon of the 2/2nd Machine Gun Battalion, a troop of the

The Saucer, photographed from Barrel Hill in 1942. The Blockhouse is clearly visible in the background. One caption to this photo says it shows 'Blockhouse tank battle'. (IMAGE COURTESY OF DAVID PEARSON)

2/3rd Anti-Tank Regiment and the Rhodesian 289th Anti-Tank Battery. They could fire on part of the main road, but were not astride it. To the 2/32nd men looking at that position at dawn on 31 October, it resembled a saucer, and the 'Saucer' is what it was called thereafter. At first light, the 2/32nd had taken more than 100 prisoners in mopping up their area. Some recalcitrant defenders of dugouts in the railway embankment were entombed with grenades, others shot at as they sought to run. The threat to the railway gap was thus removed.

The Saucer contained three landmarks: Barrel Hill, to the north-west; the Blockhouse, on the railway to the south-east; and the railway gap, some 275 metres west along the railway. Much of the ground was rocky, and the sand was thin and unsuited to digging the slit trenches that were so necessary. For the next three days this area was raked by shells and machine-gun bullets, which hit the living and the dead. Any German breakthrough there would jeopardise Montgomery's plans for a decisive British penetration further south by threatening the key British positions on the coast road and drawing away valuable resources. As General Leese put it, 'If the front of that Division had been penetrated ... the whole success of the 8th Army plan could have been prejudiced'.[212]

The Saucer, photographed from the same southward-looking angle in 1997. (AUTHOR'S COLLECTION)

Early in the morning, Rommel sent a message to his 125th Panzergrenadier Regiment, east of the Saucer: 'Regiment hang on; I am coming with strong forces to relieve you'. He was determined also to push the Australians south of the railway. He visited the 90th Light Division command post to discuss the forthcoming German counterattack with its commanders, as well as those of the artillery and flak, and the 21st Panzer Division's Kampfgruppe Pfeiffer. The Afrika Korps commander, von Thoma, and his chief of staff had to leave operations further south to attend this meeting too. [213]

Through Ultra, Montgomery learnt of Rommel's plans for 31 October, but only on 1 November. Ultra had little direct influence on the dispositions or tactics of any particular Allied unit. The time involved in decrypting and disseminating the intercepts meant they

could give no warning of an enemy operation unless orders were distributed long before. Nevertheless, Ultra could convey the state of mind of an opposing commander. Montgomery could read in Rommel's orders and reports both his desperation and his determination to counter the Australian thrust in the north.

At dawn on 31 October, the 2/3rd Pioneer Battalion occupied ground north of the Saucer. D Company, furthest north, sent a fighting patrol to investigate enemy movement further north. The patrollers were ambushed and suffered heavy losses. Any movement in

Members of the 2/3rd Pioneer Battalion shelter on the embankment of the railway, 31 October.
(IMAGE COURTESY OF TED CARTER AND DAVID PEARSON)

the company's positions brought close-range 'withering fire' from small arms and two anti-tank guns.[214] In mid-morning, a German officer approached D Company with a white flag. Hopes that this was an enemy surrender were dashed when the officer stated, in quite good English, that the Australians were almost surrounded and invited them to surrender rather than die. The reply, in the tradition of the 300 Spartans, was: 'If you want us, come and get us'; the suggestion as to where the emissary could put his flag was more in an Australian tradition.[215]

The German returned to his lines, and the fight resumed. Captain Stevens moved back to C Company, looking for ammunition. While he was away, the enemy laid down a smoke screen in front of D Company's positions. The acting company commander believed that Stevens had been killed, and on hearing that two enemy companies had been seen through the smoke preparing to attack, ordered the company to retreat. Stevens returned and with other officers tried unsuccessfully to halt the withdrawal. A large number of men fled. German fire pinned down C Company, now comprising little more than a platoon. Most were captured, as was Stevens' company headquarters. Stevens lay in a slit trench all day, feigning death. He endured enemy kicks in the ribs to check for life, and at one point lay between two tanks. The following night, he escaped.

Lieutenant Colonel Gallasch now ordered the battalion to withdraw to Barrel Hill. Unplanned and under pressure, it was a disorderly withdrawal and some retreated south of the railway, where they 'were disorganised for some time'. In the 2/48th Battalion positions, Warrant Officer Legg saw them coming: '... the whole 2/3 Pioneer Bn ran away from the Eyeties [sic], streaming down over a ridge we had to hold. I stemmed the rush, but twice again they ran back'.[216]

In fact, some courageous members of the 2/3rd Pioneers had not run. Ted Mulley was wounded a second time in mid-morning but again refused to leave his section. When his battalion fell back, he organised his section, including the other wounded. In the process he was wounded a third time but carried on as the men set up in new positions. Then, while moving between them, he sustained a fourth wound. This time he had to be carried to the RAP and evacuated. Some members of the battalion remained on the forward slopes of B11, exposed to enemy mortar and machine-gun fire. Then suddenly they bore the brunt of new gunfire, from German tanks. Both Stevens, lying out in the abandoned D Company positions, and Rosevear, commanding B company on Barrel Hill, saw fifteen or sixteen tanks of *Kampfgruppe Pfeiffer* drive towards the ridge across flat ground between the main road and the coast, at about midday.[217]

The 6-pounders in the area were all behind Barrel Hill and unable to see the tanks, which from about 900 metres out peppered the ridge with machine-gun fire. Considering the position of the Pioneers lying on the exposed slopes of B11 as hopeless, Rosevear ordered them to withdraw 30 metres to the reverse slope. They could go no further, as men of other battalions already occupied the ground.

Then, rolling up towards the Pioneers came British tanks of the 40 RTR. They halted on the reverse slope as little as 15 metres from the Pioneers, and opened fire on the German tanks as they came up over a ridge about 275 metres to the west. Those on B11 were now in the midst of a tank battle. Anti-tank shells screamed over their heads.

Four Valentines quickly caught fire, but the tide soon turned. From about 200 metres further south, anti-tank guns destroyed five of the German tanks.[218] The surviving Panzers retreated north. Their supporting infantry also withdrew, pounded by artillery fire. This attack was the first serious threat to the Saucer area that day.

The main enemy attack of 31 October began in the early afternoon and was directed at Barrel Hill. Its 11-metre height barely entitled it to the name 'hill', but it offered its occupant a vantage point over enemy territory. German tanks now drove towards the men of the B Company, 2/32nd Battalion, assigned to defend it. After the Pioneers had withdrawn, this company felt exposed on both flanks. One defender remembered some officers of this company telling the men to hold the ridge, and then leaving the scene.[219]

Some tanks were reportedly destroyed, but most reached the Australians. Threatening the defenders with their machine guns, and even driving over their positions, the Panzer commanders called out to the Australians to give themselves up. Most of the company – up to thirty-seven men – were captured. This event echoed its experience on 22 July: 'Our B Company [was] again just about wiped out', ran the sad diary entry of a D Company soldier.[220] Some evaded capture by hiding in their slit trenches or, as they were being

Captain Bill Campbell took this photograph of B11 from the Blockhouse, probably on 31 October. Tanks can be seen in the background. (IMAGE COURTESY OF BILL CAMPBELL)

rounded up, running when friendly artillery fire came down.

The tank battle raged anew, with up to twenty-five tanks on each side. The British tanks were attacked not only by the Panzers, but also by anti-tank guns the enemy had brought forward, and by artillery fire described in the 40 RTR War Diary as 'the fiercest the Battalion had been through'. Private Fred Fewtrell of the 2/32nd counted twenty-one destroyed Valentines, one of which was only a cricket pitch away, its driver's head blown off. [221]

Three 6-pounders – two Rhodesian and one Australian – were also destroyed. The Australian crew, located near B11, were all killed or wounded. The experiences of Gunner Albert Schwebel speak to the intensity of the fighting. He was hit in the arms and legs, but carried his two wounded crewmates through enemy fire and into the Blockhouse. He then

returned to his damaged gun and, after salvaging parts from other unserviceable 6-pounders, brought it into action again. Once more enemy fire hit his gun, and he received another wound, to the head. Undeterred, he took a Bren gun and joined the infantry defence.[222]

Artillery, the British tanks and the anti-tank guns eventually drove off the attackers, who left behind one burning Panzer III and at least five other immobilised tanks.

2/32 Battalion holding German counter-attack, El Alamein, 31 October 1942, by William Dargie.
Men of B Company of the 2/32nd Battalion facing a German tank attack on 31 October.
(1943, oil on hardboard, 39 x 45.4cm, AWM ART22251)

The 90th Light Division's war diary claimed that its spearheads came within 800 metres of the 'Hut', or Blockhouse, in this attack, and noted that patrols made contact with the 125th Regiment in the dunes north of the road. However, the contact was not firm, thanks to heavy fire from the 'Hut' area.[223]

Soon after 4.00pm the Germans launched a last attempt to recapture the Saucer. Several of the eighteen tanks employed were reportedly long-barrelled Panzer IVs. They used their superior 75mm armament, fired from hull-down positions north of the road, to force the 40 RTR to withdraw. However, they could not shift the Australian infantry, and lost twenty-five prisoners and at least eight tanks in withdrawing. They also left behind an 88mm gun and tractor which sought to support the attack: the gun was destroyed and the tractor set alight by a 6-pounder.

The 2/48th said of the oft-criticised British tanks that day, '40 RTR fought their tks magnificently'.[224] The machine gunners of B2 Platoon praised the tanks too, and these gunners were well qualified to comment on bravery. Located in the 'hot corner', on the north-western edge of the Saucer, they were intermingled with C Company of the 2/32nd Battalion, which started the day with only twenty-two men. Theirs was 'a desperate position', under fire from three sides.[225] Enemy tanks approached their location three times that day, and its defenders were immensely grateful for the work of four Rhodesian 6-pounders dug into the railway embankment behind them.

Australians, two of whom are wearing souvenired binoculars, pose in front of a German 88mm gun and tractor destroyed near the Blockhouse on 31 October or 1 November.
(IMAGE COURTESY OF TED CARTER)

(top to bottom)
An Australian poses after the battle with one of the Valentines destroyed in the fight near the Blockhouse on 31 October. (IMAGE COURTESY OF TED CARTER)

British tanks destroyed in the 31 October battle near the Blockhouse. (IMAGE COURTESY OF TED CARTER)

AUSTRALIA

For up to ten hours, heavy and almost continuous shellfire hit the men packed into the Saucer. They lay or crouched in shallow weapon pits as hot shrapnel rained down on them. Many who were hit were taken to the Blockhouse, though that building was not safe either. An enemy shell penetrated the roof, and others landed around the building. A dive-bombing raid hit one ambulance, killing the driver and wounding two men. The 26th Brigade report later criticised the Saucer's defenders for tending to huddle, instead of showing the flexibility necessary for a 'really effective defensive scheme'. If this criticism was tactically valid, it perhaps underestimated the precariousness of life in this small and exposed position.[226]

Stukas made this a 'bad day' for some Australian artillerymen, who had anti-personnel 'butterfly' bombs and larger bombs dropped around them. Nevertheless, the guns again provided crucial support in breaking up attacks. Even the prosaic official artillery report reveals the labour and the drama of the day: 'Counter attacks were from East, North East, North, North West and West at different times'.[227]

One account of the 2/48th's day described as 'the most nerve-racking experience possible to imagine', their ordeal lying in their pits as enemy artillery and tank fire burst overhead. An 88mm shell which struck a slit trench killed the already thrice-wounded adjutant, Captain Reid, and wounded Captain Bryant, the last remaining company commander. Another soldier lost both legs when a direct hit destroyed his trench. Two comrades braved enemy tank fire to rescue and carry him to the aid post. The 2/24th Battalion felt the strain too. A great shock was the loss of two sergeants, killed when the machine gun on an apparently derelict tank opened fire in front of the battalion positions.[228]

The German official report on the battle gave credit where it was due to the defenders of the 'Hut' area. It twice called the defence 'stubborn' and also 'very strong'.[229] The 90th Light Division War Diary acknowledged that its 361st Regiment, which had provided most of the attacking infantry, was 'terribly disorganised' by the British shellfire, and was pinned down till after dark.[230] Von Thoma and his chief of staff recommended to the *Panzerarmee* that the 125th Panzergrenadier Regiment be withdrawn immediately, but they were ordered to continue their attacks the following day.

The 26th Brigade headquarters planned to regroup the Saucer's defenders in the night of 31 October. Before the plan could be implemented, good news arrived from division. The 2/24th and 2/48th Battalions were to be relieved by the remaining two battalions of the 24th Brigade – the 2/28th and 2/43rd.

(Opposite) Captain Don Bryant of the 2/48th Battalion was awarded a Military Cross for his courage at Tel el Eisa. His comment 'She's sweet', while under enemy tank attack, entered battalion folklore. Just 24 years old when pictured, he survived his wounds at Alamein and remained in the post-war Army, receiving an MBE and retiring in 1969 as a lieutenant colonel. (AWM 041971)

AUSTRALIAN AND BRITISH TROOPS

In all of their campaigns in the Middle East, Australian troops fought alongside British soldiers. From September 1942, the Scots of the 51st Highland Division were beside the 9th at Alamein. The Australians 'fostered in' these newcomers to the desert. Initially, small groups of Scots accompanied the Australians on patrol, and eventually the Scots' brigades took it in turns to share the Australian sector. Relations between the two groups were generally excellent, and the Scots were grateful for many lessons. The Highland Division commander, Major General Douglas Wimberley, considered the Australians 'magnificent', but emphasised to his officers the importance of ensuring that the Scots did not emulate the more relaxed Australian approach to discipline. Some Australians were astonished by what they saw as excessive British attention to parade-ground drill in forward areas.

The opening barrage made Australians feel 'intensely British', according to one battalion newsletter published during the battle. Scots and Australians helped each other on the fringes of their advance that first night, though the Australians were not so impressed by the efforts of the British armour they witnessed. British anti-tank gunners, employing 6-pounders, were more impressive to the Australians, who saw

Australian and British soldiers (including Scots) inspect wrecked German equipment after Alamein. (IMAGE COURTESY OF REX LANGTHORNE)

them knocking out more than a dozen Axis tanks on 25 October. Three days later, one Australian recorded the generosity of Scottish troops who, on relieving his platoon at night, insisted they sleep and then provided them with a welcome breakfast. By then, the Scottish division had suffered more casualties than the 9th (1956 to 1668). British artillery supported Australian infantry during advances on 28–29 October, as it did throughout the battle. British tank support for the 2/23rd advance that night was imperfect, and this prompted Morshead to refuse British tank support for his next attacks, on 30–31 October. On 29 October, one Australian complained about the excessive expectations being put on the Australians, writing: 'Why can't our chaps be relieved? ... I wonder what the top brass really want from a human being? It is about time the Poms had a go'. Yet on 31 October, during a German Panzer attack on the Blockhouse area, outgunned British tanks arrived and fought a fierce tank battle that helped to save the day and won plaudits from previously sceptical Australians. Cooperation with British forces was constant in the medical field. Just 10 per cent of the casualties which Australian field ambulances brought to the 2/3rd Australian Casualty Clearing Station were Australian, while most of the other Australian casualties were treated in British medical units. By 3 November, the largest group of patients in Australian medical units were Scots of the Highland Division. Hundreds of Australians were treated in Commonwealth field ambulances, casualty clearing stations and hospitals stretching all the way back to Gaza.[231]

26th Brigade moves out and 24th Brigade moves in: 31 October, night

When darkness fell, reorganisation began in the Saucer. The 2/32nd Battalion was moved south of the railway. So too were the 2/3rd Pioneers, who were to help close the gap between the 2/32nd and 2/15th Battalions. The exhausted and depleted 2/24th and 2/48th Battalions were at last to leave the line. The 2/24th Battalion history records the amazement of a transport officer who, having brought some twenty trucks up to take out the battalion, saw that the survivors would barely fill four. A large convoy of trucks had been required to bring 2/48th Battalion into action on the night of 30–31 October, but just two vehicles were needed to remove the survivors the following night. The survivors of the 2/24th seemed to an observer to be hanging on because of Benzedrine tablets and an 'instinctive sense of duty'. Perhaps the state of these men is best summed up by the 2/48th's Warrant Officer Legg, who wrote in his diary of his condition after being driven to Tel el Eisa: 'So "done" that I trembled uncontrollably for ½ hr'.[232]

When planning the operations of the night of 30–31 October, Morshead had decided that the 24th Brigade would relieve the 26th Brigade on the night of 31 October – 1 November. So far, the overall plan had gone astray, and if the relief were to go ahead it would be in vastly different circumstances than those originally envisaged. The decimated battalions of 26th Brigade were holding a tiny bridgehead under great pressure from the enemy. In the late afternoon, Morshead learned the details of this confused situation. He could have been excused for hesitating to attempt a changeover, which was bound to be risky and administratively chaotic. However, he decided immediately to carry out the relief, with orders issued at about 7.30pm.[233]

Various Australian writers have portrayed Morshead's order to relieve the 26th Brigade with the 24th Brigade as a bold masterstroke. The Division's own report on the battle rather immodestly announced that: 'The decision to effect this relief saved this flank and probably saved the battle'.[234]

Morshead's decision has been characterised as difficult, for the changeover supposedly left the British defences between the coast and the railway cutting perilously exposed to a German armoured thrust. One battalion historian put it that the 'front door to Alexandria had to remain ajar' until the 26th Brigade could close it. There were, indeed, few Australian forces defending that coastal area while the changeover was made during the night: two squadrons of the 9th Division Cavalry, with Crusader and Honey tanks, the supporting arms of the 24th Brigade, and some 2/8th Field Regiment staff.[235]

However, even if the Germans had somehow known this, it would have been a perilous foray by their tanks to drive towards these positions in a night attack. They probably had insufficient infantry support or fuel to turn such an attack into a battle-winning manoeuvre. Their official records of the time reflect a preoccupation with rescuing or even withdrawing the 'cut-off' troops to the east of the Saucer, rather than an eastwards advance. If Morshead was truly worried about this area, he also had at his disposal the 2/23rd Battalion, which was then idle near the Fig Orchard. Morshead's decision was risky, both at the coastal end and during the changeover in the Saucer itself. He needed to make such a decision because of faults in the plan that had decimated the 26th Brigade and left it holding on desperately in the exposed Saucer. If the Germans had attacked during the relief, they may have broken the Australian line, and this would probably have upset British plans for Supercharge. Morshead's calculated risk was vindicated, for the new defenders of the Saucer needed every man they had in the fighting to come.

The 2/43rd Battalion moved out across the railway at Tel el Eisa at 8.15pm, followed by the 2/28th Battalion. Neither unit had time for a preliminary reconnaissance. The 2/28th had been rebuilt into a 'first-rate combatant unit' since its virtual annihilation in July.[236] Its convoy now drove south towards Ruin Ridge and out of the divisional area, then west past burning British armoured vehicles, and finally north into the Saucer. On debussing, the men had to use maps and compasses to find their way through the darkness. Ignorance of what they were approaching dampened enthusiasm.

The 2/43rd also had a hastily prepared circuitous drive, conducted in silence and with no smoking. After debussing, they dispersed and rested for a few minutes. Led by guides, they crossed the railway, saw dimly the low grey concrete Blockhouse to their right and found the 2/48th, which they were to relieve. The plight of their fellow South Australians saddened them. The 2/28th were glad to find the 2/24th, but the dilapidated appearance of the Victorian battalion's remnants must have added to anxieties – so too must the comment of the departing troops to their replacements: 'Start digging, you b_____s, or you'll be sorry!'[237]

Confusion arose because four battalions were crowded into the small space between the road and a point just south of the railway. Moreover, the strong 2/28th and 2/43rd took over from battalions so weakened that they were holding little more than company-size areas. Lieutenant Colonel Jack Loughrey of the 2/28th took the lead in arranging new boundaries between his and the neighbouring battalions. More men were now placed north of the railway and some were again overlooking the main road.

The arrangements made in the dark and chaos between midnight and 4.00am were certainly unorthodox. Methodical consolidation of the type the division had trained in and been applying so successfully in recent days was not possible. When Lieutenant Phil Adnams of the 2/43rd reconnoitred a position for his platoon, he was concerned that it would be difficult to retrace his steps when he brought the men forward, so as a landmark he used a haversack attached to a severed arm. Such sights, and warnings that the enemy was likely to attack at any time, spurred men on to dig enthusiastically if they could not occupy existing positions. The men in the foremost sections of Adnams's platoon were on the forward slope of Barrel Hill, where the ground was rocky shale, and few holes were deeper than sixty centimetres. Brigadier Arthur Godfrey, who would be overseeing the defence, now took over from Brigadier Whitehead and set up his command post in a dugout south of the railway and within sight of the Saucer.[238]

The defence of the Saucer had so successfully drawn the enemy's attention to themselves that the pressure on the 20th Brigade diminished on 31 October.

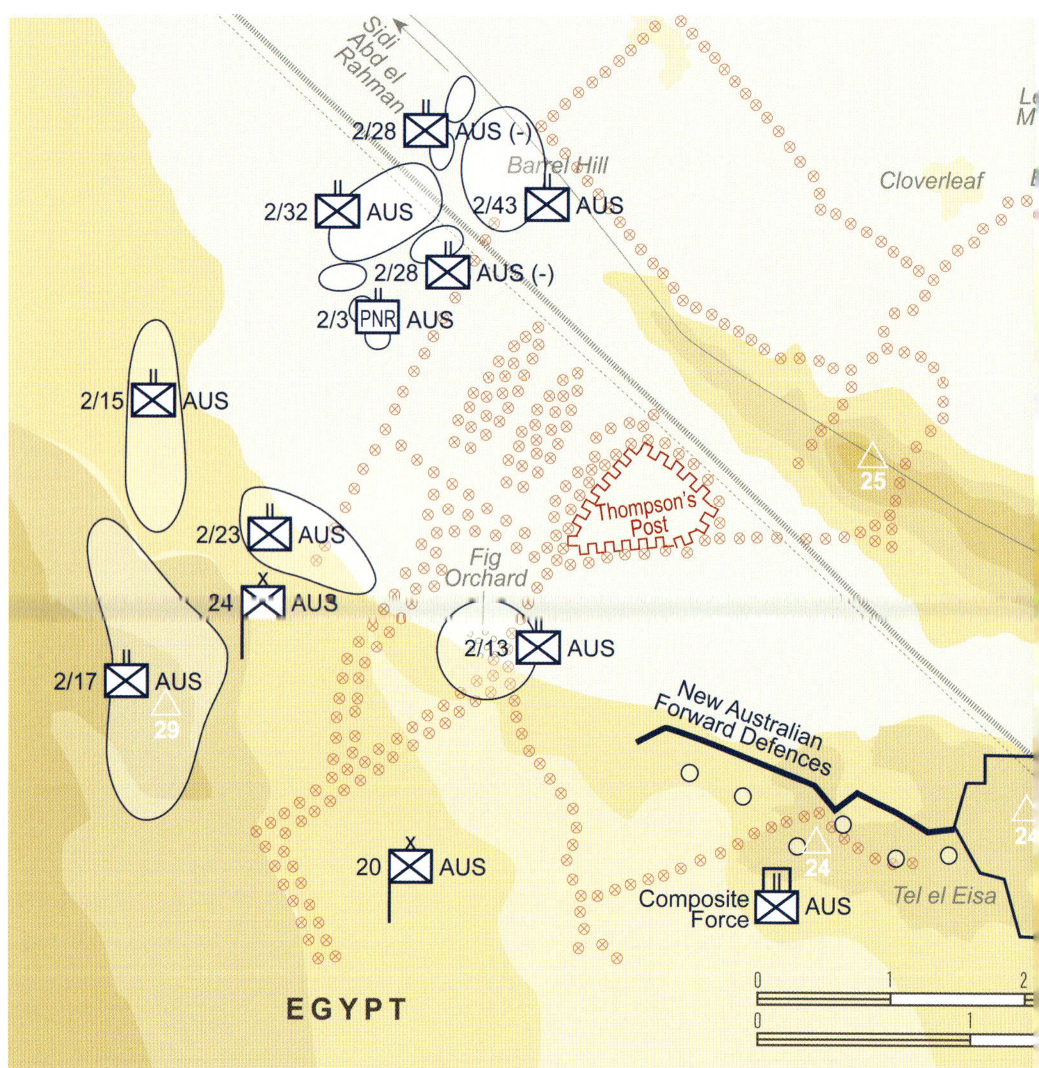

The 2/17th continued to fight small groups of enemy ensconced around the battalion's defences at Trig 29. Both sides in the area allowed the other's ambulances to remove their dead and wounded amid dust clouds.[239] Eric Lambert of the 2/15th reflected that death and wounds were a daily event, wondered if his turn was coming, and pencilled down the question being asked by 300,000 desperate men on that battlefield: 'When is this madness going to end?'[240]

The answer lay partly in Australian hands. The 9th Division had by now inflicted casualties on all four German divisions engaged in the battle. The Germans had expended many of their reserves against the Australians, and although they had re-established contact with the 125th Regiment, they had achieved no significant penetration. The British had not

Map 24. Australian dispositions after the 26th Brigade's relief, dawn, 1 November 1942

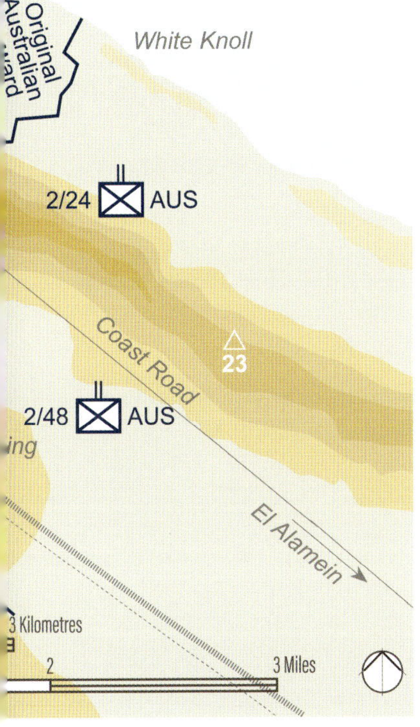

achieved their hoped-for great breakthrough either, but the major attempt, Supercharge, was slated for the night of 1–2 November. If the Australians could hold off the German attacks for one more day – 1 November – then victory could well be in sight.

'The most determined attack': the Saucer on 1 November

At dawn, neither the 2/28th nor the 2/43rd Battalion had telephone lines to brigade headquarters, so communication from the Saucer to brigade depended on fitfully working radios and on one phone line from the 2/32nd Battalion, which was in turn connected to B2 Machine Gun Platoon on the north-west of the salient.

Four platoons of the 2/43rd Battalion, as well as a few Vickers guns and two 2-pounder anti-tank guns, occupied the 200 metre-long Barrel Hill. The remainder of the 2/43rd was in the Saucer south of B11. Fairly safe from small-arms fire, its task was defending the area against attacks over the hill or from the east.

On the exposed western side of the Saucer, between road and railway, were two companies of the 2/28th Battalion. The battalion's other two rifle companies were south of the railway, behind the 2/32nd Battalion. The 2/32nd, like the 2/3rd Pioneers, had not been relieved the night before. The men of these two battalions had barely slept since the night of 30–31 October. Some 2/28th men were on the 2/32nd's immediate left, to which the 2/3rd Pioneers were adjacent on the extreme left of this 24th Brigade line.

The units in and forward of the Saucer had no overhead cover and little or no barbed wire in front of their positions, although a minefield had reportedly been laid in front of the 2/28th Battalion and the 2/32nd. The hard and sparsely vegetated ground offered little cover, and the Germans on the high ground at Sidi Abd el Rahman, approximately 7 kilometres to the north-west, had a superb overview of the area. Even brigade and battalion headquarters were visible to the enemy, and were fired on by artillery or mortars.

The brigade was soon aware that the enemy was close. Dug-in German troops were just

750–1000 metres away, in an arc from north-west to south-east. Until mid-morning, the enemy directed little fire on the area. Men had time to read mail, smoke and eat a breakfast of bully beef and biscuits. Ominously, dead and mutilated bodies lay mingled with burnt-out vehicles and guns.[241]

By 10.00am what the 24th Brigade report called 'continuous fire' was pouring into the Australian positions.[242] It was not literally continuous, but was prolonged and fearsome. It came from small arms, mortars, at least eight 88mm guns firing airburst, 105mm guns and anti-tank guns. Most fire came from the west and north-west, but 105mm fire also came from the north-east, and 88mm and anti-tank fire from the south-east.

British shelling continued to be even heavier than the enemy's, but to the Australians on the ground, the Germans' rumoured ammunition shortage appeared a bad joke. Moreover, the 2/28th had no artillery officer with them to direct defensive fire, and the first German salvos cut the telephone line of the artillery officer with the 2/43rd on Barrel Hill. Thus, for vital hours the hill's defenders did not receive the close artillery support that direct observation from B11 might have allowed.

Australians on B11 saw German lorries and smaller vehicles on the main road at about 10.00am. With smart professionalism, the Germans dismounted from their vehicles and quickly disappeared from view. Artillery fire caught at least 300 of them in the open – thus helping the incommunicado men on Barrel Hill – but their heavy casualties did not deter enemy commanders from continuing to send troops south-east from the Sidi Abd el Rahman area. Clearly, the Germans were preparing a major assault.

Earlier that morning, a message was received that the Eighth Army's 'Y' intercept service had heard of an impending attack on the 'Hut'. Rommel was at the headquarters of the 90th Light Division at about 8.30am, and was heard by the wireless intercept service, exhorting his men to overrun the 'depleted' garrison defending the area. He was unaware that the units defending the area were no longer depleted. At about 10.20am the Australian battalions learnt of this message, which said the enemy believed that they were opposed by just one strongpoint astride the railway, and that this would soon fall to the crack 90th Light Division.[243]

The threatened large-scale assault began at about noon, supported by heavy artillery concentrations and sustained mortar and machine-gun fire. An intelligence summary called this the 'most determined attack' faced by the 9th Division in the campaign. Smoke and dust soon enveloped the battlefield. Approximately one battalion of infantry attacked between the road and the railway in the west, and about two companies south of the railway. Tanks supported these assaults against both the 2/28th and 2/32nd Battalions. Soon afterwards, infantry and about twelve tanks attacked the 2/43rd from the north. The three 2/43rd platoons on Barrel Hill now fought what one of their officers called 'a private war on our own'.[244]

Lieutenant John Coen's platoon, on the top and forward slopes of B11, had already suffered heavy casualties from shelling before the tanks arrived. The Panzers covered the advance of their accompanying infantry with their machine guns. Eight Australians continued firing until a tank and supporting infantry reached the lip of the hill and forced their surrender. A chivalrous German NCO gestured towards the Blockhouse, allowing a wounded Bren gunner to go back to treatment and safety. The Germans did not fire either at other platoon members who hobbled over the brow of the hill. The enemy remained on the forward slopes of the hill rather than brave whatever might be fired at them if they went to the summit. Coen, his batman and a sergeant, despite being wounded, all did what they could with rifles to maintain the impression that coming over the hill would be dangerous. For some time, the squeaking tracks of two tanks could be heard, and their masts and turret tops seen, but the Germans did not advance to the top of Barrel Hill in this area.

Adnams's platoon, to the left of Coen's and near the centre of B11, also faced tanks and infantry. Tanks quickly destroyed a 2-pounder anti-tank gun sited to support Adnams's men. Two Vickers guns suffered the same fate when the tank crews threw grenades into the machine gunners' pits. The tanks then fired at the platoon's slit trenches from about 100 metres, inflicting many casualties. The Australians kept firing. Crewmen of the remaining 2-pounder ran from cover, forced a shell into the breech, ran back to their dugout and pulled the lanyard, only to see their shell bounce off a tank like 'a tennis ball off a brick wall'.[245] The tanks destroyed this gun and advanced. German infantry riding on the tanks captured the Australians still forward of the hilltop. Only five men in Adnams's platoon were still standing by the end of the day.

On Adnams's left was Sergeant 'Alby' Joy's platoon, the northernmost unit of the 24th Brigade. Aircraft, machine guns and artillery halted the infantry and tanks advancing towards it. On the left of the 2/43rd men on Barrel Hill was a company of the 2/28th Battalion. One of its officers, Lieutenant Roger Price, was wounded early in the day, but remained on duty. The Germans approached his position in small groups, 'rifles slung, looking for all the world like spectators drifting away from a minor football game'.

Another 2/28th man saw about eight tanks and 500 or more infantry advancing very slowly towards the Australians. By firing automatics and rifles 'like mad', the Australians checked the infantry advance. When fighter-bombers and artillery fire came down, the attack wilted. On all sides, artillery fire drove off most of the enemy infantry with heavy casualties. From hull-down positions the surviving tanks sought to reduce the defences. Some intrepid Germans climbed into derelict Valentine tanks and directed their 2-pounder guns at the Australians, until destroyed by medium artillery.[247]

At about 1.25pm, the forward German tanks as well as 'intense' artillery support helped enemy infantry press their attack. The anti-tank guns concentrated on the tanks, while Australian small arms fire inflicted heavy casualties on the infantry. These infantrymen were able to find just one point of penetration, where a group overran one of the 2/43rd Battalion platoons defending B11. Assisted by tanks, they used their height advantage and fired point-blank on the Australians on the slopes below.[248]

Within about ten minutes of this blow, the 2/43rd launched a counterattack which

AIR SUPPORT

Tactical airpower was directed from a central headquarters with Air Support Controls (units at corps level comprising army and air force personnel) based on lorry transport and carrying radio and radar. These Controls liaised with army units further forward, via wireless-based 'tentacles', and air units further back. The Royal Air Force had air superiority over the battlefield throughout the battle, enabling light bombers to operate effectively in daylight against targets of opportunity; air support sorties regularly arrived within forty minutes of the initial request. There were at least two air support 'tentacles' with the 9th Division for the October battle – one at its tactical headquarters and another with the 26th Brigade's headquarters – and its post-operations report acknowledged that timely provision of air support had broken up enemy counterattacks and affected Australian and enemy morale.[249]

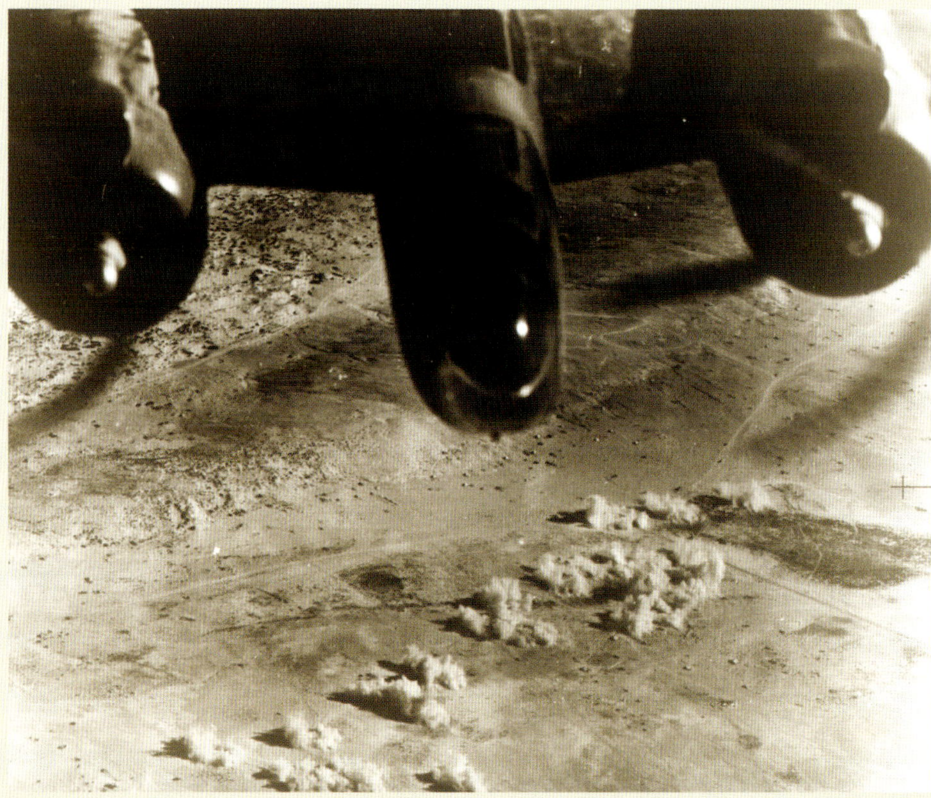

During a bombing raid by No. 223 Squadron RAF in support of the Alamein offensive, a Martin Baltimore Mark III overflies the target, the German-held landing ground at El Daba. (IWM HU 52289)

regained the vital ground of Barrel Hill. Several other successes could be counted around the Saucer. Anti-tank fire had destroyed one Panzer IV, two Panzer IIIs and an 88mm gun north of the 2/43rd. The latter was towed, in full view of the Rhodesian gunners, into a position on or near the main road, presumably in the hope of knocking out the Australian defences at close range. Instead, it was dispatched after firing just two rounds, and burned for some time.

Credit for defeating the tanks belonged mainly to the Rhodesian and Australian anti-tank gunners. In the Saucer, Allan Jones was very close to a Rhodesian gun, which was firing at tanks driving in from the west towards the 2/28th Battalion. He saw the Australians stand up and applaud every time the Rhodesians scored a hit, to the puzzlement of the serious gunners.[250]

By mid-afternoon the Rhodesians had lost eight guns, the primary targets of the Panzers. The four guns of A Troop of the 2/3rd Anti-Tank Regiment, in vulnerable positions on B11, had also been destroyed. Tank support was requested all the way up to corps level but was not available. Luck and courage brought another troop of Australian guns through enemy fire to replace the Rhodesians between the railway and B11. Once sited, they destroyed two tanks. An additional Rhodesian troop came over, but during the day all of its guns were destroyed and its commander killed.[251]

At about 3.00pm, artillery defensive fire routed enemy infantry on the railway. On B11, though, the tanks returned soon afterwards and, with infantry support, forced Sergeant Joy's platoon back. Through his binoculars, the Pioneers' Major Rosevear saw 2/43rd men being driven off the ridge; he believed that had his battalion still been north of the ridge it would have been 'annihilated'. Allan Jones, on the flat behind Barrel Hill, also saw men coming over the crest, including one running with his clothes on fire.[252]

Jones then saw the men go back up the hill, bearing 'expressions of resolute endeavour'. Helped by Captain Collin Newbery of the 2/28th Battalion, and Captain Ivan Hare of the 2/43rd, Joy had halted the retreat. He reorganised his platoon and, under heavy fire, led his men back to recapture all but one of the posts they had lost. Eventually the Germans withdrew from even the one remaining position. Hare was killed leading a similar but unsuccessful counterattack.[253]

Some details of the fighting on B11 remain obscure. After about 3.50pm, apparently neither side controlled the summit, which was untenable for either. An Australian machine gunner saw a German officer standing on the ridge and coolly observing the Australian dispositions before being shot dead and dragged out of sight. The Germans controlled most of the forward slopes, and by the end of the day perhaps all of those slopes. The Australians, five of whose sections had been overrun, controlled all of the southern, reverse slopes.[254]

The RAF shared the confusion. At one stage in the afternoon they strafed and bombed the Australians on B11. No Australians were hurt, unlike the Germans caught by the bombers' eighteen-strong 'football team' north and north-east of Barrel Hill. The 2/28th was also bombarded for fifty-five minutes by 'friendly' artillery.[255]

Lieutenant Coen's experience typifies that of many Australian casualties that day. On the reverse slope of B11, shrapnel wounded him early in the morning. By the afternoon his damaged leg was numb, and he needed treatment. He crawled out of his weapon pit and headed for the Blockhouse. He had made little progress when two stretcher-bearers came from the Blockhouse to get him and, though nearby shelling caused them to drop him once, carried him inside. At the western end, the battalion chaplain greeted him. Inside the 'cool and dim' building, he received a quick but sympathetic examination from his Regimental Medical Officer, Captain Mick Colyer, and after a cup of tea which he suspected was laced with something, he fell asleep. Twenty-four other members of his platoon were taken to the Blockhouse that day.

Rommel probably saw some Australians enter the building, for in the early afternoon he went to look over the area from Point 16, near Sidi Abd el Rahman. 'Visibility was excellent', he wrote. He could see a Red Cross flag flying from the 'Hut', which was surrounded by seven wrecked tanks. He claimed that he could see thirty to forty more British wrecks further on. 'The British were obviously getting their wounded out, and our artillery had accordingly ceased fire.' This was evidence of what the official history calls Rommel's 'scrupulous adherence to the rules of war'. However, an Australian in the Saucer noticed an unscrupulous use of the Red Cross by Germans on the same day, when he saw a German ambulance bring forward a machine gun.[257]

To reach the sanctuary of the Blockhouse, the wounded from Barrel Hill had to pass

A German Marder III self-propelled gun at Alamein, probably one of two destroyed in the battle for the Saucer on 1 November. (IMAGE COURTESY OF JACK BULLEN)

across the flat ground in between. This area was terribly dangerous. Lieutenant Price of the 2/28th said that it seemed impossible for anyone to survive one particular bombardment. He was amazed at how few were hit. Yet many were, including most of the stretcher-bearers in Price's company. Numerous soldiers owed their lives to bearers, such as the 2/28th's Private John Carey, who made eleven trips of more than 600 metres each, carrying wounded to the RAP. Gunner Schwebel, whom we last saw taking a Bren gun to join the infantry following the loss of his anti-tank gun, also rose to walk across the Saucer. He was carrying a wounded comrade 450 metres to the Blockhouse. Schwebel tried to return to the action, but was detained when someone realised he had a bullet wound to the head.

At 4.00pm the Germans launched simultaneous and determined attacks from the north-west, north and south-east. Some tanks had infantry riders, but Vickers guns soon shot them off or forced them to ground. Artillery fire drove back the attackers. From the north-west, a Marder III self-propelled gun and several tanks advanced down the main road. They fired just three rounds before the Marder and one tank were destroyed. Twenty minutes later, an identical fate befell another Marder in the same area. Sergeant Joy said of these self-propelled guns, 'they looked fearsome iron monsters to us small chaps in our "holes"'.[258] This assault withered within an hour.

At about 3.15pm, the 90th Light Division commander told Rommel that he could neither hold the newly won line nor launch a new attack. Rommel refused to use any of the *Panzerarmee* reserves or to withdraw the 125th Regiment. Instead, he gave instructions that

The Blockhouse, photographed from the southern side on 1 November. (IMAGE COURTESY OF JACK CASTLE)

(Top to bottom) An 88mm gun emplacement, with a dead crewman in the foreground. He was killed by tank machine-gun fire, while eight of his compatriots lay dead in the pit. Victims of this gun are visible in the background. (IMAGE COURTESY OF ALAN SANDBACH)

Axis shells land around 9th Division positions in the late afternoon of 1 November. (AWM 042082)

the enemy must be diverted from the coastal area of operations by feint attacks and artillery concentrations further south. He did not realise that the key diversion was the one that had kept his attention on the coast, rather than the south.[259]

At the 24th Brigade command post, Brigadier Godfrey had reason to be pleased with the performance of his men. Late in the afternoon, though, disaster struck. The Germans clearly identified the area of his headquarters as a worthwhile target, and after being shelled continuously for half an hour, the headquarters received a direct hit. Godfrey was mortally wounded in the stomach. Five other officers were killed or wounded. The Brigade Major, Donald Jackson, took command.

Just after 5.30pm, the enemy attacked from east and west, trying to obey Rommel's reiterated order that 'the Hut was to be taken today'. Five or six tanks led infantry from the Ring Contour 25 area towards the 2/43rd and 2/32nd Battalions, but their assault petered out under the pressure of artillery and aircraft. In the west, about 100 German infantry braved heavy artillery fire to attack the 2/28th Battalion between the road and railway. Small arms and mortar fire halted them.[260]

The Germans used the dust and smoke, and their high ground on B11, to assemble secretly an attacking force of at least three tanks and fifteen truckloads of infantry north-east of the Saucer. At last light (about 6.30pm), this group sought to take advantage of the poor visibility by attacking simultaneously from this direction and the west. They used the standard German practice of attacking out of the setting sun. Both attacks were pressed into the hours of darkness.

At 9.30pm, Lieutenant Colonel Evans of the 2/23rd arrived to take over the 24th Brigade command. Soon afterwards, a German prisoner stated that the attack was to continue, so at irregular intervals the artillery fired on the enemy assembly areas. Sounds of enemy movement were everywhere in that dark night, and the Australians repulsed enemy troops whenever they approached. Only at 2.30am did enemy fire cease, signalling an end to Rommel's hopes of a breakthrough.

'A critical day': conclusions on 1 November

Few defenders of the Saucer on 1 November wrote detailed accounts of the day, perhaps because they found it too difficult. All had an impression of prolonged action. A few days after the battle, a corporal in the 2/28th wrote that on the 1st a Panzer division had attacked them for over eight hours. This Tobruk veteran considered it the 'most concentrated attack I have ever been in'. Corporal Jones of the 2/43rd wrote two weeks afterwards: 'On November 1st we were continuously attacked with tanks, artillery and infantry for fifteen hours'.[261]

With 103 casualties, 1 November was the 2/43rd's bloodiest day of the war. The casualties included its CO, Lieutenant Colonel Wain, concussed by a shell which blew him out of his command post. In the fighting in and around the Saucer between 30 October and 1 November, the 24th Brigade and its four battalions had suffered nearly 500 casualties.[262]

ICONIC IMAGE OF INFANTRY CLOSE COMBAT?

This photograph is probably the most famous image of the battle of El Alamein. Its caption says it shows Australian infantry storming a German strongpoint. In fact, it is one of many reconstructed battle scenes photographed by 'Chet's Circus', a team of British cameramen led by a former newspaper photographer, Sergeant Len Chetwyn. Obtaining genuine action photographs in the desert was virtually impossible – especially with so much night action. Some other cameramen did take frontline photographs, though, and resented the way Chetwyn's team produced slick and plausible shots using base troops and special effects. Evocative though it is, this photograph actually depicts Australian soldiers recreating a charge outside a cookhouse well behind the lines on 3 November 1942, by which time the 9th Division's fighting had effectively ended.[263]

(AWM 042070)

For the Germans, too, it had been a terribly costly day in human life – as Australians discovered when, in subsequent days, they examined the ground in front of their lines.

A few days later, when the XXX Corps Commander visited the 24th Brigade, he made it clear that 1 November had been 'a critical day in the Battle of ALAMEIN', and that the brigade's successful defence had provided the opportunity for the breakthrough further south. How close had the Germans come to their own breakthrough in the Saucer? One author estimates that the 24th Brigade's casualties equalled the total manpower remaining in 26th Brigade when it was relieved, and that by bringing in fresh troops Morshead had 'saved the day'. At the sharp end, it certainly seemed a close-run thing.[264]

Morshead, in his cable to Blamey concerning the day's operations, began: 'One of the most determined attacks ever made against 9 AUST DIV was launched at 1215 hrs'. He said too that 'the issue was NOT decided until night'. On 12 November, he reflected in a letter that virtually the entire German force was eventually concentrated against the Australians. Then he added '"concentrated" is not the word, for had they really concentrated it might have been a different story'. In other words, an opponent using better tactics on 1 November might have defeated the Australians. Instead, as he concluded: 'They all came against us at one time or another, but not in as great strength as they should, and so they were beaten in detail'.[265]

According to one eyewitness, the consensus among senior officers who visited the Saucer after 1 November was that the ground was 'theoretically untenable'. The Australians had occupied the position in haste, and lacked a significant reserve force. The Germans should have broken through. They did re-establish firm contact with the beleaguered troops on the coast, but uncharacteristically poor coordination between tanks and infantry, and their piecemeal commitment, contributed to their failure to smash the Saucer. Rommel's assurance that they would face little opposition that day probably created false hopes, and when these were dashed it must have been hard for the much-harassed Germans to maintain their self-belief and determination. Ultimately, though, determined defence in the Saucer was essential to the German failure. The Australians in charge there had shown effective and determined leadership, steadying and rallying their men whenever necessary, and demonstrating willingness to counterattack to regain lost ground. Artillery fire and well-sited anti-tank defences had also been critical. Impressive evidence of the intensity of the combat is one company's ammunition expenditure on 1 November: 19,000 small-arms ammunition rounds, 15,000 Thompson submachine-gun bullets, and about 250 3-inch mortar bombs.[266]

The morale of the Australians on this most testing day was clearly high. On entering the Saucer for their first major involvement in the battle, 24th Brigade members had felt that 'if the 26th Brigade could take it, we could hold it'. Men of the 2/32nd Battalion, who had enjoyed little or no rest since 30 October, showed great determination. One wrote proudly on 2 November, 'Battalion doing a terrific job. We have had the responsibility of holding the right flank for the whole army over the last few days'. No doubt a desire to

ENEMY COUNTERATTACKS

Obtaining definitive data on enemy counterattacks during the October battle is impossible, but this table, from the collection of the 9th Division CRA, Brigadier Alan Ramsay, is instructive.

Figure 6:

AXIS counterattacks on 9th division during battle / 23 Oct – 5 Nov 1942

DATE	TIME	AGAINST	COMPOSITION
24 Oct	0700 hrs	2/48 Bn	15 tks and lorried inf
	1200–1800 hrs	2/13 and 2/48 Bns	Tks and lorried inf – 3 times
25 Oct	0630 hrs	2/48 Bn	12 tks and 50 MT
	1500 hrs	26 Bde northern flank	–
	1412 hrs	2/13 and 2/17 Bns	20/30 tks astride 297 grid
26 Oct	0430 hrs	20 Bde	Northing grid 2895. Got within 400 yds of FDL
	0715 hrs	–	Tks and inf 86602983
	0955 hrs	2/13 Bn and 51 HD	Inf only
	0815 hrs	26 Bde	Tks and inf massing 87003015
	1815 hrs	2/17 Bn	Inf debussed 863299. Four tks and MG fire
Patrol	1915 hrs	2/48 Bn	Enemy patrol of 50
27 Oct	0415 hrs	20 Bde	15 tks and lorried inf
	0515 hrs	2/48 Bn	50 inf
	1400–800 hrs	2/17 Bn Pt 29	Armd Cs, inf and tks. Regtl – 2 up 1 res bn
	2345 hrs	During relief	One bn
28 Oct	1130 hrs	2/17 Bn Pt 29	Inf supported by tks
29 Oct	0715 hrs	2/23 Bn	300/400 inf
	1200–2030 hrs	20 Bde	Four attacks tks and inf
30 Oct	0200 hrs	2/15 Bn	Inf – two attempts
	0515 hrs	2/15 Bn	Inf – one attempt
31 Oct	0630 hrs	26 Bde	Inf from east and from west south of the rd
	0 hours	20 Bde Pt 29	Inf
	1200 hrs	20 Bde	Tks and MT
	1410 hrs	26 Bde	Tks from NW north of rd
	1600 hrs	20 Bde and 2/32 Bn	Tks and inf between rd and ry
	1730 hrs	26 Bde	18 Mk III and inf
1 Nov	1215 hrs	24 Bde	One bn and two coys from north and NE simultaneously (between rd and ry)
	1425 hrs	2/43 Bn	Tks and inf
	1456 hrs	24 Bde	27 tks and inf from north
	2030 hrs	24 Bde	Attacks being pressed
2 Nov	0230 hrs	24 Bde	–
	0830 hrs	20 Bde	30 tks withdrew

(FROM THE PAPERS OF ALAN RAMSAY,
COURTESY OF ALAN SANDBACH).

It gives a good sense of the intensity of a battle in which the Australians were often attacking, but in which they also had to defend against counterattacks that the Axis forces launched every single day, including '25 separate organised attempts to recapture Pt 29'.

RESULT AND HOW REPULSED
Broken up by arty fire Broken up by arty and med arty
Broken up by arty and 40 RTR Attack not pressed home Repulsed with loss of 16 tks
Repulsed by inf fire Engaged by arty and did not develop Arty and inf fire Arty Repulsed by arty fire
Allowed to approach and then dispersed by inf fire
Arty, mortar and SA fire Inf weapons Arty and with inf weapons Arty and SA fire
Arty
Arty Arty and inf
Arty and inf Arty and inf
Arty and inf Inf RAF bombing 40 RTR knocked out five Arty, 40 RTR and inf Inf repulsed. Tks gain ridge east of 26 Bde. 40 RTR forced to withdraw
Everything. Northern attack repulsed 2/43 driven off high ground between rd and ry – counter attacked and regained posn Arty
Attacks finally repulsed. 24 Bde pushed back from high ground and hold ry only A tk guns

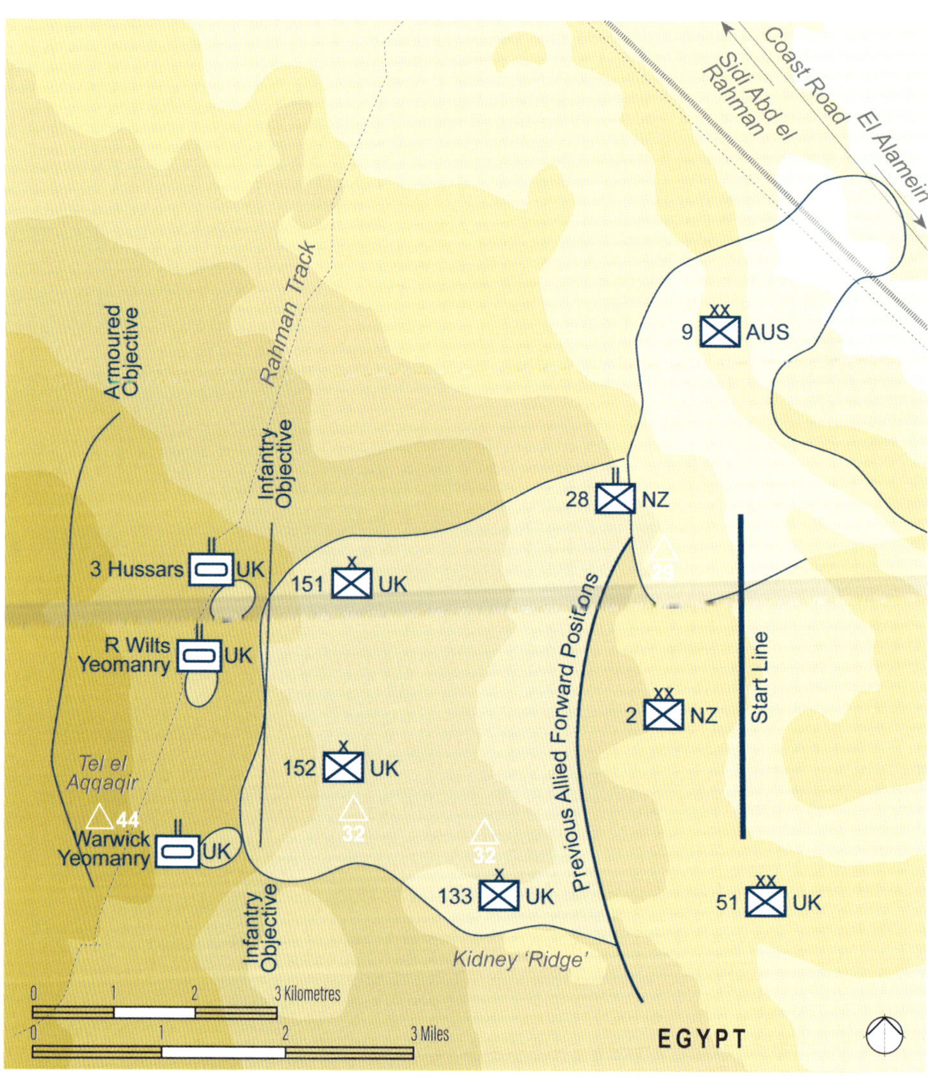

(Left to right)
Map 25: Operation Supercharge, 2 November 1942
Map 26: The Supercharge breakthrough, 2–4 November 1942

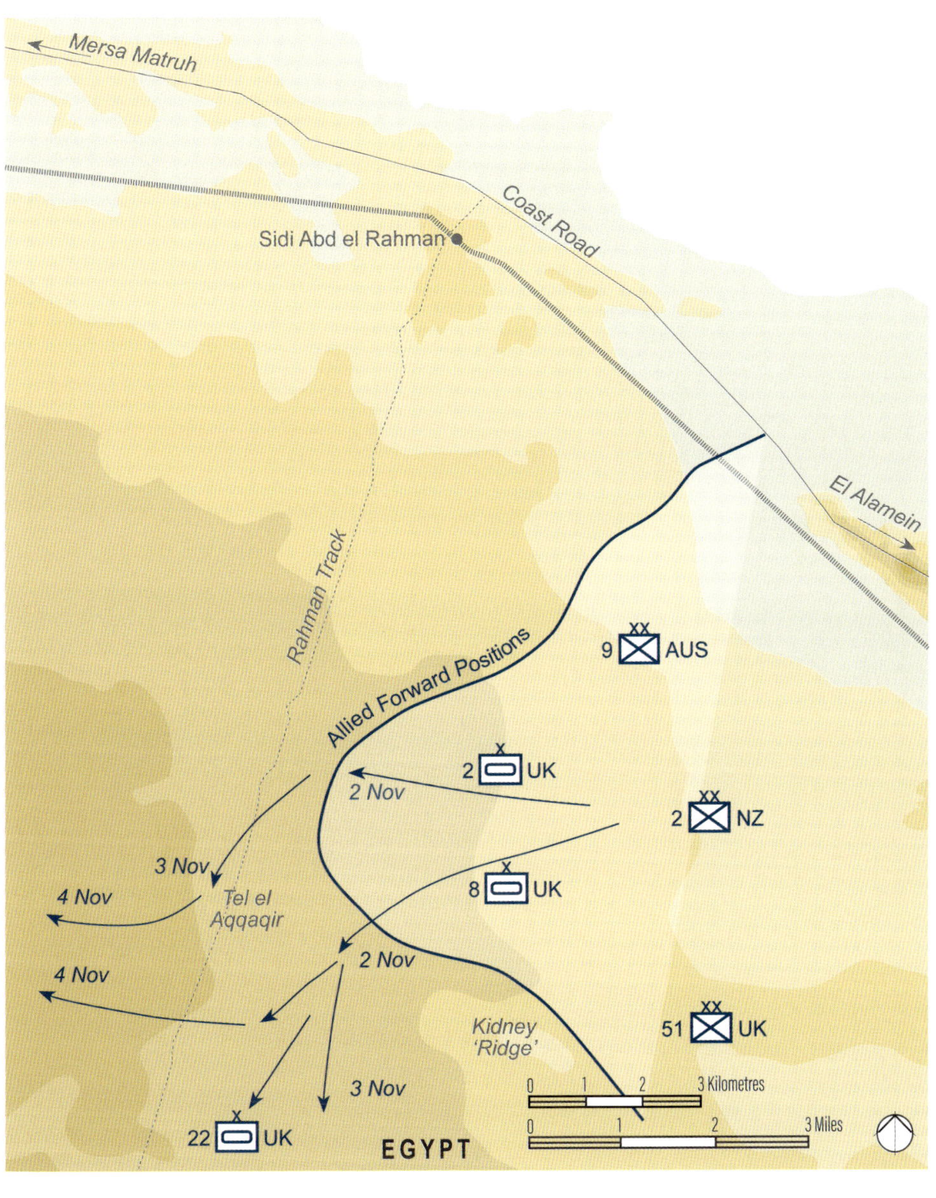
Mersa Matruh
Coast Road
Sidi Abd el Rahman
El Alamein
Rahman Track
Allied Forward Positions
9 AUS
2 UK
2 Nov
2 NZ
3 Nov
4 Nov
Tel el Aqqaqir
8 UK
2 Nov
4 Nov
Kidney 'Ridge'
51 UK
3 Nov
22 UK
EGYPT
0 1 2 3 Kilometres
0 1 2 3 Miles

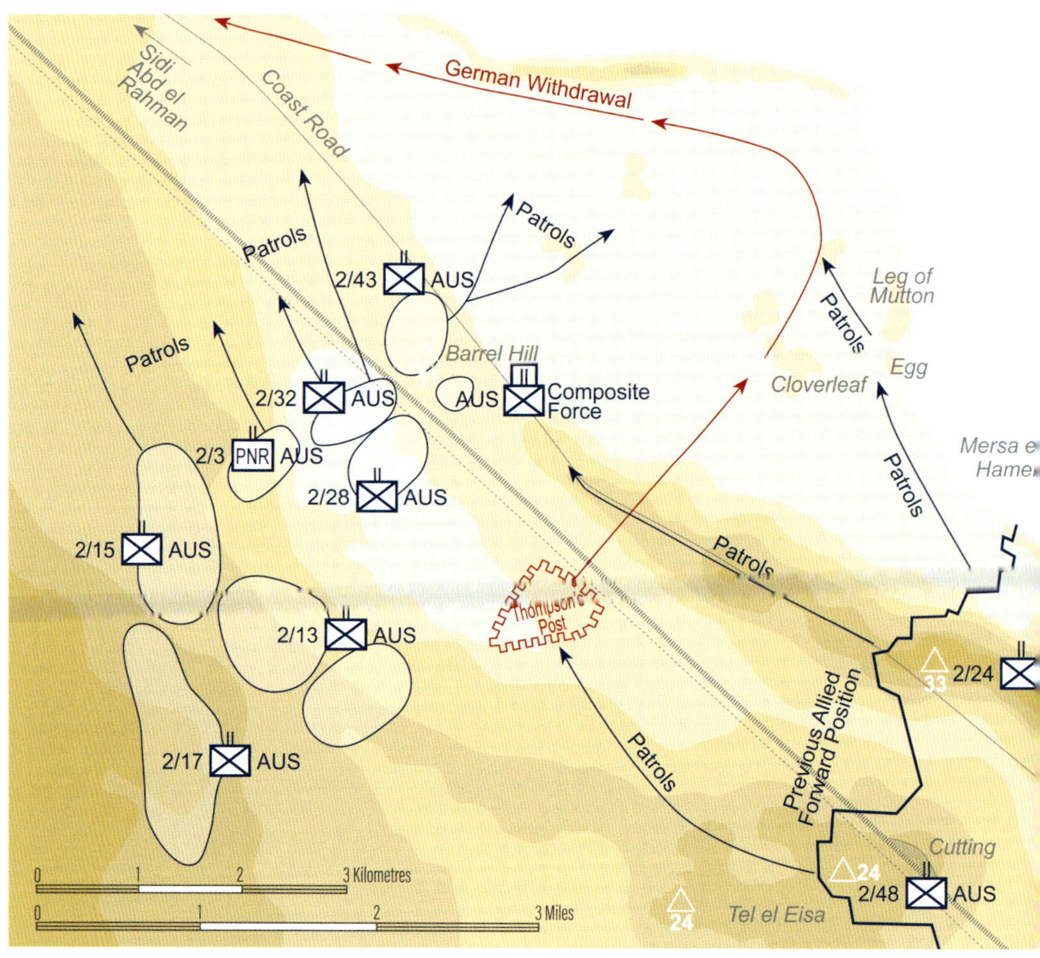

Map 27: The Australian sector, 3 November 1942

match their sister brigade's performance, and especially a sense of the importance of what they were doing, maintained morale among these troops. Morshead, in the letter quoted above, said he was struck by a comment made by 'a real digger' as he went round the line: 'Yes Sir it's tough all right and real willing but we've at last got these bloody Germans by the knackers'.[269]

Some men, however, found the strain of the day unbearable. At the frantically busy Divisional Rest Centre, a diarist complained that the number of time-consuming psychiatric casualties was a problem.[270] But the great majority of Australians at the front had somehow held their nerve, and the Saucer.

terranean Sea

EGYPT

El Alamein

Supercharge

The Australians' skilful, determined and costly defence of the Saucer had been designed to enable the breakthrough further south. That breakthrough, Operation Supercharge, was timed to commence at 1.05am on 2 November. Its right flank was protected by the 28th (Māori) New Zealand Infantry Battalion, which needed to attack through the 2/17th lines. The 2/15th Battalion was to give Vickers machine-gun fire support, guides and other aid to the New Zealanders. Part of the 2/17th Battalion had to withdraw, so as to ensure that the attackers knew that all in front of them were enemy. This was not popular with the Australians, some of whom were wounded by enemy shelling as they withdrew.

The Supercharge attack opened according to plan. The flanking fire was provided. New Zealand wounded were evacuated through the 20th Brigade, which also assisted in handling prisoners captured in the advance.

The Australians welcomed the thought of other Commonwealth infantry bearing the brunt of the fighting. Once the New Zealanders and British infantry achieved a breakthrough, the tanks of X Corps passed through, and a huge tank battle followed around Tel el Aqqaqir. Eventually and at great cost, the enemy tanks and anti-tank guns were overcome. The Australians avidly followed news of this battle, and were pleased when Montgomery sent them a message, via Morshead, congratulating them for 'the magnificent work' they had done 'on the right of the line'.

On the night of 2 November, four Australian battalions sent out raiding parties – forty men and two officers in each case – to determine the strength of the enemy forces still in the coastal sector and to prevent them from leaving. These proved a costly waste of time: twenty-one Australians were killed, and the enemy withdrawal proceeded smoothly that night. The Australians probed forward cautiously on 3 November. By 4 November, Rommel had accepted defeat and ordered a general withdrawal. On 6 November, the corps commander, General Leese, stated in a letter to Morshead, soon distributed to the 9th Division, that the Australians had played an 'immense part' in the victory. Referring to the fact that the Australians would, from their slit trenches, not have been aware of 'the magnitude of their achievement', especially as the breakthrough had occurred further south, he said that 'this breakout was only made possible by the homeric fighting over your Divisional sector'.[271] Montgomery never forgot the contribution of the Australians to his most famous victory. In 1967, on the 25th anniversary of the battle, he wrote:

> *When all did so well it would hardly seem right to single out any for special praise. But I must say this – we could not have won the battle in 12 days without that magnificent 9th Australian division.*[272]

Māori infantry in the Western Desert. (NATIONAL LIBRARY OF NEW ZEALAND 1/4-019365-F).

PART 3

AFTERMATH AND ASSESSMENT

General view of the parade of the whole of the 9th Australian Division on 22 December 1942 at Gaza airport for inspection by the Commander-in-Chief, Middle East forces, General Sir Harold Alexander, KCB, CSI, DSO, MC. 9th Australian Divisional Cavalry Regiment is in the foreground.
(AWM 050142)

CHAPTER 8

AFTERMATH

THE AUSTRALIAN ARTILLERY AND machine guns fired the division's last rounds at the Germans on the night of 4–5 November. Carriers of the 2/15th pushed on to Sidi Abd el Rahman, the Cavalry Regiment's tanks and carriers to Ed Daba. That was as far west as the Australians advanced from Alamein, for the division was by inter-governmental agreement to return to Australia soon. Rommel's forces retreated west, doomed never to return. The Eighth Army would be present at their final defeat the following year and would cross the Mediterranean to Sicily, then Italy. At Alamein, the Australian troops pottered around the battlefield, salvaging and training, or souveniring, resting and taking photographs. Immediately after the battle, three common reactions among the Australian survivors were exhaustion, pride and sorrow. An awareness of their contribution to victory spread through the division. Late in November a 2/8th gunner was able to write to his father of 'a smashing victory, in which the old Div played a major part. It is all over thank God'.[273]

Some also felt pity for their defeated enemies, especially the hard-fighting Germans. Lieutenant Andrew Hirst expressed ambivalence about them when he wrote to his wife on 6 November of seeing lines of captured Germans:

> *Lots of the prisoners are boys of sixteen and seventeen years and it is tragic to realise that they have been trained from birth to such a grisly role. Two days ago they were shelling us mercilessly with the most vicious guns in the world, one in particular, his 88mm almost got me three times in one day. Today they are marching back into our lines, beaten. One Jerry Major complained that our artillery barrages were inhuman – I'll say no more.*[274]

Australians of the 2/15th Battalion look over a captured 88mm gun position after the battle. Two dead Germans lie in the foreground. (AWM P06258.020)

MEDICAL ARRANGEMENTS

Australian medical units dealt with large numbers of casualties inflicted by the high intensity conflict at Alamein. Typical cases were described in the diary of Sergeant Jack Williams, a theatre assistant in a surgical unit on 22 July: one man with his jaw and tongue blown away; another with a hole in his skull and a sizeable portion of brain hanging out; a third with left arm and leg so badly shattered they had to be amputated; a fourth with a broken femur, his kidney severed by a bullet, and multiple flesh wounds. There were, he said, dozens of equally severe cases and a 'terrific' number of deaths.[275]

During the October battle, the wounded were passed along a well-established evacuation route from company stretcher-bearers to regimental aid posts, to field ambulances (where emergency surgery such as that witnessed by Williams occurred), to casualty clearing stations where there were nurses, doctors and orderlies. Two of the division's three field ambulance units acted as Main Dressing Stations (MDS) with surgical teams attached, the third as a Divisional Rest Station that took the lightly sick or wounded and psychological patients. More than 3000 wounded and sick were admitted to, and in most cases evacuated from, the forward medical posts. The division had thirty-two ambulances, while a similar number of trucks were provided to move the walking wounded. The ambulance drivers were nearing exhaustion at the battle's end. A check post did the vital work of routing ambulances and trucks to the MDS that could best handle them at that time. There was no full-scale advanced dressing station (ADS) operating during the battle, though four temporary ADSs were established, including one at the Blockhouse.

Only stretcher-bearers were authorised to carry wounded from battle. In daylight hours, stretcher-bearers were often the only Australians walking around above ground at the front.[276] Sometimes just ten to fifteen bearers in a battalion were coping with 100 casualties. More than sixty Australian Army Medical Corps personnel were killed or wounded in the battle. The medical report on the battle wrote proudly of the service's attempt to 'give the fighting troops the best service they had ever received', by giving adequate surgery to more wounded earlier than ever before. This would be done by bringing 'Harley Street ... almost to the front line'. In practice, 659 operations were performed in the two Main Dressing Stations between 24 October and 7 November. These included 218 compound fractures, 119 abdominal wounds and 28 amputations.[277]

(Opposite, top to bottom) Nursing Sister Berenice Morrisby looks at a newspaper with one of her patients at the 2/6th Australian General Hospital at Gaza Ridge in August 1942. The soldier, Sergeant John Philp of the 2/3rd Anti-Tank Regiment, had been wounded in the legs in July. (AWM 024927)

Map 28: Australian medical facilities at El Alamein at the opening of the October battle. (From Allan S Walker, *Middle East and Far East*, p. 379)

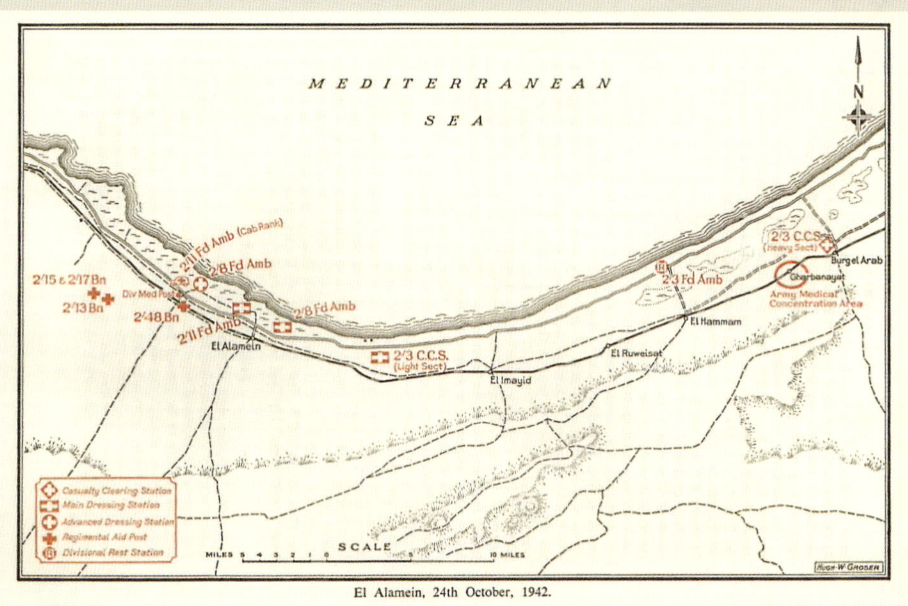

El Alamein, 24th October, 1942.

Hirst felt sorry for the German boys as products and victims of an aggressive system, but like so many Australians who had been at the receiving end of German technology, he had limited sympathy when Germans complained about what they themselves were suffering.

The Australians' own survival was food for thought. Just a few hours after the battle, Sergeant Ahearn of the 2/32nd wrote, 'I'm alive – something to ponder and be thankful for'.[278] Tom Derrick, in whose 2/48th Battalion the rifle companies numbered just seventy-one men, reflected that 'one must feel very lucky to be on the active list'. Those lucky ones would never forget the 'continuous close calls with death' they had experienced.[279] Reinforcements came forward to help rebuild the decimated battalions.

'Don't forget to say a good word to the cooks', Morshead told his commanders, at a conference following the battle. He was aware that victory at Alamein was a team effort. These men are cooks from the 2/11th Field Ambulance. (AWM 043213)

Though it represented just under 10 per cent of the Eighth Army's strength, the 9th Division had suffered over 20 per cent of its casualties in the October–November battle. Thirteen per cent of the 9th Division's men had been killed or wounded – exactly double the British percentage, and three times that of the other Dominion formations. The Army's official casualty figures for the entire Alamein campaign, from July to November, recorded it had cost the lives of 1,177 Australians, plus 193 missing. Assuming most of those missing were not recovered, total Australian dead were over 1,300. An additional 3,629 were wounded, with 795 captured – a total of 5,794 casualties for a division with a notional strength of about 15,000. Alamein was the single costliest Australian operation in the two years of operations in the Mediterranean.[280] In the Pacific war, only the Malayan and Papuan campaigns would cost more Australian lives in battle.

When the 9th Division left the desert early in December, most of its men seem to have been more preoccupied with the losses rather than the gains. Crawford felt 'infinitely saddened, broken, homesick'.[281] As time passed, the sense of loss was probably eased by knowing that this battle was special, and that the Australians' role in it had been exceptional.

On 22 December 1942, the 9th Division assembled at Gaza Airport for the first parade it had mounted as a complete formation. General Alexander took the salute.

After the German retreat from El Alamein, the 2/3rd Casualty Clearing Station, including its nurses, was sent forward to Garawla, near Mersa Matruh. The official medical history acknowledges that they did 'useful work'. Here a group, including the CO (Lieutenant Colonel John Gillespie, centre), pauses nearby on 7 November. (AWM P02212.077)

PSYCHIATRIC CASUALTIES AT ALAMEIN

The Australian Army entered the Second World War conscious that war involved psychiatric casualties, but from 1941 realised that more skilled psychiatric assistance was needed to deal with 'combat exhaustion' and other mental health problems. By September 1941, it was estimated that 20 per cent of men with combat exhaustion – often diagnosed as 'fear state' in Tobruk – could be treated in the forward area before returning to their units. This estimate was raised in later campaigns. At Alamein, the flow of wounded slowed in the first week of November but the number of 'NYDN' (not yet diagnosed nervous) cases, men overcome by strain, increased. On 29 October the Divisional Rest Centre admitted 167 men with 'fear states' and 'exhaustion', and was 'almost snowed under'. After several days there, soldiers returned to their units or were sent to the rear. By 2 November, with 418 men in the

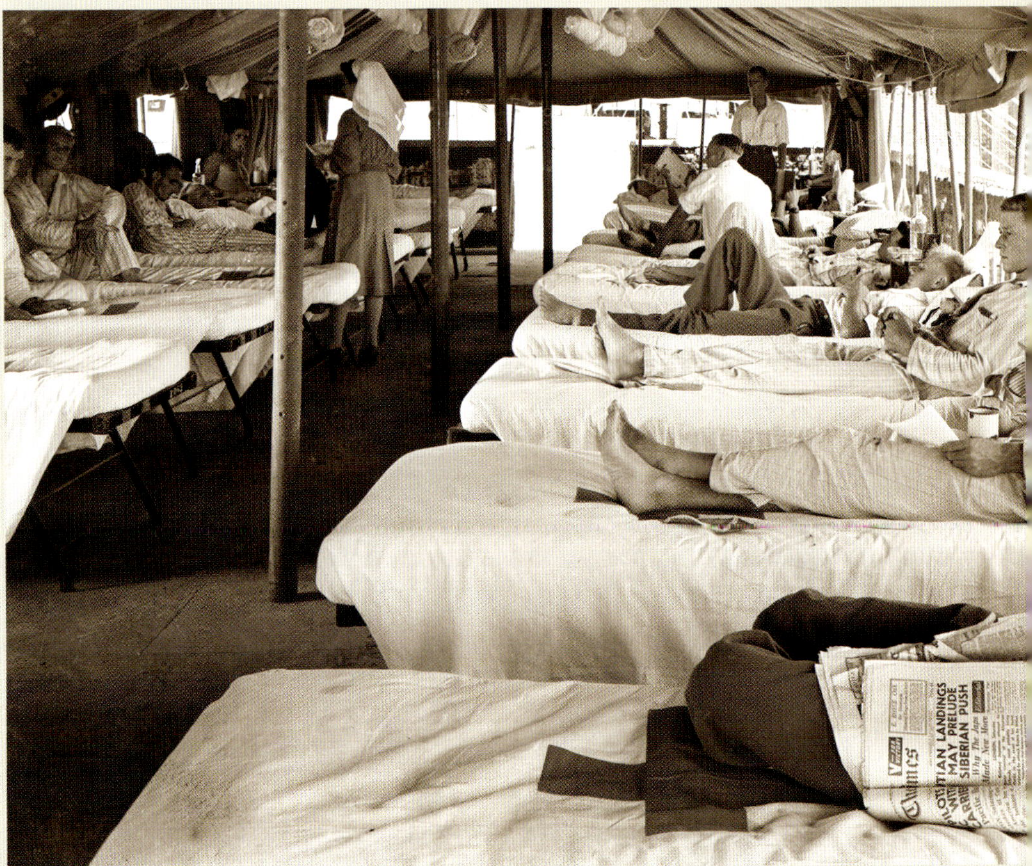

centre and a further 131 admitted, the unit's war diary confessed that 'nerve cases are a problem' because 'we cannot spare time for treatment'. A trained psychiatrist, Major Allan Stoller, only arrived when the battle was almost over, by which time over 900 men had passed through the centre. The psychiatric first aid post set up under Stoller was the first such Australian facility of the war. The official medical historian, Walker, asserted that Stoller's follow-up on men treated in forward areas showed that very few continued to display severe psychiatric symptoms, thus confirming the value of early treatment. Walker also noted accusations that some medical authorities were too reluctant to apply the term 'fear', preferring to send men to medical boards classified with 'anxiety neurosis' or 'depressive state' when treatment for 'fear state' further forward would have sufficed. If any battle was likely to leave mental scars on its participants, surely Alamein was one. Two weeks after the battle, Acting Sergeant John Lovegrove wrote of men around him as sombre and grieving. He reflected on the heavy casualties suffered by his platoon on the battle's first night, when he was among the wounded:

> *I am totally shattered and could weep as I look back now and feel just so strongly for my men ... We had virtually all been together since enlistment 2 ½ years ago and entwined with a bond of respect and comradeship that mere words can't adequately describe – every bit as strong as a family 'blood' relationship and the horror of that night will live with those of us who survived for the remainder of our days ...* [282]

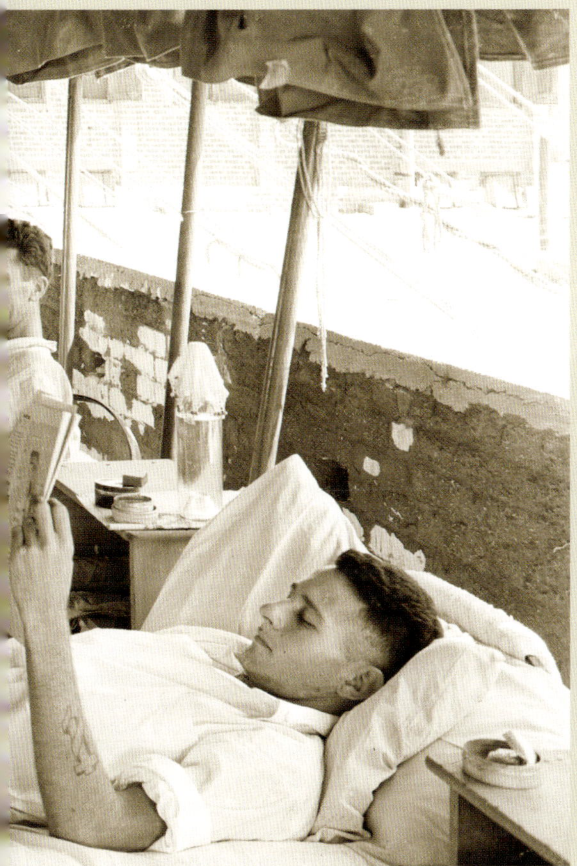

Australian casualties of Alamein recovering in a desert hospital in November 1942.
(PHOTOGRAPHER: FRANK HURLEY, AWM 013654)

In a speech, he described the Australian part in the battle concisely: 'The battle of Alamein has made history, and you are in the proud position of having taken a major part in that great victory'. The parade, a great source of pride to the participants, signalled the end of the Australian commitment to the land war in the Middle East and against Germany.

Prime Minister Curtin had, since the fall of Singapore in February, been periodically urging the return of the 9th Division to Australia. He had been temporarily placated by an explanation that the recall of the 9th Division could imperil the Persian oil that comprised 60 per cent of Australia's supply. By mid-October, Curtin, urged on by Blamey and General Douglas MacArthur, Allied commander in the South West Pacific Area, was pressing more insistently than ever for the 9th's return. Despite entreaties from Churchill and Roosevelt to change his mind, Curtin got his way after the battle of El Alamein, and by mid-December a January 1943 departure had been arranged. On 24 December, General Montgomery sent this message to the division: 'Please convey to all ranks in 9 Aust Div my best wishes

for Christmas and my very best regards. I cannot adequately tell you how much I miss your Division, it was a great blow when you left my Army'.[283]

The victory at Alamein helped to transform Allied fortunes. On 8 November, Anglo–American forces landed in north-west Africa in Operation Torch. In May 1943, six months after Alamein and Torch, and following much hard fighting, the First and Eighth Armies met in Tunisia and the entire Axis army in Africa surrendered.

Some writers have criticised Montgomery's conduct of Alamein, and indeed of his later battles, as too slow and cautious. As Alec Hill – an astute member of 9th Division and postwar professional historian – observed, Montgomery could not launch a 'British blitzkrieg' at Alamein. His armour, artillery and air were not fully integrated 'in the German fashion'; while on the other side of the hill, his opponents were not the old-fashioned armies of 1939–40 Poland and France, but the Afrika Korps. Its anti-tank screen could not be broken until the very end of the battle.[284]

Australians of the 2/48th Battalion drink Canadian beer from a dump they passed on the way to Alamein in July. All but one of the pictured soldiers would be wounded in the forthcoming desert fighting. (Image courtesy of Bill McEvoy)

BRAVERY AWARDS TO AUSTRALIANS

The British XXX Corps commander, General Leese, referred to the 'homeric fighting' that the 9th Division engaged in during the October battle. This recalled the heroes of Homer's *Iliad*. It is interesting to consider whether this generosity was reflected in decorations awarded for Australian bravery in the battle. As always, divisional commanders requested more decorations than were allowed, but in addition, General Alexander stated to Morshead that he had to award decorations in proportion to a formation's size, rather than the duration or extent of its contribution to the battle. Morshead had, according to Alexander, requested decorations 'greatly in excess' of the number laid down for a division. It seems that the Australians were entitled at this time to six bravery awards per month for every 5000 troops in an operational command; and periodical awards, usually for meritorious service or leadership over a longer period, were available at a rate of one per 250 troops every six months. This presumably entitled the division to about twenty awards in the July battles, and then again in the October battle. However, the Australians received many more awards than this: approximately twice as many in each period. This probably included 'unused' awards allocated in other months, such as June. Morshead clearly requested still more, for he had to resubmit his initial request to conform to the quota.[285]

As mentioned in the text, three Australians received Victoria Crosses for the July and October fighting. Stan Gurney earned his on 22 July, Percy Gratwick on 26 October and Bill Kibby on 23–31 October. All three were members of the 2/48th Battalion, and all three awards were posthumous. The 2/48th also received numerous other awards, including four DCMs in July and another four in October. By war's end, it would be the most decorated battalion in the Second AIF. The 9th Division received at least thirteen DCMs in July and at least sixteen in October–November.[286] There were large numbers of Military Crosses and Military Medals too – at least fourteen Military Crosses in October, for example. Of course, even higher was the number of extraordinary acts of bravery that no-one reported or even witnessed. The 26th Brigade report on the October battle concluded: 'Throughout this report there has been little mention of the determination and outstanding gallantry of the troops – the operations speak for themselves'.[287] Up to a point, the bare facts of the operations do reflect the 'outstanding gallantry' of the Australians, but sadly neither those operations nor the individuals who executed them are well known today.

(Clockwise from top left)
Private Stan Gurney, VC. (AWM 100639)
Private Percy Gratwick, VC. (AWM 100640)
Sergeant Bill Kibby, VC. (AWM 061364)

CHAPTER 9

INSIGHTS FROM BATTLE – WHY STUDY ALAMEIN?

AT FIRST GLANCE, THE large-scale positional warfare at El Alamein in 1942 might seem of limited relevance to modern operations. While this book was being written, however, the outbreak of war in Ukraine reminded us that positional warfare – with its obstacle belts, entrenched positions, concentrated fires from both air and land based platforms, intensive combat and high casualty rates – is not confined to the pages of Second World War history books. Different social, political and organisational contexts, as well as changing technology, make drawing explicit lessons from history a fraught process. Nevertheless, reflecting on the factors contributing to the outcome at El Alamein provides many insights into the conduct of both the attack and defence.

To consider the attack first, the Australians achieved and benefited from surprise in the night actions that opened their fighting on 10 July and 23 October. The use of a brilliant deception plan before the October battle was critical, and its success vindicated the extensive security measures applied within the whole Eighth Army. Later in the battle, the Australian attacks in the north exploited Rommel's known concerns and drew in so many German forces as to make a surprise and decisive penetration possible, further south in Supercharge. Those same attacks achieved one of the modern principles of offensive operations – namely, forcing the enemy to commit their reserve. The 9th Division drew Rommel's reserves to the north and wore them down to a point where they could not meet a new threat.

The Australians' ability to advance at a high tempo and take critical ground, such as at Trig 29, and then to reorganise quickly and efficiently against the inevitable counterattacks, was also a key to Australian successes in October. Such tempo owed much to battle drills and abbreviated administrative procedures born from experience and training. Previously lacking these attributes, but also committed to attacks largely in daylight, the Australian brigades and battalions had often struggled to quickly reorient from attack to defence in July.

Penetration of the enemy's deep defences required much obstacle clearance. Indeed, the October battle featured the most extensive set of breaching operations in the history of the Royal Australian Engineers and demonstrated the need for increased engineering resources in positional warfare; while the 9th Division's engineers accomplished their tasks, several additional sub-units had to be improvised to assist, and there was no redundancy. The Alamein fighting also highlighted the nature of breaching as a combined arms task. The engineers depended on the infantry for close protection, and lauded the suppressive effect of their supporting artillery, which spared them heavier casualties as they breached the minefields. Despite the engineers' efforts, however, the obstacle belts still curtailed manoeuvre, and hard experience taught the difficulties of assaulting through relatively narrow minefield breaches with tanks and infantry at night.[288]

The Australians' experiences of night operations at Alamein were mixed. Many of their successes were achieved at night, including the seizure of the Trig 33 ridge on 10 July and the capture of Trig 29 on 25–26 October. Moreover, some of their biggest disasters happened in daylight, notably in late July. Other Eighth Army formations, such as the New Zealanders, also received bloody noses in the daytime. Australian, and indeed all British and Dominion, units tended to see themselves as superior night fighters to the Germans, so they generally entered these actions more confidently than in daylight. They probably also felt that night actions were preferable to day ones, as they nullified the advantages that German tanks, 88s and other direct-fire weapons possessed in the open expanses of the desert. Indeed, after the battle, the 15th Panzer Division war diary acknowledged the Eighth Army's infantry were 'superior' in night fighting.[289] Nevertheless, Australian night operations sometimes proved costly too: Ruin Ridge in July, the tank rider debacle of 28–29 October and the night of 'ifs' (30–31 October) were chastening examples. In each case, there were problems unrelated to night – poor and unrealistic planning and faulty inter-Allied and inter-arms cooperation – but the uncertainties inevitable when operating with limited vision also contributed.

Perhaps the Germans' reluctance to fight at night was a recognition on their part of the inherent difficulty of night operations and the potential for them to end in confusion. At night, once contact was made and fighting began, it was especially difficult to maintain direction for the right distance and at the appropriate pace, as well as to send back information needed by higher commanders and also by those whose task was to send forward supplies, consolidation stores and other vital units. Control of the battle was also made difficult when observation was limited to a few metres. On the other hand, clearly the desert, with its largely featureless terrain, gave the defender great advantages in a daylight battle.[290]

Although British armour was crucial to victory at Alamein, infantry validated its traditional title as 'Queen of Battle'.[291] Armour might dominate the battlefield, but it could not operate until minefields were cleared and while anti-tank guns remained firing.[292] Just as today, infantry had the indispensable role of capturing and holding ground. Even though it lacked substantial armour, the 9th Division could make a profound contribution to the outcome of battles because its infantry was able to oust Rommel's forces from critical locations such as Trig 33, Trig 29 and the Saucer, and hold these places that the enemy believed they could not afford to lose.

Australian infantry was crucial to the Eighth Army's victory, but a vital element of nearly every successful Australian attack at Alamein was fire support. Some of this came from the air, especially in October after improvements in air–ground liaison. The British victory is rightly most associated with artillery fire support, not only in attack but also defence. The doctrine of vesting control of artillery in the highest possible commander was validated. Programmed supporting fire from thirteen or more field regiments and three medium regiments could be organised within six and a half hours of the infantry commander informing the divisional CRA of a pending attack. Defensive fire from the 9th Division's artillery – three field regiments and an attached British medium regiment – could be delivered very quickly and usually proved sufficient to halt the strongest attacks. The artillery regiments suffered their own losses but a pool of replacement guns was established, so that even though eighteen guns were taken out of the line during the battle for various reasons, only on two brief occasions were all ninety-six guns comprising the divisional artillery not in action.[293]

Concentrations of fire from 25-pounder guns often drove off enemy tanks at long range, and one specialist artillery historian has noted that the effectiveness of Allied artillery against mechanised attacks on Trig 29 was 'the beginning of an accepted wisdom that it was possible to master tanks with guns', and that British and American artillery later validated this perception in North-West Europe.[294] The 9th Division, however, was more circumspect in its report after the battle and implicitly called for more discernment in the use of indirect fire in defensive battles. It noted that pre-arranged defensive fire barrages were often called for when observed artillery fire would have been more economical in the use of ammunition. Additionally, artillery fire often drove off enemy tanks before they came within the shorter range of the more destructive anti tank guns, and the dust and smoke it created obscured the fields of fire of all direct fire weapons.

In whatever degree responsibility for the success of the British offensive battle at Alamein is apportioned to armour, infantry or artillery, the unprecedented degree of cooperation between the arms was clearly indispensable to success. Crucial as each arm was, none could win the battle alone. The fact that the Eighth Army had been forced to fight so close to their base owed much to Axis expertise at combined arms operations. Only when the British made profound improvements in the same field could they hope to force the enemy back permanently.

The Alamein fighting also validated longstanding principles of defence. The value of defence in depth was proved by the way the unexpectedly deep Axis defences contained the initial assault in October, prevented the desired breakthrough, and necessitated another attempt with Operation Supercharge at the beginning of November. The breakthrough only came eleven days after it was planned to occur. The value of using terrain effectively – such as on Trig 33 in July and Trig 29 in October – was apparent even in the relatively flat desert, as was the importance of mutual support and all-round defence. The tenacity of the German defenders impressed their opponents even during the fighting. The mutually supporting defences the Australians encountered at Ring Contour 25, Thompson's Post, the Fig Orchard, Trig 29, and even behind their front line on 30–31 October, were superbly sited and defended. Moreover, the German propensity to launch counterattacks to regain vital ground demonstrated the utility of maintaining reserves and ensured that the Australians could never afford to be complacent.

One of the main pillars of Australian success at Alamein was thorough preparation. Victory in the October battle proved the value of 'dress rehearsals', which trained men in the exact operations they would be undertaking, under similar conditions and with the appropriate supporting arms. These rehearsals revealed many unforeseen difficulties which would otherwise have only arisen during the battle. Troops often referred to aspects of the battle as 'just like an exercise'. One unit's warning order, 'battalion attacks tonight administration normal', demonstrated the influence of training and well-established standard operating procedures on the battle. Rommel gave as one of the reasons for his defeat at Alamein the 'extremely high rate of training' in the British forces.[295]

The division's post-operations report emphasised the importance of maintaining pressure on the enemy. It stated: 'So often in history, the battle has gone to the side which had the will or the strength to hang on just long enough to outlast the opponent'. Indeed, Montgomery's entire conduct of the battle rested on allowing the enemy no respite – switching focus from one part of the battlefield to another as necessary, but forcing the commitment of all available enemy forces to bring about their destruction. Clearly, the high morale of the Australians was crucial here, particularly as the battle dragged on. So was the quality of leadership, a topic that emerges on many pages of this book and one on which Alamein provides many insights.

By October, the standard of leadership in the division had improved by practice in training, and by the experience gained in the early days of the Alamein campaign (July–August) as well as in Tobruk. 'The men were well led, and knew it', according to the post-battle report, 'and the officers knew that all the men required was sound leadership'.[296] That is an exaggeration. Leadership counts for little if men are facing a tank attack with inadequate weapons and ammunition. Nevertheless, it accords with an observation by John Lovegrove, an NCO who led numerous patrols in Tobruk and was wounded in heavy fighting on 23 October, that soldiers were always 'looking eagle-eyed towards their N.C.O. or officer for guidance and perhaps above all for example'.[297]

Garth Pratten, in his authoritative book on Australian battalion commanders, reflects that 'the exercise of command at Alamein, and in particular the October battle,

Parade of the 9th Division at Gaza Airport, 22 December 1942. (AWM 050142)

demonstrated a maturity and refinement that was absent in many of the engagements in 1941'. He observes, too, that it can be argued that 'Alamein marked the high point of Australian battalion command'. Eight of the fourteen battalion commanders who served in the Alamein battles received DSOs for their efforts there. They came into the battles experienced: four had previously commanded battalions in action, six had been 2iCs, four had been decorated for bravery, and at least six had undertaken studies at the Middle East Tactical School.[298] Similar levels of competence and confidence can be identified right along the command chain. John Coates refers to more than fifty cases in the 9th Division's history when privates commanded platoons in action, and more than twenty where NCOs led companies.

This ability of more junior-ranked soldiers and officers to step up and take command was essential in the victory at Alamein, where casualties occurred in every rank of leader all the way up to brigadier – an enduring feature of high-intensity conventional operations. In reflecting on the battle, the CO of the 2/48th Battalion, Heathcote 'Tack' Hammer, counselled commanders at all levels to avoid rash heroics: 'Fight wisely,' he advised, 'keep Comds alive – they will come to the front when things are tough'. That could only be followed to a point, as the decimation of officers in his battalion during the battle and his own wounding on the battlefield show. The casualty rate among Australian battalion COs at Alamein was unusually high, testifying to the intensity of the battle. The sources of their wounds – gunshots, shrapnel, mines and booby traps – demonstrated that they were not safe anywhere on the battlefield. An XXX Corps report emphasised that one of the battle's lessons was 'the value of siting HQ of every level well forward', but the death of the commander of the 24th Brigade, Arthur Godfrey, in an overly exposed command post should add a note of caution to this principle.[299]

When battalion commanders felt that circumstances compelled them to go forward to rally their men or to lead them, this had mixed results: Evans on 28–29 October made a difference in leading remnants of his battalion, but Magno leading the 2/15th into battle on the same night resulted in his death. Lieutenant Colonel Weir was wounded leading from the front on 30–31 October. The exercise of personal example and intervention was not always possible – for example, when intensive artillery fire pummelled the Saucer – and in such situations, where men were isolated from commanders, or commanders were killed, the 9th Division's resilience was demonstrated.[300] Despite very heavy losses, such as in the 2/24th and 2/48th Battalions, unit cohesion was maintained throughout the battle. Pratten points to such continuing cohesion as going against a tendency, noted by British historian David French, for British battalions, with a war establishment smaller than the Germans', to lose cohesion after sustaining only relatively light casualties.[301]

The 9th Division's post-operations report stated that the high standard of leadership in the battle 'engendered mutual trust and respect between the officers and men', which in turn led to 'excellent teamwork'. In the fighting of July–August 1942, the 9th Division's artillery, machine gunners and pioneers fought together with the infantry for the first time

– they had not been at Tobruk – and in doing so, 'developed complete battle confidence between the various arms'. The respect and confidence thus engendered led to a higher level of teamwork, so by the time of the October battle, the division had become 'an efficient and formidable fighting machine'. Its development as a combined arms team was symptomatic of the way the entire Eighth Army had progressed in combating the enemy's superiority in that vital area. In his notes on the battle, Hammer concluded from hard-won experience that 'Team work pays handsome dividends', and insisted that 'unselfishness' was a golden rule that applied to platoon and company commanders as well as battalion commanders, who should do all they could to help units on their left and right.[302]

Despite the 9th Division's impressive capabilities and robust cohesion, hindsight shows that at times during the July and October fighting, this formation and its constituent units were allocated objectives that were beyond them. This raises questions about whether commanders at the time recognised this, and whether they attempted to do anything about it. On several occasions, brigade and battalion commanders expressed concerns about the viability of orders, especially concerning ground they had to capture or hold. However, these leaders showed a willingness to follow orders to attack, even when they felt the tasks beyond their units and when the consequence might be heavy casualties. Examples include the 2/23rd Battalion on 16 July, all three 26th Brigade battalions on 22 July, the 2/15th on 1 September, and the 2/24th and 2/48th Battalions on 30–31 October. That their commanders went ahead without apparently raising serious doubts, even when they had them (although we can never be sure they were not broached verbally), was of course part of the contemporaneous military ethos of following orders without question, but was probably also partly due to personal and unit pride, the aggressive ethos of the AIF and, in October, the belief that they were fighting a turning-point battle.[303]

Arguably, some Australian commanders should have questioned harder. Questioning voices at the brigade level, for example, might have led to a more realistic plan for 30–31 October. Commanders and their staffs, however, were increasingly exhausted as this marathon battle progressed. Perhaps this made it even more imperative for subordinates to take it upon themselves to say, 'Are you sure about that, Sir?' On the other hand, questioning 'Ming the Merciless' Morshead, who had not responded favourably to doubts raised by subordinates at Tobruk, may have been easier said than done. Moreover, his subordinate commanders and staff at Alamein were fatigued too. Over eighty years from the battle, we will never know exactly why some decisions were taken, but it is well to consider the human frailties of even the toughest commanders under the prolonged stresses of high-intensity combat.

In his important book on Alamein, British historian Niall Barr states that 'the lessons learned in the bare deserts of Egypt were not necessarily of value elsewhere'. He acknowledges the development of lasting improvement in the artillery and engineers, and he could have added air–ground liaison, but talks in particular of the fact that the detailed preparation put into the lead-up to the October battle was not replicated later. Thus, in the British army, inexperienced units continued to be thrust into battle in other theatres.

Ideally, the experience and knowledge gained in the desert campaigns would have been used to aid untried units in subsequent campaigns. Similarly, he notes that the great coalition force assembled for Alamein was split up with the departure of the Australians and South Africans in its aftermath.[304] He might have acknowledged that the 'British Army' that fought in Italy from the following year remained a coalition force, including New Zealanders, Canadians, South Africans and Poles. Despite Barr's objections, the British and Australian achievement at Alamein remains in many ways a model of the qualities that armies should strive for when faced with an expert and determined enemy. Those qualities, demonstrated at a high level by Australians as part of the Eighth Army, include expertise based on preparation and experience; rehearsed teamwork within and between coalition forces; confidence in weapons, tactics and leaders; and determination to risk all for cause and comrades.

(Opposite)
Buglers of the 9th Australian Division playing the *Last Post* during the tribute to fallen comrades by the whole of the 9th australian division on parade at Gaza on 22 December 1942 for the inspection by the Commander-in-Chief, Middle East forces, General Sir Harold Alexander, KCB, CSI, DSO, MC, who praised and thanked the division for the part it played in the battle of El Alamein. (AWM 050133)

CONCLUSION

EL ALAMEIN WAS a pivotal Second World War battle. Look up any reference on the battle and the description 'turning point' will almost certainly be used. For example, *The Oxford Companion to the Second World War* concludes in its article on the battle that 'El Alamein was the climax of the Western Desert campaigns and one of the turning points of the war'.[305] Winston Churchill argued that it might be said that: 'Before Alamein we never had a victory. After Alamein we never had a defeat'.[306]

Alamein was also a high point in Australian military history. Australians would fight in large numbers in the Pacific thereafter, but not as part of large, fully engaged formations as the 9th had within the Eighth Army at Alamein. It was Australia's last great set-piece battle – that is, one involving hundreds of thousands of men on both sides, and tanks and guns employed on a vast scale. The *Australian Army Journal* said in 1967 that for those who survived Alamein, the battle would remain their 'St Crispin's Day': that is, as Henry V told his men on the eve of the battle of Agincourt on that day in 1415, an experience that they would never forget, which others would envy them for, and that would be remembered until the end of the world.[307]

General Morshead became a corps commander in March 1943, and although he fulfilled that role with skill and dedication till war's end, he experienced this period after Alamein as an anti-climax.[308] The 9th Division also went on to further successes after Alamein, against an enemy it ranked lower than the Germans and for objectives of diminishing strategic significance. Its war ended in three brigade operations in Borneo.

While the battle of El Alamein was in some ways the end of an era for Australia, it retains its relevance because of its enduring impact, its extreme severity and the exceptional performance it drew from Australian troops. Before, and especially during, the battle those troops set the bar tremendously high in leadership, mutual trust, training, discipline, esprit de corps, courage and initiative.[309] The Australians made a crucial contribution, but were part of a coalition, and one which used its advantages in intelligence and material to outfight and out-think the opposing alliance. Examples of successful coalition warfare continue to be relevant to the Australian Army, which can justly look back at its contribution to Allied victory at Alamein as one of its finest achievements.

Three headstones that exemplify the sacrifice involved in earning the right to say that Australian troops took a leading role in a turning-point of history.

(Clockwise from top left)
'Our Jack' Doyle, killed in action on 22 July 1942, aged 17. (AUTHOR'S COLLECTION)

Captain Lance Bode, MC, killed in Operation Bulimba on 1 September 1942. (AUTHOR'S COLLECTION)

Lance Corporal George Markham, 2/24th Battalion, killed in action on 31 October 1942. (AUTHOR'S COLLECTION)

ENDNOTES

1 Churchill, *Second World War,* Volume 4, p. 536.

2 Leese to Morshead, 6 Nov 1942, Appendix H to 9 Div Report on Operations Alamein, CAB 106/777, TNA.

3 Anonymous British officer, 'Behind the British Victory in North Africa', *Foreign Affairs*, January 1944. foreignaffairs.com/articles/north-africa/1944-01-01/behind-british-victory-north-africa

4 Liddell Hart, *Rommel Papers*, p. 132.

5 *Rommel Papers*, pp. 225–6.

6 Lewin, *Life and Death of the Afrika Korps*, p. 23.

7 Ibid., p. 52.

8 This metaphor is from Alec Hill, review of Maughan, *Tobruk and El Alamein,* in *Australian Army Journal*, No. 215, 1967, p. 49.

9 Bean, *The A.I.F. in France*, Volume V, University of Queensland Press, St Lucia, 1983, p. 301.

10 Wilmot, *Tobruk 1941*, p. 87.

11 Compares favourably: In Middle East Field Censorship Report 1–7 April 1942, AWM54, 883/2/97, AWM. Last war: in the entry on Morshead in Dennis et al. *Oxford Companion to Australian Military History*, p. 408. Driving to limit: Hill, 'Morshead, Sir Leslie James (1889–195)', *Australian Dictionary of Biography*. Ali Baba: Maughan, *Tobruk and El Alamein*, pp. 620, 638.

12 Coates, *Bravery Above Blunder*, p. 34.

13 Barr, *Pendulum of War*, p. 33.

14 LT G Combe, letter 11 July 1942, MJC.

15 Maughan, p. 552.

16 On Blamey's charter: Long, *To Benghazi*, p. 101. Johnston and Stanley, p. 99. Barr, *Pendulum of War*, p. 156.

17 Combe, *Second 43rd*, p. 98. Johnston and Stanley, p. 54.

18 Lieutenant General Morshead letter to Colonel Rasmussen, August 1944, AWM54, 522/1/2, AWM.

19 Derrick, diary 10 July 1942, in Johnston (ed.) *Derrick VC in his own words*, p. 220.

20 Derrick DCM citation, AWM.

21 Ali Baba's battle restrictions: Goodhart, *Turning Tide*, p. 162. Sources of all the quotations in this section can be found in Johnston, *Fighting the Enemy*, Chapter 1.

22 Superhuman: 26 Bde Narrative of Ops 5–29 July 1942, p. 2, AWM54, 526/6/16, AWM.

23 Baillieu, *Both Sides of the Hill*, p. 14.

24 Coup: Anthony Cave Brown, quoted in Baillieu, *Both Sides of the Hill*, p. 22. Overcoming resistance: Serle, *The Second Twenty-Fourth*, p. 165. Baillieu, pp. 7–8, 14. Bronzed giants: *Furphy Flyer in Mufti*, August 2000, p. 6. Done for: Baillieu, p. 13. Direct information: Boog et al, *Das Deutsche Reich*, vol. 6, p. 661n.

25 Sources of all the above quotations can be found in Johnston, *Fighting the Enemy*, Chapters 2 and 3.

26 In Masel, *The Second 28th*, p. 111.

27 Derrick, diary 10 July 1942, in *Derrick VC in his own words*, p. 221.

28 Maughan, Introduction to Baillieu, *Both Sides of the Hill*, pp. viii–x.

29 Barr, *Pendulum of War*, p. 111.

30 Calculated from Table 5 in Appendix 1 to Johnston, *That Magnificent 9th*.

31 AWM, S0055, Interview with Victor Knight for the Keith Murdoch Sound Archive of Australia in the War of 1939–45.

32 Hail: 2/2 MG Bn Report on July Ops, AWM 526/6/4, AWM. Oakes, *Muzzle Blast*, pp. 101–3. Knight received an immediate award of the DCM.

33 Pratten, *Australian Battalion Commanders*, p. 114. Maughan, *Tobruk and El Alamein*, p. 661 mistakenly says it was six guns.

34 Mutual support and 13 July attack: 'Report on Ops by RAA 9 Aust Div in El Alamein Area', p. 3, AWM54, 526/6/4, AWM.

35 In Parsons, *Gunfire!*, p. 101. Cutler was killed in an OP on 1 November 1942.

36 Schlachtbericht, 13.–14.7.1942, AL 866/1, IWM. The *Panzerarmee*'s report on the day's fighting said that the concrete defences were sited in depth and protected by minefields. AL 866/6, 14 July.

37 Stokes, 'Taradale to Tarakan', pp. 198, 204, 205.

38 Pratten, *Australian Battalion Commanders*, pp. 127–8.

39 Ibid., p. 169.

40 Ibid., p. 170.

41 LT L Thomas, 2/43 Bn, diary 17 July 1942, MJC.

42 SGT SR Ferrier, 9 Div Cav Regt, letter 9 or 10 July 1942, MJC.

43 Chamberlain and Ellis, *British and American Tanks of World War II*, p. 38.

44 Ferrier, letter 8 November 1942. *Alamein: The Australian Story*, pp. 255–6. Handel, *Dust, Sand and Jungle,* p. 28.

45 Maughan, *Tobruk and El Alamein*, p. 579. Barr, *Pendulum of War*, pp. 155–6.

46 Serle, *Second Twenty-Fourth*, pp. 180–2.

47 Crawford, 'Forward from El Alamein', p. 204.

48 Maughan, *Tobruk and El Alamein*, p. 586.

49 Johnston and Stanley, *Alamein: The Australian Story*, p. 94.

50 Ibid., p. 96.

51 Ibid., p. 99.

52 Pratten, *Australian Battalion Commanders*, p. 118.

53 Johnston and Stanley, *Alamein: The Australian Story*, pp. 108–110.

54 In Maughan, *Tobruk and El Alamein*, p. 598.

55 Ibid, p. 599.

56 Maughan, *Tobruk and El Alamein*, p. 599.

57 Pratten, *Australian Battalion Commanders*, p. 114.

58 Ibid., pp. 113–4.

59 Crawford, 'Forward from Alamein', p. 43, 3 DRL 368, AWM.

60 Johnston and Stanley, *Alamein: The Australian Story*, p. 128.

61 Pratten, *Australian Battalion Commanders*, p. 117.

62 In Lewin, *Montgomery as Military Commander*, p. 15. See also Chapter 1 of Lewin's book on the impact of the First World War on Montgomery.

63 Johnston and Stanley, *Alamein: The Australian Story*, p. 129.

64 Johnston, *Australian Band of Brothers*, 185–6.

65 Ibid., p. 633.

66 Johnston and Stanley, *Alamein: The Australian Story*, p. 141.

67 This account is based more on McLachlan's testimony, reprinted in the battalion history, than on his DCM citation. Austin, *Let Enemies Beware*, pp. 139–141.

68 Winters, *Beyond Band of Brothers*, p. 94.

69 Morshead to Colonel Rasmussen, p. 57, AWM54, 522/2/2, AWM.

70 Hill, 'Lieutenant-General Sir Leslie Morshead', in Horner (ed), *The Commanders*, p. 191.

71 LCPL J Craig, 2/13 Bn, diary 27 Sep, 10 Oct 1942, MJC.

72 Leslie Watkins, 'As I remember it', p. 61, AWM MSS 1587, AWM.

73 'Engineer Lessons from recent operations', 11 Sep 1942, War Diary, Commanding Engineer, Eighth Army HQ, WO 169/3942, TNA. 'Report on Tank destruction', 7 Sep 1942, War Diary, Commanding Engineer, Eighth Army HQ, WO 169/3942, TNA. Hammer, 'Re-Organisation', p. 4, in 2/48 Bn War Diary, November–December 1942, AWM. McNicoll, *Royal Australian Engineers*, p. 110.

74 2/17 Battalion War Diary, 27 September 1942, AWM52, 8/3/7/14, AWM.

75 40 RTR War Diary, 14, 28, 29 September, 1–17 October 1942, WO 169/4518, TNA.

76 Drills: Maughan, p. 650; Pratten, p. 116. Bush hats: Johnston and Stanley, p. 145. PTE J Butler, 2/23 Bn, diary, 20 October 1942, 3 DRL 3825, AWM.

77 Pratten, *Australian Battalion Commanders*, pp. 115–7.

78 Ibid., pp. 121–2. Hammer, 'Re-Organisation Alamein', p. 4.

79 Barr, *Pendulum of War*, p. 259.

[80] Boog et al, *Das Deutsche Reich und der Zweite Weltkrieg*, vol. 6, p. 698.

[81] Bidwell, *Gunners at War*, pp. 186–190. Barr, *Pendulum of War*, pp. 287–8, 292–3.

[82] Terraine, *Right of the Line*, p. 379.

[83] Barr, *Pendulum of War*, p. 276.

[84] Smith, *Battle Winners: Australian Artillery in the Western Desert,* pp. 232, 235.

[85] Bidwell, *Gunners at War*, p. 245

[86] Citino, *Death of the Wehrmacht*, p. 275.

[87] Hamilton, *Monty*, p. 466. Maughan, *Tobruk and El Alamein*, pp. 653–4, 660.

[88] Maughan, *Tobruk and El Alamein*, p. 663.

[89] Pratten, *Australian Battalion Commanders*, pp. 117–8. Maughan, *Tobruk and El Alamein*, p. 662. Fearnside, *Bayonets Abroad*, p. 261.

[90] Morshead circular, 10 Oct 1942, 3 DRL 2632, item 46–7, AWM.

[91] Fearnside, *Bayonets Abroad,* pp. 253–4.

[92] Quoted in Pratten, *Australian Battalion Commanders*, p. 113.

[93] WO CL Craig, 2/13 Bn, letter Dec 1942, MJC.

[94] Maughan, *Tobruk and El Alamein*, p. 661.

[95] Appendix A to 9 Aust Div Intelligence Summary No. 353, AWM54, 423/11/18, Part 5, AWM.

[96] Craig, letter Dec 1942. Memoir by PTE W Fairbrother, MJC. Joseph Stokes, 'Taradale to Tarakan', p. 221–5.

[97] Maughan, *Tobruk and El Alamein*, p. 651. Most information for this box is from McNicoll, *Royal Australian Engineers*, pp. 109–117.

[98] Hammer, 'Re-Organisation', pp. 1–5, in 2/48 Bn War Diary, November–December 1942, AWM. Maughan, *Tobruk and El Alamein*, pp. 610, 705.

[99] 'Notes 23 and 24 October 1942', CAB 106/785, TNA.

[100] Next to go: LCPL C Mears, 2/17 Bn, diary 24 (actually 25) Oct 1942, PR84/379, AWM. Bearers: Crawford, p. 149. Signallers: Anson, diary 25 Oct 1942, MJC.

[101] Watkins, 'As I Remember It', p. 66.

[102] Maughan, *Tobruk and El Alamein*, p. 661.

[103] Johnston and Stanley, *Alamein*, pp. 181–2.

[104] Careful siting: citation for MC in WX5057, Wallder Alfred Frederick, B883, NAA.

[105] Rodriguez, Thomas Angelo, WO 373/23/511, TNA. The unnamed officer is quoted in the citation. Smith, *Battle Winners*, pp. 260–1.

[106] Pike, *What we have we hold*, p. 163.

[107] WO2 F Legg, 2/48 Bn, Diary 25 October 1942, PRG 466. 2/48 Bn War Diary. Glenn, *Tobruk to Tarakan*, p. 149.

[108] Glenn, *Tobruk to Tarakan*, p. 167. Wigmore, *They Dared Mightily*, p. 241.

[109] 9 Div Report El Alamein 23 Oct – 5 Nov, p. 26, AWM54, 527/6/9, AWM. DAK War Diary, 25 Oct, AL 834/1/1–2, IWM.

[110] WO Frank Legg, 'Taking of Trig 29', *Radio Call*, 22/9/1943.

[111] Oakes, *Muzzle Blast*, p. 143. 9 Div Report. 26 Bde Report on Operations Oct–Nov 42, AWM54, 527/6/9, AWM.

[112] Ibid. Pike, *What We Have*, p. 165.

[113] RAE 9 Div Report, AWM54, 527/6/11, AWM. 9 Div Report.

[114] 9 Div Report. 26 Bde Report. 2/48 Bn War Diary. Glenn, *Tobruk to Tarakan*, p. 148. Isaksson, 'Key to the Victory – The Battle for Trig 29', *RUSI Bulletin*, Dec 1997, p. 17.

[115] 2/48 Bn War Diary. 9 Div Report. 26 Bde Report. Glenn, *Tobruk to Tarakan*, p. 153. Argent, *Target Tank*, p. 228. According to 9 Div Intelligence Summary 338, during that night's fighting on Trig 29 and the surrounding area, 173 Germans and 69 Italians were captured.

[116] Lewin, *Afrika Korps*, p. 214.

[117] Berry: National Archives of Australia, B883 VX31716.

[118] The issue of whether the feature called Hill 28 by the Germans was in fact 'Kidney Ridge', as stated in various British accounts, or Trig 29 has long been an issue of implicit dispute. On this issue see: Maughan, *Tobruk and El Alamein*, p. 692;

Lucas Phillips, *Alamein*, p. 249; Clissold, 'The Australians' Attack at El Alamein – on Trig 29, Hill 28, or Kidney Ridge?', *Sabretache*, April–June 1995, pp. 26–34. Perusal of any contemporary German map of the battlefield makes it clear that Hill 28 was Trig 29. See, for example: the map copied from Rommel's personal map in Caccia-Dominioni, *Alamein*, p. i; Baillieu, *Both Sides of the Hill*, p. 23. Definitive are German maps held at the Imperial War Museum: the 164 Lt Div map in IWM AL 881, p. 106 and the Afrika Korps situation maps in IWM AL 834/4.

119 Johnston and Stanley, *Alamein: The Australian Story*, p. 188. Maughan, *Tobruk and El Alamein*, p. 698.

120 France: Oakes, *Muzzle Blast*, p. 146. Pte F M Paget, 2/28 Bn, diary 27 October 1942, MJC.

121 Anson, diary 28 October 42. 2/17 Bn War diary, 28 October 1942, AWM52, 8/3/17, AWM. Pike, *What We Have*, p. 168.

122 9 Div Report. Maughan, *Tobruk and El Alamein*, pp. 698–9.

123 Maughan, *Tobruk and El Alamein*, p. 699.

124 '2/15 Bn Narrative of Ops 23 Oct – 5 Nov 42', AWM54, 526/6/10, AWM.

125 '2/15 Bn Narrative of Ops 23 Oct – 5 Nov 42', AWM54, 526/6/10, AWM. Recommendation for Strange's DSO: Strange, Bruce Dowsett, WO373/23/498, TNA.

126 90 Lt War Diary, 28 Oct 42, AL 879/1, IWM. 20 Bde Report.

127 PTE E Lambert, 2/15 Bn, diary 28 Oct 42, MS10049, SLV.

128 Dreadful: SGT KB MacArthur, 2/15 Bn, diary 29 Oct 42, PR86/121, AWM. Lambert, diary 29 October 1942.

129 C Craig, 2/13 Bn, letter – Dec 42, MJC. Craig's company was in former German positions, while the adjacent B Company was hemmed in on its right by a wire fence laced with booby traps.

130 2/13 Battalion War Diary, October 1942, p. 232, AWM52, 8/3/13, AWM. CPL L Clothier, 2/13 Bn, diary 29 October 1942 in Gillan, *We Had Some Bother*, pp. 99–100.

131 Wirewhiskers: Butler, diary 28 Oct 1942.

132 46 RTR War Diary, WO 169/4523, TNA. 26 Bde Report. Share, *Mud and Blood*, pp. 217–219. Butler, diary 28 Oct 1942 on the Germans on the start-line. Barr, *Pendulum of War*, p. 367.

133 Joyce, 'As I Saw It', p. 21.

134 Share, *Mud and Blood*, p. 220. 46 RTR War Diary, WO 169/4523, TNA. On conflicting evidence about what happened here, see *Alamein: The Australian Story*, p. 290 n19.

135 Share, *Mud and Blood*, p. 221.

136 26 Bde Report on Operations Oct–Nov 42, AWM54, 527/6/9, AWM. The confusion is also apparent in 46 RTR War Diary, WO 169/4523, TNA.

137 Ibid., p. 222. This may have been the tank referred to by Sergeant Carleton, who wrote of twelve men of a section of fourteen being wounded when their tank hit a mine. Sgt F Carleton, wartime memoir, p. 51, PR91/0033, AWM.

138 Share 222.

139 Butler, diary 28 October 1942. Carleton, wartime memoir, p. 51.

140 Butler, diary October 1942.

141 Joyce, 'As I Saw It', p. 22. 46 RTR War Diary, WO 169/4523, TNA. Carleton, Memoir, p. 53.

142 SGT F Carleton, wartime memoir, p. 51, PR91/0033, AWM. Share, *Mud and Blood*, p. 223.

143 Schlachtbericht, 28 October, AL743/1/1, IWM. Tank strength: Ultra intercept, 29 October 1942, HW 1/1021, TNA. More tanks became available on subsequent days: *Rommel Papers*, p. 336.

144 Schlachtbericht, 28 October, Anlage 82, AL743/1/1, IWM.

145 Lewin, *Afrika Korps*, p. 218.

146 Fearnside, *Bayonets Abroad*, p. 286.

147 20 Bde Report, 2/15 Bn Narrative.

148 Lambert, diary 29 October 1942.

149 Diary 28 (actually 29) Oct 42, PR84/379. The 90th Light Division believed that the defenders of Trig 29 were 1000 New Zealanders. This belief was apparently based on a prisoner's testimony. 90 Lt War Diary, AL 879/1, IWM.

150 Goodhart, *We of the Turning Tide*, p. 175. On codenames: Maughan, p. 661. Smith, *Battle Winners*, p. 252. Code words were for Australian and Irish towns, and birds.

151 Goodhart, *We of the Turning Tide*, pp. 169, 216.

152 Battle winning: Middle East Training Memoranda, 'Lessons from Operations October and November 1942', War Diary

GHQ ME Military Training Branch, WO 169/3901, TNA. How to use it: Lambert, diary 1 November 1942. Curtain: Royal Artillery notes, CAB 106/785, TNA. Jap gun: quoted in Coates, *Bravery Above Blunder*, p. 46.

153 Hieroglyphics: Crawford, 'Forward from El Alamein', p. 177. Mears, 2/17 Bn, Diary 28(29) October 1942. 'Beast': Anson, diary 29 October 1942.

154 Butler, diary 29 October 1942. Share, *Mud and Blood*, pp. 224–225. DAK Messages in, 29 Oct, AL834/2/2, IWM. Morshead Messages to Blamey, 3DRL 2632, AWM.

155 Schlachtbericht, 26–29 Oct, AL743/1/1, IWM. No longer corsetting: Maughan, *Tobruk and El Alamein*, p. 707.

156 Johnston and Stanley, *Alamein: The Australian Story*, p. 209.

157 9 Div Report, p. 34, AWM54, 527/6/9, AWM.

158 Morshead, Messages to Blamey, 3DRL 2632, AWM. The second experience he had in mind is not clear.

159 Ibid. Maughan, *Tobruk and El Alamein*, p. 708. 90th Light Division, which held the area opposite the 9th Division, had twenty-three troops of field guns and seven of AA, including 88mm guns, on the 30th. This group would almost certainly have comprised more than 100 guns. 90 Lt War Diary, appendices, p. 3, AL 879/1, IWM.

160 Phillips, *Alamein*, p. 312.

161 *We of the Turning Tide*, p. 197.

162 Abraham, diary 30 Oct 42, MJC. 2/48 Bn War Diary 29–30 Oct 42. Later, the War Diary says 292 men took part in the attack. 30–31 Oct 42, AWM 52, 8/3/36, AWM.

163 Ultra intercept, 29 October 1942, HW 1/1018, TNA.

164 2/32 Bn War Diary, AWM52, 8/3/32, AWM. CPL J Castle, 2/32 Bn, diary 30 Oct 42, MJC

165 QX4060, MacDonald, Duncan, B883, NAA.

166 26 Bde Report on Operations Oct–Nov 42, AWM54, 527/6/9, AWM. 2/32 Bn War Diary, AWM52, 8/3/32, AWM.

167 Walker, *Middle East and Far East*, p. 382.

168 2/32 Bn War Diary.

169 2/32 Bn War Diary. 26 Bde Report.

170 Infantry fighting: 90 Lt War Diary appendix, p. 7, AL 879/1, IWM. Horrifying tales: Captain Bolger 4th/46th Artillery Group, in Caccia-Dominioni, *Alamein*, p. 230. On alcohol, see Johnston, *At the Front Line,* p.65. There is no indication of alcohol consumption in the 2/32nd records. Tanks: 90 Lt War Diary, 31 Oct and Appendix p. 7, AL 879/1, IWM.

171 Castle, diary 30 October 1942.

172 2/48 Bn War Diary, AWM52, 8/3/36, AWM.

173 WO2 F Legg, 2/48 Bn, diary 30 Oct 42, PRG 466. Glenn, *Tobruk to Tarakan*, p. 164.

174 Serle, *The Second Twenty-Fourth*, p. 216. 26 Bde Report. Maughan, Tobruk and El Alamein, p. 713n.

175 Serle, *The Second Twenty-Fourth*, pp. 218–9. 26 Bde Report.

176 Serle, *The Second Twenty-Fourth*, p. 218. Cameron was awarded a Military Cross, a rare distinction for a warrant officer.

177 Maughan, *Tobruk and El Alamein*, p. 712.

178 Ralla: Glenn, *Tobruk to Tarakan*, p. 169. Riley: Lt J.T. Gregory, 2/48 Bn, letter 29 November 42, MJC.

179 'Forty-One Aussies Fight On', *Radio Call*, 6 Oct 43. The War Diary says they fought on the final objective, but this is unlikely.

180 Abraham, diary 31 October 1942.

181 2/48 Bn War Diary.

182 'Forty-One Aussies Fight On'.

183 'Forty-One Aussies Fight On'.

184 WO2 F Legg, 2/48 Bn, diary 30 Oct 42 (sic), PRG 466.

185 2/48 Bn War Diary, AWM52, 8/3/36, AWM. The 26 Bde Report says there were forty-eight men.

186 'Forty-One Aussies Fight On'.

187 Another consideration may have been knowledge or a belief that 2/24th were withdrawing too: the sources do not agree.

188 Serle, *The Second Twenty-Fourth*, p. 220.

189 2/48 Bn War Diary.

190 Anderson & Jackett, *Mud and Sand*, 1st edn, pp. 296–7.

191 Ibid., p. 301.

192 Ibid, pp. 301–2.

193 Major Rosevear, diary 30 Oct 42, in Anderson & Jackett, *Mud and Sand*, 2nd edn, p. 89.

194 Ibid.

195 Only to go ahead if other phases succeeded: 2/3 Pnr Bn War Diary, 30 October 1942, summary, AWM52, 8/6/3/10, AWM.

196 Rosevear, p. 89. Maughan, *Tobruk and El Alamein*, p. 718. 26 Bde Report.

197 Anderson & Jackett, *Mud and Sand*, 1st edn, p. 308.

198 9 Div Report.

199 90 Lt War Diary, 30 Oct, AL 879/1, IWM. Also Rommel Papers, pp. 311–2. The Australians' belief may have been based on the interrogation of the OC of II/125 Regiment, captured on the night of 25 October. 9 Div Intelligence Summary 338, AWM54, 423/11/18, AWM.

200 Maughan, *Tobruk and El Alamein*, p. 720.

201 Prisoners: Johnston and Stanley, *Alamein: The Australian Story*, p. 224. Morshead Message to Blamey, 3 Nov 42, 3DRL 2632, AWM.

202 Message to Blamey, 3 Nov 42, 3DRL 2632, AWM.

203 *Tobruk and El Alamein*, p. 719.

204 Hill, 'Lieutenant-General Sir Leslie Morshead', in Horner (ed), *The Commanders*, p. 195.

205 Knowing enemy defences were strong: Moore, *Morshead*, p. 148.

206 26 Bde Report.

207 These arguments owe much to Alec Hill, letter to the author 12/8/98.

208 90 Lt War Diary, 31 Oct 42, AL 879/1, IWM. *Rommel Papers*, p. 315. Schlachtbericht, 31 Oct 42, AL743/1/1, IWM.

209 'Forty-One Aussies Fight On'. Glenn, *Tobruk to Tarakan*, p. 171. Goodhart, *We of the Turning Tide*, p. 200.

210 Ibid. There were apparently still more than 260 men in BHQ and HQ Company. Annexure 3 to Appendix A in 26 Bde Report, Brigadier Ramsay's copy. MJC.

211 Annexure 3 to Appendix A in 26 Bde Report, Ramsay copy shows two officers and seventy-two men in the rifle companies, 225 and 7 in BHQ and HQ Company. MJC.

212 Hamilton, *Monty*, p. 832.

213 Hang on: Schlachtbericht, Anl. 119(1), AL743/1/1, IWM. Orders to 90 Lt, 31 Oct 42, AL 879/1, IWM. Schlachtbericht, 31 Oct 42, AL743/1/1, IWM. DAK War Diary, 31 Oct, AL 834/1/1–2, IWM. The War Diary calls this instruction 'incomprehensible'.

214 Withering: Major Rosevear, diary, in *Mud and Sand*, p. 90.

215 'Come and get us': Anderson & Jackett, *Mud and Sand*, p. 310.

216 Disorganised: 26th Brigade Report. Legg, diary 31 October 1942. The attackers were Germans. The 2/32nd War Diary recorded it differently, saying the Pioneers 'fought their way through' to the road, silencing enemy machine-gun nests with the bayonet as they came.

217 There is implicit debate as to whether there were two tank attacks or one in the late morning/early afternoon.

218 Rosevear, in *Mud and Blood*, p. 90. 9 Div Intelligence Summary 343 of 1 November gave the credit to the British tanks. AWM54, 423/11/18, AWM.

219 Phone interview with Fred Fewtrell, 3 April 1998 and 16 August 1998.

220 Castle, diary 31 October 1942.

221 Interview with Fred Fewtrell, 16 August 1998. The 40 RTR did lose twenty-one tanks on this day, as well as thirteen men killed or died of wounds. 40 RTR War Diary, WO 169/4518, TNA.

222 Argent, *Target Tank*, p. 253. Maughan, *Tobruk and El Alamein*, p. 722. It is possible that this happened on 1 November. See Argent, p. 246.

223 90 Lt War Diary, AL 879/1, IWM.

224 2/48 Bn War Diary, AWM52, 8/3/36, AWM. Also Legg diary 31 October 1942.

225 2/2 MG Bn B Coy report on 'Lightfoot', AWM54, 526/6/4, AWM.

226 26 Bde Report.

227 Bad day: Goodhart, *We of the Turning Tide*, p. 209. Official report: Summary of Artillery Operations in 9 Aust Div, AWM54, 526/6/4, AWM.

228 'Last Day at Alamein', *Radio Call*, 13/10/43.

229 26 Bde Report. Schlachtbericht, 31 Oct, AL743/1/1, IWM.

230 90 Lt War Diary, AL 879/1, IWM.

231 All quotations in this section from Johnston, *Anzacs in the Middle East*, pp. 182–197.

232 Serle, *The Second Twenty-Fourth*, p. 222. 'Last Day at Alamein'. Glenn, *Tobruk to Tarakan*, p. 171. Masel, *The Second 28th*, p. 107. Legg, diary 1 November 1942.

233 Maughan, *Tobruk and El Alamein*, p. 723.

234 9 Div Report. Oakes, *Muzzle Blast*, p. 155. Argent, *Target Tank*, p. 244. Goodhart, *We of the Turning Tide*, p. 207. Glenn, *Tobruk to Tarakan*, p. 171. Masel, *The Second 28th*, p. 104.

235 Goodhart, *We of the Turning Tide*, p. 207. Oakes, *Muzzle Blast*, p. 155. Front door: Masel, *The Second 28th*, p. 106. 24 Bde Report, AWM54, 526/6/12, AWM. There were also Vickers guns to the west of Tel el Eisa, overlooking the area. In addition, the artillery further south could have been called into play.

236 Maughan, *Tobruk and El Alamein*, p. 723.

237 Serle, *The Second Twenty-Fourth*, p. 222.

238 Telephone conversation, 17 Sep 1998, with R Sangster, who was in Godfrey's HQ. Maughan, *Tobruk and El Alamein*, pp. 723–4 says the HQ was in the Saucer

239 'Forward from El Alamein', p. 188.

240 Lambert, diary 31 October 1942.

241 Combe, *The 2/43rd*, pp. 126–8. On the 2/43rd on 1 November, see also Johnston, *An Australian Band of Brothers*, pp. 220–230.

242 24 Bde Report.

243 Impending attack: Summary of 9 Div Artillery Operations. 24 Bde Report. Depleted: Masel, *The Second 28th*, p. 108; Phillips, *Alamein*, p. 317; Yeates and Loh, *Red Platypus*, p. 47; DAK War Diary, AL 834/1/1–2, IWM. One strongpoint: Yeates and Loh, *Red Platypus*, p. 47; Combe, *The 2/43rd*, p. 122.

244 Determined attack: 9 Div Intelligence Summary 345. One battalion: 2/32 Bn War Diary. Private war: in Combe, *The 2/43rd*, p. 127.

245 Combe, *The 2/43rd*, pp. 123, 127, 128.

246 In Masel, *The Second 28th*, 1st edn, p. 111.

247 Fairbrother, 2/28 Bn, diary and reconstructed account of 1 November 1942. Like mad: Masel, *The Second 28th*, p. 111. Intrepid Germans: Morshead, Message to Blamey, 3 Nov 42, 3DRL 2632, AWM.

248 24 Bde Report.

249 Report on Operations, p. 49. Terraine, *Right of the Line*, p. 385. '9 Aust Div OO No. 21 – Lightfoot', pp. 4–5. Gladman, 'Development of Tactical Air Doctrine', p. 193.

250 'Volunteer's Story', p. 199. Phillips describes a Rhodesian gun which successively destroyed a Pz.Kpfw. III, an 88 gun and a portee carrying a captured 6-pounder, all in quick succession. He continues:

'There followed a demonstration that must be almost unexampled on a modern battlefield. The surrounding Australians, transfixed with admiration for this cool and superlative shooting, stood up in their doovers and burst into cheers, as though they were applauding a century in a Test Match'. *Alamein*, p. 321. He suggests that this happened on 2 November.

251 2/32 Bn War Diary.

252 *Annihilated: In Mud and Sand*, p. 91.

253 Combe, *The 2/43rd*, pp. 123, 129.

254 CPL W Fairbrother, 2/28 Bn, reconstruction of 1 November. He dated this as 2 November, but this is highly unlikely.

255 Combe, *The 2/43rd*, p. 123. The Germans called the British bomber formations 'Parteitage' – Rally Days, after the perfect formations seen at Nazi rallies. 9 Div Intelligence Summary 348. A German report says that the area between Sidi Abd el Rahman, Trig 29 and 125th Regt was attacked thirty-four times on 1 November by the eighteen bombers. Schlachtbericht, 1 Nov 42, AL743/1/1, IWM.

256 In Combe, *The 2/43rd*, p. 126.

257 *Rommel Papers*, p. 315. Maughan, *Tobruk and El Alamein*, p. 710. Masel, *The Second 28th*, p. 41n.

[258] Combe, *The 2/43rd*, p. 128.

[259] *Alamein: The Australian Story*, p. 295, n. 79.

[260] DAK War Diary, AL 834/1/1–2, IWM.

[261] Concentrated: Fairbrother, 2/28 Bn, diary Nov or Dec 43, Jones, letter 15 November 42, MJC.

[262] By the end of the following day, the total would exceed 500. Maughan, *Tobruk and El Alamein*, p. 728 erroneously says the figure was 487 for October 30 to 2 November. In fact, the figure for that period is 487 *other ranks* and thirty-one officers. Calculated from 24 Bde Report.

[263] Gilbert, *The Desert War*, pp. 184–5.

[264] Critical day: 24 Bde Report on 5 November 1942. Saved: Masel, *The Second 28th*, p. 112.

[265] Determined: Morshead Messages to Blamey, 3 Nov 42, 3DRL 2632, AWM. Concentrated: Letter to DL Bowdell, 12 November 1942, in AWM 3/2562, AWM.

[266] Untenable: Masel, *The Second 28th*, 1st edn, p. 113. Expenditure: Yeates and Loh, *Red Platypus*, pp. 47, 49.

[267] Allan Jones, in Combe, *The 2/43rd*, p. 129.

[268] Castle, diary 2 November 1942.

[269] Hold it: Allan Jones, in Combe, *The 2/43rd*, p. 129. Terrific job: Castle, diary 2 November 1942. Knackers: Morshead, letter to DL Bowdell, 12 November 1942.

[270] 2/3 Fd Amb War Diary, AWM52, 11/12/12, AWM.

[271] Montgomery's message can be found in most Australian unit war diaries on and following 2 November.

[272] In Derek Jewell (ed), *Alamein and the Desert War*, Sphere Books, London, 1967, p. 93.

[273] Airgraph 14406, ORME0077, Reel 8, AWM.

[274] LT AG Hirst, 2/3 AT Regt, letter 6 November 1942.

[275] SGT JD Williams, 2/7 AGH, Diary 22 July 1942.

[276] Johnston and Stanley, *Alamein*, pp. 181–2.

[277] 'Medical Aspects of the Alamein Battle', AWM52, 481/12/59, AWM. Walker, *Middle East*, p. 386.

[278] Shelton Smith, *The Boys Write Home*, p. 59.

[279] Alive: ibid. Active: Derrick, Diary Memo for end of November 1942. Close calls: Watkins, 'As I Remember It', p. 69.

[280] Table, 'Operations in the Middle East', A5954, 529/9, NAA. After cross-referencing a number of sources, including databases maintained by the Memorial and the Commonwealth War Graves Commission, Craig Tibbitts of the Australian War Memorial has produced a figure of 1259 Australian army fatalities in the El Alamein fighting. Tibbitts, 'El Alamein 80 Years on'.

[281] Crawford, 'Forward from El Alamein', p. 210.

[282] 2/3 Fd Amb War Diary, AWM52, 11/12/12, AWM. Walker, Middle East, p. 383. Walker, *Clinical Problems*, p. 687. Lovegrove, diary 14 November 1942.

[283] Reproduced in 2/48 Bn War Diary, November–December 1942, p. 231. On the division's return to Australia, see Johnston and Stanley, *Alamein: The Australian Story*, pp. 129–130.

[284] Hill, review of Maughan, *Tobruk and El Alamein*, in *Australian Army Journal*, 215, 1967, p. 55.

[285] Statistics and entitlements: Bryce Abraham, emails to the author 6 May and 31 May 2022 and based on his outstanding thesis on, and forthcoming book about, Australian awards, nova.newcastle.edu.au/vital/access/services/Download/uon:36329/ATTACHMENT01?view=true, p. 142. Morshead's requests: Alexander to Morshead, 23 Dec 1942, 3 DRL 2632, item 16, AWM.

[286] There were at least the following: for July nine MCs, thirteen DCMs and sixteen MMs, and in October fourteen MCs, sixteen DCMs, and six MMs, but there were almost certainly more. My calculations are based on research for my forthcoming book on Australian medal recipients in the Second World War.

[287] 'General Conclusions and Lessons', 26 Bde Report, AWM.

[288] Report on Operations – 9 Div – El Alamein – 23 Oct – 5 Nov 42, p. 46, AWM54, 527/6/9, AWM.

[289] Harper, *Battle for North Africa*, p. 241.

[290] I owe some of the arguments here against night fighting to a fine New Zealand historian, Shaun Mawdsley. See also Hamilton, *Monty*, p. 466. Maughan, *Tobruk and El Alamein*, p. 653–4, 660.

[291] The 9th Division's report on operations invoked a 'prewar infantry training manual' when it described the infantry as the 'Queen of the Battlefield'. The term has much older origins and stretches back at least to the 18th Century. One theory

of its origin relates to the position of the Queen as the most powerful piece on the board in a game of chess. Report on Operations, p. 48; US Army, 'Infantry Online', moore.army.mil/infantry/magazine/FAQs.html, accessed 20 May 2024.

292 Report on Operations, p. 48.

293 Ibid. Summary of Artillery Operations in 9 Aust Div, p. 8, AWM54, 526/6/4, AWM.

294 Smith, *Battle Winners*, p. 299.

295 Report on Operations, pp. 46–47. Rommel Papers, pp. 328–9.

296 Report on Operations, p. 45.

297 SGT J Lovegrove, 2/43 Bn, diary 12 September 1942 and letter to the author, late 1990.

298 Pratten, *Australian Battalion Commanders*, p. 112.

299 XXX Corps draft report, p. 1 in 'Report on Operations'.

300 Pratten, *Australian Battalion Commanders*, pp. 123, 125.

301 Fifty cases: Coates, *Bravery Above Blunder*, pp. 7–8. Continuing cohesion: Pratten, *Australian Battalion Commanders*, p. 125.

302 Teamwork and fighting machine: Report on Operations, p. 45. Hammer, 'Re-Organisation', p. 4.

303 As suggested in part by Pratten, *Australian Battalion Commanders*, p. 128.

304 Barr, *Pendulum of War*, pp. 411–2.

305 Dear, *The Oxford Companion to the Second World War*, p. 238, Oxford University Press, Oxford, 1995.

306 Churchill, *Second World War*, Volume 4, p. 541.

307 Coady, 'The 2/48th Battalion at El Alamein', p. 3, *Australian Army Journal*, No. 221, October 1967.

308 Hill, 'Lieutenant-General Sir Leslie Morshead', p. 197.

309 Loosely based on Coates, *Bravery Above Blunder,* p. 12.

BIBLIOGRAPHY

Note: 'MJC' refers to items in the author's collection.

PERSONAL WARTIME TESTIMONIES

PTE JH Abraham, 2/48 Bn, diary, donor: Mrs Joan Abraham.
PTE R Anson, 2/17 Bn, diary, donor: RJ Anson.
PTE JM Butler, 2/23 Bn, diary, 3 DRL 3825, AWM.
CPL F Carleton, 2/23 Bn, wartime memoir, PR91/0033, AWM.
SGT L Clothier, 2/13 Bn, diary, PR00588, AWM.
LT GD Combe, 2/43 Bn, letters, donor: Gordon Combe.
WO2 C Craig, 2/13 Bn, L-/12/42, donor: Jack Craig.
CPL J Craig, 2/13 Bn, diary, donor: Jack Craig.
CPL and SGT TC Derrick, 2/48 Bn, diary 1942, PR82/190, AWM.
CPL W Fairbrother, 2/28 Bn, diary and memoir, donor: Winston Fairbrother.
CPL J Castle, 2/32 Bn, diary, donor: Jack Castle.
SGT SR Ferrier, 9 Div Cav Regt, letters, donor: SR Ferrier, via John Barrett.
LT JT Gregory, 2/48 Bn, letter, donor: Monica Jeffries.
LT AG Hirst, 2/3 AT Regt, letters. Donor Kathleen Hirst.
PTE to CPL AA Jones, 2/43 Bn, letters. Donor: Allan Jones.
PTE E Lambert, 2/15 Bn, diary, MS 10049, State Library of Victoria.
WO2 F Legg, 2/48 Bn, diary, PRG 466, Mortlock Library of South Australia.
SGT JH Lovegrove, 2/43 Bn, diary, MJC.
SGT K MacArthur, 2/15 Bn, diary, PR86/121, AWM.
PTE C Mears, 2/17 Bn, diary, PR 84/379, AWM.
LTGEN L Morshead, letters, AWM54, 522/1/2 and 3/2562, AWM.
PTE FM Paget, 2/28 Bn, diary, donor: FM Paget.
LT LH Thomas, 2/43 Bn, diary, donor: Janet Hayes.

OFFICIAL RECORDS

Australian War Memorial

AWM52, AIF unit and formation war diaries: 8/3/13, 2/13 Bn; 8/3/17, 2/17 Bn; 8/3/32, 2/32 Bn; 8/3/36, 2/48 Bn; 8/6/3/10, 2/3 Pnr Bn; 11/12/12, 2/3rd Fd Amb.

AWM54, Written Records, 1939–1945: 423/11/18, 9 Division Intelligence Summaries; 526/6/4, 2/2 MG Bn Report on July Operations; 526/6/4, 2/2 MG Bn B Coy report on 'Lightfoot'; 526/6/4, Report on Ops by RAA 9 Aust Div in El Alamein Area; 526/6/4, Summary of Artillery Operations in 9 Australian Division in Sidi Abd el Rahman from 23 October to 4 November 42; 526/6/10, 20 Bde Report on Ops 'Lightfoot'; 526/6/10, 2/15 Bn Narrative of Ops 23 October – 5 November 42; 526/6/12, 24 Bde Report on October battle; 526/6/12, 9th Australian Division Operations in the El Alamein Area July 1942; 526/6/16, 26 Bde Narrative of Ops, 5–29 July 1942; 527/6/9, Part 2, Report on Operations 9 Aust Div – El Alamein 23 October – 5 November 42 ; 527/6/9, 26 Bde Report on Operations Oct–Nov 1942; 526/6/16, 527/6/11 Part 2, RAE 9 Div Report.

3 DRL 2632, Morshead Messages to Blamey, July–November 1942.

Imperial War Museum

AL743/1/1, 'Schlachtbericht der Deutsch–Italienischen Panzerarmee, 23, Oktober 1942–23, Februar 1943', vol 1.
AL833/1, War Diary of the German *Afrika Korps*, June–July 1942.
AL 834/1/1–2, War Diary of the German *Afrika Korps*, 3 August – 22 November 42.
AL 834, DAK messages in.
AL 834/4, DAK Situation Maps.
AL866/1, 'Schlachtbericht über die Kämpfe der Panzerarmee Afrika', 26 May – 27 July 42.
AL 866/6, 'Appendices to German War Narrative', June–July 1942.
AL 879/1, 90 Light Division War Diary, 5 September 42 – 31 December 42.
AL 881, 164 Light Division Reports, July–December 1942.

National Archives of Australia

A5954, The Shedden Collection: 529/9, Operations in the Middle East. Allied offensive in North Africa, October, 1942. (AIF casualties in ME campaigns).

B883, Second Australian Imperial Force Personnel Dossiers, 1939–1947: QX4060, MacDonald, Duncan; WX5057, Wallder, Alfred Frederick.

The National Archives, United Kingdom

CAB 106, Cabinet Office: Historical Section: Archivist and Librarian Files: 777, Western Desert: report on operations of 9th Australian Division at Alamein 1942 Oct. 23 – Nov. 5; 785, Western Desert: notebook of the official narrator Lieutenant-Colonel M. E. S. Laws; notes 1942 Oct. 23–24 HW1, Government Code and Cypher School: Signals Intelligence Passed to the Prime Minister, Messages and Correspondence: 1018, North Africa; 1021, North Africa.

WO 169, War of 1939 to 1945, War Diaries, Middle East Forces: 3901, GHQ ME Military Training Branch; 3942, Commanding Engineer, Eighth Army HQ; 4518, 40 Royal Tank Regiment; 4523, 46 Royal Tank Regiment.

WO373, War Office and Ministry of Defence: Military Secretary's Department: Recommendations for Honours and Awards for Gallant and Distinguished Service (Army): 23/51, Rodriguez, Thomas Angelo; 23/498, Strange, Bruce Dowsett.

UNPUBLISHED POSTWAR REMINISCENCES

Crawford, JA, 'Forward from El Alamein', 3 DRL 368, AWM.
Joyce, Ken, 'As I Saw It … From Tobruk to Tarakan 1940–1945', 1995, donor: Pat Share.
Stokes, Joseph Placid, 'Taradale to Tarakan', n.d. AWM MSS 1120.
Watkins, L, 'As I Remember It', MSS 1587, AWM.

INTERVIEWS

Fewtrell, Fred, 2/32 Bn, phone interviews 3 April 1998 and 16 August 1998.
Knight, Victor, 2/2 MG Bn, interview for Keith Murdoch Sound Archive, AWM S0055.
Sangster, Robert, 24 Bde HQ, phone interview 17 September 1998.

SECONDARY SOURCES

Abraham, Bryce, 'Valore Australis: Constructions of Australian Military Heroism from Sudan to Vietnam, 1885–1975', PhD thesis, University of Newcastle, Australia, 2019.
Anderson, JA and Jackett, JGT (eds), *Mud and Sand: the Official War History of the 2/3 Pioneer Battalion A.I.F.*, 1st edn, 2/3rd Pioneer Battalion Association, Sydney, 1955.
——*Mud and Sand: 2/3 Pioneer Bn at War, 2nd edn*, 2/3 Pioneer Battalion Association, Sydney, 1994.
Anonymous British Officer, '*Behind the British Victory in North Africa*' Foreign Affairs, January 1944.
Argent, JNL, '*Target Tank*'. *The History of the 2/3rd Australian Anti-Tank Regiment, 9th Division*, AIF, Parramatta, 1957.
Austin, Ron, *Let Enemies Beware! 'Caveant Hostes': The History of the 2/15th Battalion, 1940–1945*, 2/15th Battalion and Slouch Hat Publications, McCrae, 1995.
Baillieu, Everard, *Both Sides of the Hill: The Capture of Company 621*, 2/24 Battalion Association, Melbourne, 1985.
Barr, Niall, *Pendulum of War: The Three Battles of El Alamein*, Pimlico, London, 2005.
Bean, CEW, *The A.I.F. in France*, Volume V, University of Queensland Press, St Lucia, 1983
Bidwell, Shelford, *Gunners at War: A Tactical Study of the Royal Artillery in the Twentieth Century*, Arrow Books, London, 1972.
Boog, Horst, et al., *Das Deutsche Reich und der Zweite Weltkrieg*, vol. 6, Deutsche Verlags-Anstalt, Stuttgart, 1990.
Caccia-Dominioni de Sillavengo, Paolo, *Alamein 1933–1962: An Italian Story*, Allen & Unwin, London, 1966.
Chamberlain, Peter, and Ellis, Chris, *British and American Tanks of World War II*, Arco, New York, 1981.
Churchill, Winston S., *The Second World War*, Volume 4, Cassell, London, 1951.
Citino, Robert, *Death of the Wehrmacht: The German Campaigns of 1942*, University Press of Kansas, Lawrence, 2007.
Clissold, Barry, 'The Australians' Attack at El Alamein – on Trig 29, Hill 28, or Kidney Ridge?', *Sabretache*, April/June 1995.
Coady, CF, 'The 2/48th Battalion at El Alamein', *Australian Army Journal*, 221, October 1967.
Coates, John, *Bravery above Blunder: The 9th Australian Division at Finschhafen, Sattelberg and Sio*, Oxford University Press, Melbourne, 1993.
Dear, ICB (ed), *The Oxford Companion to the Second World War,* Oxford University Press, Oxford, 1995.
Dennis, Peter et al, *The Oxford Companion to Australian Military History,* Oxford University Press, Oxford, 1995.
Fearnside, GH (ed.), *Bayonets Abroad, A History of the 2/13th Battalion A.I.F. in the Second World War*, Waite and Bull, Sydney, 1953.
Gilbert, Adrian, *The Imperial War Museum Book of the Desert War*, Sidgwick & Jackson, London, 1992.
Gillan, H (ed.), *We Had Some Bother: 'Tales from the Infantry'*, Hale and Iremonger, Sydney, 1985.
Gladman, Brad, 'The Development of Tactical Air Doctrine in North Africa, 1940–43' in S Cox and P Gray (eds), *Air Power History: Turning Points from Kitty Hawk to Kosovo*, Frank Cass, Abingdon, 2002.
Glenn, John G, *Tobruk to Tarakan: The Story of the 2/48th Battalion A.I.F.*, Rigby, Adelaide, 1960.
Goodhart, David, *We of the Turning Tide*, FW Preece Ltd, Adelaide, 1947.
Hamilton, Nigel, *Monty: The Making of a General, 1887–1942*, Hamish Hamilton, London, 1982.
Handel, Paul, *Dust, Sand and Jungle: a history of Australian armour during training and operations, 1927–1948*, RAAC Memorial and Army Tank Museum, Puckapunyal, 2003.
Harper, Glyn, *The Battle for North Africa: El Alamein and the Turning Point for World War II,* Massey University Press, Auckland, 2017.
Hill, AJ, 'Lieutenant-General Sir Leslie Morshead: Commander, 9th Australian Division', in DM Horner (ed.), *The Commanders: Australian military leadership in the twentieth century,* Allen & Unwin, Sydney, 1992.
——Review of Maughan, *Tobruk and El Alamein,* in *Australian Army Journal,* 215, 1967.
Isaksson, O, 'Key to the Victory – The Battle for Trig 29', *RUSI Bulletin*, Dec 1997.
Jewell, Derek (ed.), *Alamein and the Desert War,* Sphere Books, London, 1967.
Johnston, Mark, *An Australian Band of Brothers,* NewSouth, Sydney, 2018.
——*Anzacs in the Middle East: Australian soldiers, their allies and the local people in World War II,* Cambridge University Press, Port Melbourne, 2012.
——*At the Front Line: Experiences of Australian Soldiers in World War II,* Cambridge University Press, Cambridge, 1996.
——(ed.), *Derrick VC in his own words,* New South, Sydney, 2001.
——*Fighting the Enemy: Australian soldiers and their adversaries in World War II,* Cambridge University Press, Cambridge, 2000.
——*That Magnificent 9th,* Allen and Unwin, Sydney, 2002.
——and Stanley, Peter, *Alamein: The Australian Story,* Oxford University Press, Melbourne, 2002.
Legg, Frank, 'Forty-One Aussies Fight On', *Radio Call,* 6 October 1943.
——'Last Day at Alamein', *Radio Call,* 13 October 1943.
——'Taking of Trig 29' *Radio Call,* 22 September 1943.

Lewin, Ronald, *Montgomery as Military Commander,* Stein and Day, New York, 1971.
——*The Life and Death of the Afrika Korps,* Corgi Books, London, 1979.
——*Ultra Goes to War,* Grafton Books, London, 1988.
Liddell Hart, BH (ed.), *The Rommel Papers,* Hamlyn Paperbacks, London, 1984.
Long, Gavin, *To Benghazi,* Collins/Australian War Memorial, Sydney, 1986.
Lucas, James, *War in the Desert: The Eighth Army at El Alamein,* Beaufort Books, New York, 1982.
Masel, Philip, *The Second 28th,* 1st edn, 2/28th Battalion and 24th Anti-Tank Coy, Perth, 1961.
Maughan, Barton, *Tobruk and El Alamein,* Australian War Memorial, Canberra, 1966.
McNicoll, Ronald, *The Royal Australian Engineers 1919 to 1945: Teeth and Tail,* Royal Australian Engineers, Canberra, 1982.
Moore, John, *Morshead: A Biography of Lieut. General Sir Leslie Morshead,* Haldane, Sydney, 1976.
Moorehead, Alan, *African Trilogy,* Hamish Hamilton, London, 1965.
Oakes, Bill, *Muzzle Blast: Six Years of War with the 2/2 Australian Machine Gun Battalion,* A.I.F., 2/2 Machine Gun Battalion War History Committee, Sydney, 1980.
Parsons, Max, *Gunfire! A History of the 2/12 Australian Field Regiment,* Globe Press, Cheltenham, 1991.
Phillips, CE Lucas, *Alamein,* Heinemann, London, 1962.
Pike, P and others, *'What We Have ... We Hold!': A History of the 2/17 Australian Infantry Battalion,* 2/17 Battalion History Committee, Balgowlah, 1990.
Pratten, Garth, *Australian Battalion Commanders in the Second World War,* Cambridge University Press, Port Melbourne, 2009.
Serle, RP (ed.), *The Second Twenty-Fourth,* The Jacaranda Press, Brisbane, 1963.
Share, Pat (ed.), *Mud and Blood: 'Albury's Own' Second Twenty Third Australian Infantry Battalion,* Heritage Book Publications, Frankston, 1978.
Shelton Smith, Adele, *The Boys Write Home,* Consolidated Press, Sydney, 1944.
Smith, Alan H, *Battle Winners: Australian artillery in the Western Desert 1940–1942,* Barrallier Books, Geelong, 2014.
Terraine, John, *The Right of the Line: The Royal Air Force in the European War 1939–1945,* Sceptre, Sevenoaks, 1988.
Tibbitts, Craig, 'El Alamein 80 years on', *Wartime: Official magazine of the Australian War Memorial,* No. 101 (2023).
Walker, Allan S, *Clinical Problems of War*, Australian War Memorial, Canberra, 1952.
——*Middle East and Far East,* Australian War Memorial, Canberra, 1956.
Wigmore, Lionel, *They Dared Mightily,* Australian War Memorial, Canberra, 1963.
Wilmot, Chester, *Tobruk 1941,* Angus and Robertson, Sydney, 1945.
Winters, Dick, *Beyond Band of Brothers,* Ebury Press, Reading, 2006.
Yeates, JD and Loh, WG (eds.), *Red Platypus: A Record of the Achievements of the 24th Australian Infantry Brigade Ninth Australian Division 1940–45,* Imperial Printing, Perth, 1946.

INDEX

Notes:
Italics denote non-English language terms, and titles of works.
Page numbers in **bold** denote illustrations.
Titles starting with 'The' are filed under the next word.
e.g. '*The Royal Engineers Clearing the Mine Fields*' is filed under R.
Army units are filed numerically under the national army.
e.g. Australian Army, 2/2 Machine Gun Battalion

N

O

P

W

Y